BonSens.org is a non-profit association recognized to be of public utility under the 1908 French law on association.

By virtue of the French Constitution and our fundamental right to know the truth, our commitment at BonSens.org is rooted in :

– the teacher's duty to speak,

– the journalist's duty to speak,

– the scientist's duty to speak,

Because to do so is common sense,

Because to do so is our duty,

Whatever the cost.

Cover image: © Pravin Chakravarty | Dreamstime.com
Photo of Hélène Banoun: Christophe Lepissier
ISBN: 978-1-913191-63-4

Talma Studios
231, rue Saint-Honoré
F-75001 Paris
www.talmastudios.com
info@talmastudios.com

Hélène Banoun
with the collaboration of
Pryska Ducœurjoly

SCIENCE VS THE ABUSE OF POWER
How Biopolitics Dictated
COVID-19 Policy

Translated from French
by Nina Vugman

Preface to the English translation

This book is the English version of my publication in French *La Science face au Pouvoir: Ce que révèle la crise Covid-19 sur la biopolitique du XXIᵉ siècle* (November 2023). Nothing has been added apart from a few updated links.

Developments in health biopolitics since that publication have validated the soundness of my interpretation of how the COVID-19 crisis was managed.

I supplemented and further elaborated the latest evidence proving the artificial origin of the SARS-CoV-2 virus in a preprint. The US Senate hearings investigating the origin of COVID-19 have confirmed the hypothesis that the virus was manufactured and leaked from a laboratory. Only the exact origin of the leak remains undetermined (China or elsewhere: possibly the USA?).

Recently disclosed documents from the Robert Koch Institute in Germany confirm that the political management of the crisis tended to artificially inflate the disease burden to cause panic among populations and fuel anxiety in anticipation of a "providential" vaccine, as had been planned in the pandemic simulations I describe in this book. As for the COVID-19 disease itself, it is now considered increasingly likely that the natural immunity acquired post coronavirus infection protects against severe forms of the disease whereas the vaccines do not. In fact, the vaccines both facilitate and exacerbate infection and reinfection, which is partially explained by the presence of facilitating antibodies (the ADE phenomenon, which I have also studied for influenza and measles vaccinations). The toxicity of anti-COVID vaccines, and mRNAs in particular, has only recently been confirmed by the scientific literature. The possibility of vaccine excretion (mRNA and Spike) that I proposed in 2022 is compatible with clinical observations.

Throughout the past year, biopower forces have continued to obstruct any criticism of their management of the crisis, notably by sanctioning doctors who have had the courage to treat patients for COVID since 2020, as exemplified by the sanctions against Dr. Peter McCullough in 2022. In August 2024, the ABIM (American Board of Internal Medicine) revoked the medical licenses of Drs. Pierre Kory and Paul Marik: they are accused of endangering patients by treating them for COVID with ivermectin. Drs. Kory and Marik and the FLCCC (Frontline COVID-19 Critical Care Alliance) have produced 170 scientific references attesting to the efficacy and safety of ivermectin in the treatment of COVID.

Gains in function on viruses that are most certainly at the origin of SARS-CoV-2 have not ceased and may even be implicated in the recent emergence of the viruses that are now feeding the hype about a coming pandemic (avian flu and monkeypox viruses). The same processes are again used to instigate fear by exaggerating the danger of the diseases, intentionally confusing "cases" (human or animal) with the actually sick by means of fraudulent PCR tests and proposing dangerous and ineffective vaccines. As I wrote earlier, the pretext of preserving health serves to enable population control: the EU is taking the lead with the launch of a test pilot in May 2024 in five countries for a "European Vaccination Card" before its roll out in 2026.

In 2023, I also warned of the imminent proliferation of emergency authorizations for anti-infectives and vaccines. In September 2024, I published an article on Beyfortus, a monoclonal antibody against RSV bronchiolitis for newborns: this expensive product with unknown data on long-term safety is the first monoclonal antibody to be administered globally to populations of newborns. Analysis of clinical studies and the 2023-2024 immunization campaigns alert us to the possibility of ADE (facilitation/aggravation of bronchiolitis in rare cases) and the lack of cost-effectiveness of this product being administered to an entire cohort of healthy babies. I have reviewed the biological mechanisms that may explain this phenomenon. This product is recommended for all infants by the US Food and Drug Administration.

I show in this book how gene vaccines, including mRNA, have since the 2009 H1N1 flu been considered to replace conventional vaccines, and how COVID-19 provided an opportunity to develop them on a global scale. Will resistance by the population and the work of critically minded scientists and doctors prevent or slow down the widespread use of gene products? We can only hope so: in fact, development of anti-flu mRNAs seems to be lagging (no mRNA has been announced against avian flu7, and the combined influenza-COVID vaccine appears to be struggling: it does not meet the immunogenicity criteria against influenza B. The mRNA vaccine against seasonal flu is less effective than the classic quadrivalent vaccine in people aged over 65).

Acknowledgments

I would like first of all to pay tribute to the following:

In Europe and Quebec, Canada
To the doctors and paramedics who treated patients despite ban on treatment and at risk to their own professional situation (forced lay-offs, suspension and other sanctions up to potential disbarment from the French Order of Physicians (Ordre des Médecins). Included here, of course, are Professors Christian Perronne and Didier Raoult,

To the rare scientists who had the courage to speak out at risk to their career, including, but not limited to, Drs. Jean-Marc Sabatier, Laurent Toubiana, Laurent Mucchielli in France, Martin Zizi in Belgium, Patrick Provost in Quebec,

To the healthcare professionals who said No to experimental injection. They are the heroes of this crisis.

I would like to thank:

The BonSens.org association for its financial support of the work of Pryska Ducœurjoly, the freelance science journalist with whom I wrote this book. My thanks also to Corinne Reverbel, Jean-Yves Capo and the members of BonSens.org for their comprehensive and rigorous proofreading,

Pryska Ducoeurjoly for the highly pleasant and fruitful collaboration we enjoyed throughout the writing process: it enabled me to synthesize my work and make it accessible more widely, as well as to clarify many points. Pryska's contribution was essential to making the content more reader-friendly,

Prof. Patrick Provost, Dr. Jean-Marc Sabatier and Prof. Martin Zizi for their forewords to this book,

Alexandra Henrion-Caude for her support of my work as of 2021 and for the joy, empathy and benevolence she always radiates,

All those with whom I have worked for several years: AIMSIB (French acronym for International Association for Independent and Benevolent Scientific Medicine) and notably Drs. Vincent Reliquet and Eric Menat; Dr. Michel de Lorgeril for his reading and correction of my first articles; ReinfoCovid (Drs. Carole and Louis Fouché), the CSI (Conseil Scientifique Indépendant, Independent Scientific Council) and all those who make it work, including Drs. Carole and Louis Fouché, Vincent Pavan, Emmanuelle Darles, Dr. Philippe de Chazournes, as well as the technicians and guest speakers like Pierre Chaillot, for their kindness, intelligence and our fascinating discussions,

Dr. Pierre Sonigo for the exchanges on LinkedIn before my eviction from that platform, Anne-Marie Moulin and Patrick Tort for their attentive review of my text on the role of antibodies in 2021.

In the USA
Drs. Pierre Kory, Robert W. Malone, and Peter McCullough who took part in ICS 2 (International COVID Summit) at the Marseille University Hospital Institute (IHU) in March 2022,

All those with whom I have exchanged correspondence, notably Drs. Maria Gutschi, Kevin McKernan, Jessica Rose, David Weiseman, David Speicher, the members of DRASTIC (Dedicated Research and Scientific Team Investigating COVID-19), who denounced the man-made origin of the virus, Dr. Adrian Gibbs, US Right to Know, and the Children's Health Defense team.

Forewords

The COVID-19 crisis has shaken the democracies of the contemporary world as never before. Diseases and wars in the past – two of them global – have scarred and decimated generations. But never before has a global situation affected so many people, nor seen a comparable scale of global coordination by so very few.

This unprecedented scale of coordination was made possible by communications technology, the centralization of power and the intervention of supranational firms of private consultants and pharmaceutical companies, as well as of individuals with private interests more powerful than entire nations and whose activities have endangered democratic societies.

Government management of COVID-19, allegedly based on a "Science" driven not by query, but by certainties, gave rise to a political and scientific context in which science was instrumentalized to justify an agenda more political than health-related, rather than serving informed decision-making for the purpose of protecting the public first and foremost.

It can also be said that the context created a political-pharmaceutical-medical triumvirate that resulted, in particular, in the "seizure" of governments, regulatory bodies and professional orders, particularly that of doctors. This paved the way for the manipulation of government apparatus and science, and the deregulation of approval processes for new pharmaceutical products which, facilitated and fast-tracked as it was, heedlessly exposed the population to greater health risks. The actions of this triumvirate ran counter to all the rules of medical ethics and deontology expressly designed to guide decision-making in situations such as the one we experienced with COVID-19; these include the Hippocratic Oath, the Nuremberg Code, the precautionary principle, individual risk-benefit assessment, free and informed consent, and the right of refusal.

Said actions were conducted in total impunity and with highly lucrative motivations. This probably explains why our governments ignored the pandemic emergency plans drawn up by their own public health agencies, preferring instead to put their trust in consulting firms with private interests... And, also, why they purchased experimental pharmaceutical products under confidential contracts.

In this book, Hélène Banoun takes a critical, analytical look at some of the scientific aspects of this unprecedented crisis, from various perspectives. She literally takes us out of our comfort zone, sharing with us the perspective of many independent doctors, experts and scientists, whose critical thinking is sharp, bold and at odds with the official narrative. The commitment to the well-being and health of populations on the part of Hélène and her fellow "resisters" is free of any conflict of interest and rooted in a strong social conscience, itself grounded in unshakeable moral values and profound humanity.

For these professionals, protecting the public was a non-negotiable priority. The price they paid was sometimes high, but in no way did consequences detract them from their selfless conviction to "do what must be done." More than anyone else, these professionals committed to public service have honored their sense of duty, rigor, integrity and scientific probity to ensure the highest possible quality of public service.

Governments, unfortunately, have turned a deaf ear, preferring to rely on the advice of excessively influential multinationals and lobbies.

Not only have dedicated experts and scientists highly experienced in their fields seen their analyses, criticisms and recommendations ignored, but many have been publicly reprimanded for daring to contradict the authorities. The authorities have made anti-examples of them.

My colleague Hélène Banoun, whom I had the privilege of meeting owing to this crisis, is an example of rigor, integrity, perspicacity and perseverance. Like a lighthouse, she guides us through the storm.

I hope that you, like me, will be enlightened by her insights. Happy reading!

Dr. Patrick Provost
Full Professor, Department of Microbiology-Infectiology
and Immunology,
Faculty of Medicine, Université Laval
Quebec, Canada
October 2023

This book by Dr. Hélène Banoun is undoubtedly one of the most important ever published on COVID-19, on the anti-COVID "vaccine" injections (particularly with messenger RNA) and their harmful effects on the human organism, as well as on the phenomenon of "shedding." It is a must-read for anyone interested in the SARS-CoV-2 "pandemic" and its repercussions on public health, in France and abroad. I therefore highly recommend reading this work, which is particularly enlightening for people in various disciplines, be they scientific, medical or otherwise. Readers will find here a comprehensive and realistic view of the health crisis.

On a personal note, I would like to emphasize the exceptional role embraced by Dr. Banoun from the beginning of the crisis to the present day, both in terms of her information sharing (in her capacity as a key principal in the Conseil Scientifique Indépendant or CSI, and other entities), and in scientific terms (publications in international specialist journals). Finally, I salute the courage of an extraordinary woman whose boundless dedication to the greater good of all has been exemplary.

Dr. Jean-Marc Sabatier
Research Director
CNRS (Centre National de la Recherche Scientifique), France,
Specialist in proteins, toxins
and drug design
October 2024

"Follow the Science" or how to axe the vital clash between Science and Politics …

Since first standing up and gazing at the starry heavens ever so long ago, humankind has swayed between Fear and Wonder. When faced with the inexplicable, reason resorted to the magical – to survive but one more night – seeking to muster that sense of power that was so lacking within. In birth, death, and disease in between – a sense of powerlessness overtook our reasoning.

Two million years later, for all our progress and even though science and magic are now distinct, the milestones that are birth, death and disease remain revolving doors to our most profound interrogations and primary fears. We humans are all too quick to believe in our own rationality, and we have created structures in which Science and Politics are two vectors of power.

This began a long time ago, when Priest-Kings combined the two. When blood was required to sustain dawning of the Sun, and the Son of Heaven needed an underground army to help him conquer Death.

That lasted for centuries. With the "magic" of polished glass in the shape of a lens, astronomy separated from astrology. The "Galileo affair" marked a fundamental rift between magical and scientific thinking. Despite his sentencing, Galileo Galilei had torn the curtain: measure and experimentation had overtaken political narrative. The Galileo affair didn't mark the birth of rational thought; we were rational thinkers from as far back as the Greeks and through to the Mayans, via the Babylonians, Hindus, Latins, Arabs and Polynesians. No, the Galileo affair marked the end of the absolute power of the political narrative. Drawing virgin blood was no longer necessary to appease the gods... Fear had given way to Logic.

But that beast slept lightly, with one eye open. And just when our technological revolutions are accelerating, profound forces have been awakened. Birth, death, and disease in between, provide the backdrop.

Fear has returned, stirred and invoked by the Kings of our day, amplified by our mass media. In February 2020, in a mere few days, part of humanity regressed to magical thinking... and once again blood is drawn to appease unfounded fantasy. Fearmongering – and the money behind it – appears to be winning...

Dr. Hélène Banoun is the first to launch this vital debate between Science and Politics – those two necessary vectors that must remain independent of one another, because the politicization of science means the death of both scientific process and of politics as an organizing force. A lose-lose situation is spawning, and it must absolutely be aborted.

I did not know Hélène before the disastrous management of SARS-CoV-2. Now, she is doing me, the military biodefense specialist, the honor of inviting me to write this foreword to her book.

It was the crisis that brought us together, as it did scores of other scientists in all specializations. Along with so many others, we exchange ideas in an effort to alert, to save and to explain. We are not conspirators, but free and inquisitive spirits who, overnight, found ourselves on the wrong side of the axe – attacked for precisely that, for who we are. Although our views occasionally differ, we go forward together – united in the certainty that the filter of Time consolidates Science, True Science that is...

The clash between Science and Politics must continue. And this book is one step in the right direction.

Thank you, Hélène, for writing it.

Thank You for reading it…

Dr. Martin Zizi
Mountain View, CA, USA
October 2023

Introduction

This book came to be thanks to my passionate interest in biology and my wish to share the outcomes of my research, which had enabled me to decipher the coronavirus health crisis. During that time, which shook us all to the core, I drew on my scientific literacy and the knowledge available to investigate the origin of the virus, to grasp the mechanisms of the disease and to clarify the grey areas around anti-COVID-19 vaccines.

This journey through the intricacies of our biology taught me a great deal, occasionally leading me to question the validity of certain official assertions. As time went by, these assertions increasingly seemed to me to be based more on political ideology than on scientific grounds.

The aim of this book is to provide a clear and accessible overview of the current state of knowledge, to stimulate reflection and foster critical thinking. Although the COVID-19 episode seems to belong to the past, everything points to the fact that the battle against health crises is far from over. After exploring the roots of this pandemic and delving into the biology of COVID-19 and immune mechanisms, we'll look at the challenges and risks of the new biopolitical era that is now influencing our lives.

I will first share my own research, but I will also cite the contributions of fellow scientists who share a critical vision. For further, in-depth exploration, I invite you to consult my publications and those of the experts cited. Clearly, it is impossible to cover all the related subjects, hence please forgive my omissions.

From pharmacology to evolutionary theory
My scientific career began with studies in pharmacy. During my internship, I got my first taste of the fastidious world of the laboratory. I then entered the world of research, spending seven years at the Gustave Roussy Cancer Research Hospital near Paris, where I explored anti-cancer molecular pharmacology, initially as a pharmacy intern, then as an Inserm research fellow. (Translator's note: Inserm is France's public research organization entirely dedicated to human health.)

My work focused on bacterial mutagenesis; I studied how bacterial mutants are selected in the presence of potentially anti-cancerous molecules. Bacteriology had fascinated me during my internship and my work at this stage indulged my lab interest at the "workbench."

I nonetheless chose not to pursue that path because the world of research seemed too restricted for me. I was young and looking for new kinds of experience. What's more, the laboratory director had told us that he didn't believe in pharmacology as a means of treating cancer. He was pinning all his hopes on immunotherapy, an intuition that proved correct. Our laboratory focus on anti-cancer drugs was due mainly to funding received from the pharmaceutical industry. How could I invest fully in this field knowing that research was already being driven by financial interest?

I then obtained my biology certification to become a clinical biologist. I had occasion to replace a number of lab directors overseeing medical analysis. Ultimately, life directed me towards an artistic activity. Throughout all these years, however, my interest in biology never waned.

One of my favorite subjects is the study of biology from the perspective of evolutionary theory. This theory can be applied to micro-organisms, of course. Bacteria, viruses, antibodies – the media now pay them a lot of attention, and political leaders sometimes have their own motivations for interest.[1] Are viruses really an enemy? Do antibodies "want" to protect us? The anthropomorphic vision is recurrent in political (and even scientific) discourse, but its main aim is to make us adhere to a logic of a war against viruses. I will present my biologist's point of view in the second part of the book, which focuses on understanding immunity and the mechanisms of the COVID-19 disease.

Commitment to scientific information
My passion for biology found a new outlet through writing and knowledge-sharing. My commitment to accurate scientific information took root in 2017, when France announced 11 mandatory vaccines for infants. The critical backlash to that decision challenged me. At the time, I had no set opinion on vaccines. Like most healthcare professionals, I had received no specific training on the subject of vaccines, not even for my immunology certificate. Vaccines were taken for granted and seemed to pose no scientific problem.

---

1. *Les métaphores du virus COVID-19 dans les discours d'Emmanuel Macron et de Pedro Sánchez*, Isabel Negro, Universidad Complutense de Madrid, Çedille n°19, 2021.

Intrigued, I decided to explore the subject of vaccination through the lens of biological evolution, that is, in terms of the theory of evolution. Having brushed up on virology and immunology, I published my first article[2] on the AIMSIB blog,[3] a fully independent association providing medical information. My article focused on measles vaccination. Dr. Michel de Lorgeril, a member of the AIMSIB medical committee at the time, helped me considerably to refine the scientific rigor. In the article, I asked many questions about the vaccine's efficacy. While there was no sign of aggressivity in the article on my part, I received severely critical response from an immunologist with close ties to the pharmaceutical industry. I replied to his objections item by item. Since then, it seems that I have been monitored closely on social networks, to a degree akin to milk heating on a stove.

Coincidentally, just before the COVID-19 pandemic, a severe measles epidemic broke out in Samoa. It was officially attributed to a drop in vaccination coverage. In January 2020, I published a new article, which helped prepare me intellectually for COVID-19.[4] When talk began in January 2020 of a virus of potentially pandemic proportion, I approached the matter with an *a priori* distrust of official communications by authorities. Initially, they were reassuring. But, I had been warned early on by a virologist of the potential seriousness of what lay ahead. He had identified that the virus in question was a SARS very similar to that of the 2003 epidemic; and SARS-1, although not particularly contagious, had a high fatality rate.

For my own understanding, I began to scrutinize all the official information, as I did with the 2019 measles epidemic in Samoa. Soon realizing that this pandemic was being instrumentalized, I spent a lot of time checking and rechecking certain obvious inconsistencies.

I have always taken a critical approach to my own interpretations, at least until mid-2022. Whenever new information seemed to contra-

---

2. *La vaccination anti-rougeole expliquée par une spécialiste en immunoinfectiologie,* Aimsib.org, May 26, 2019.
3. Association internationale pour une médecine scientifique indépendante et bienveillante (International Association for Independent and Benevolent Scientific Medicine), Aimsib.org.
4. *Flambée* de rougeole aux Samoa, prévenez *l'OMS et l'Unicef,* Aimsib.org, January 5, 2020.
See also: Measles and Antibody-Dependent Enhancement (ADE): History and Mechanisms, Helene Banoun, https://www.xiahepublishing.com/2472-0712/ ERHM- 2022-00018

dict my findings, I questioned my own conclusions and did further research. I scrutinized the scientific studies behind the official statements, analyzing every piece of data, including those hidden in the appendices. Invariably, I detected flaws or inconsistencies that discredited the credibility of these studies. Today, I believe that I have identified the majority of the scientific biases. I no longer systematically question my own perspective in the light of every new contradictory official statement because every time I do, I always find the same biases. What's more, I am far from alone in perceiving the instrumentalization detected.

It was only natural that I should seek to share my discoveries by publishing them on the AIMSIB website, the ResearchGate platform and LinkedIn. My first articles focused on the concept of group immunity,[5] natural immunity[6] and the sometimes paradoxical role of antibodies.[7] Many other articles followed in the three years thereafter, in a reflection nourished by the emergence of other independent publications and the networking of researchers questioning the official version.

The strength of independent scientific networks
As the months went by, probing scientists naturally sought to communicate with one another and, gradually, a network had formed – initially on social media, then through face-to-face meetings. Thanks to my LinkedIn account, created in 2020, I was able to establish ties with virologists and doctors. My presence on that platform (owned by Microsoft) was short-lived: my account was abruptly deleted in May 2021 after I shared a post calling for the raw data of the Israeli healthcare system to be made public. I won't dwell on the barrage of censorship and computer-sabotage incidents that I endured. Admittedly, this eviction is a small loss compared with the number of doctors and nurses who were suspended or disbarred from practice for treating patients or publicly opposing official health policy.

In October 2020, during the second lockdown, I had the opportunity to meet Dr. Louis Fouché, an anaesthetist. At the time, he was working

---

5. *Vaccin anti-COVID-19 et immunité de groupe, c'est non... et encore non*, Aimsib.org, May 3, 2020.
6. *COVID19: Cross-Immunity with Other Coronaviruses, Immunopathological Phenomena*, ResearchGate, January 2020.
7. *Covid graves, admettre l'existence des anticorps facilitateurs*, Aimsib.org, August 23, 2020.

at the Hôpital de la Conception in Marseille, less than a kilometer from my home. During the first wave of confinement, like everyone else in France he was allowed to venture no further than one kilometer from his home, later upped to a radius of 10 kilometers in October 2020. At the time of our meeting, he was laying the ground for a new organization called ReinfoCovid, uniting some 400 doctors, researchers, other healthcare professionals and citizens, with the aim of promoting a different health policy. This collective later federated into Coordination Santé Libre,[8] or Free Health Coordination, which mainly brought together doctors who had defied the official ban on COVID treatment. This ban on treatment is still in effect as I write these lines, since the Vidal website makes no mention of the early ambulatory treatment successfully carried out at the IHU (University Hospital Institute) in Marseille and recommended by Coordination Santé Libre, along with other doctors around the world, the Front Line COVID-19 Critical Care Alliance (FLCCC) in the USA, and the Canadian COVID-19 Care Alliance (CCCA) in Canada.

In January 2021, Coordination Santé Libre doctors decided to establish an independent scientific council to disseminate "high-level scientific information totally independent of any financial or political influence." The aim was to promote debate and provide a viewpoint contesting the opinions and recommendations of the governmental scientific council ...

The challenges to this new Conseil Scientifique Indépendant, hereafter CSI,[9] began in April 2021. The first two programs were aired on Youtube and quickly censored. The CSI continued to air on Crowdbunker, an independent platform.[10] One year later, we held a live broadcast to a packed house of 650 participants in Le Fossat, near Toulouse. Two years later, celebrating CSI's 100th broadcast in May 2023, 1,700 citizens and scientists met in the town of Saintes in southwest France, reuniting there again one year later for the 150th broadcast in 2024. In the overall context of unprecedented censorship during COVID-19, CSI's growing notoriety enabled scientific debate to emerge among

---

8. https://childrenshealthdefense.eu/eu-affairs/espoir-de-changement-de-gestion-sanitaire-grace-a-la-coordination-de-milliers-de-medecins-scientifiques-et-elus-independants-france/?lang=fr
9. https://www.conseil-scientifique-independant.org
10. https://crowdbunker.com/@CSI

the general public thanks to the high-quality presentations and speakers featured.

In the meantime, I continued to publish the progress of my work on the AIMSIB blog and took part in their annual congresses, appreciating the fruitful encounters there.

Initially working in isolation, researchers from various disciplines were finally able to join forces and created a robust network, continually exchanging views on all aspects of health. Alongside doctors, our network today comprises statisticians, epidemiologists, modelers, data processors, clinical trial specialists, computer scientists, biologists, historians, lawyers, sociologists, anthropologists, psychologists, and many others. Within the CSI, we are all volunteers, as are those who run the sites and manage the technical aspects, particularly the video broadcasting crew.

All publications by independent scientists are obviously closely examined by the authorities and fact-checkers, who pounce on the slightest inaccuracy. There is zero tolerance for error or approximation: everything we say or publish must be rigorously sourced and referenced in the scientific literature.

Over the past four years (2020-2024), in contrast to the obvious and repeated contradictions of the official discourse, the coherence of the CSI discourse has been validated, with only minor corrections of no particular consequence. Another fine example of this scientific pluridisciplinary cooperation is the collective work on *The COVID Doxa* (*La Doxa du COVID-19*), published in January 2022. It brings together no fewer than 30 contributors from all walks of life, under the direction of Laurent Mucchielli, sociologist and director of research at the CNRS, the National Scientific Research Council in France.

Other collaborative groups and associations have grown out of the crisis. One such, beginning in October 2020, is the association BonSens.org, working alongside Prof. Christian Perronne, which re-informs the general public about the various issues raised by this crisis, and initiates legal action.

Science or scientism ?

Y a-t-il une erreur qu'ILS n'ont pas commise ?[11] (*Is there a mistake THEY haven't made?*) is the title of the best-selling book authored by Prof. Christian Perronne,[12] also vice-president of the BonSens.org association. It eloquently sums up the results of our collective action and underscores the utter discrepancy between official claims and the contents of impartial, high-quality scientific publications since the beginning of 2020. This discrepancy reflects the contrast between science and scientism. Understanding the distinction between the two has become vital if the general public is to find its way through the deluge of information that abounds. The concern of science is to produce objective, verifiable knowledge. Scientism, on the other hand, is an ideological posture that instrumentalizes science for its own purposes. It takes the "consensus" reached by specialists in each discipline at face value and does everything in its power to confirm it. The COVID-19 crisis demonstrated that the so-called consensus accepted by the scientific community simply refers to the current state of knowledge agreed upon by a few opinion leaders, namely experts emulated by their colleagues and echoed by the media and politicians. This scientific consensus is far from systematic "truth."

In a normal process of scientific development, the consensus is called into question when contested by observed data, compelling a revision of the theory, or even a paradigm change, as philosopher and historian of science Thomas Kuhn explains in *The Structure of Scientific Revolutions* (1962). "The development begins with the awareness of an anomaly, that is to say, with the discovery of a new paradigm, the impression that nature, in one way or another, contradicts the results expected within the paradigm that governs normal science."

This paradigm shift does not occur without some resistance, often generating a "scientific crisis," as the Copernican Revolution demonstrated. Scientists tend to consider the provisional consensus as a revealed "truth," making it virtually impossible to criticize said "truth" without being accused of heresy and virtually ex-communicated, as in the days of the Inquisition. Yet scientific truth is never a definitive, once-and-for-all result, because knowledge creation is an infinite

---

11. *Y a-t-il une erreur qu'ils n'ont pas commise ?* Christian Perronne, Albin Michel, June 2020.
12. Former head of the infectious and tropical diseases department at the Raymond-Poincaré hospital in Garches, France. His book is currently available only in French.

dynamic. Who can claim to have reached the ultimate in knowledge or in the understanding of a phenomenon? The scientific approach is not about revealing a hidden truth pre-existing all research, still less about imposing it. It involves continuous comparison between observation and theory, based on hypotheses derived from the theory; where there is a discrepancy between observations and a theory, the theory needs to be modified, not the observations rejected.

In the 19th century, the accelerated development of the natural sciences brought with it a new approach to scientific work, developed both by philosophers (notably Auguste Comte) and scientists (from various disciplines), who posited scientific knowledge as the very form of all objective rational knowledge of phenomena. It is this approach, this ideology of Science as Knowledge or absolute Truth, that is generally referred to as scientism. As the modern state (born of bourgeois revolutions) has always sought to rationalize its domination, and today strives to do so more than ever, scientism is necessarily linked to State interest, in other words it is invoked in the interests of power.

Scientism in health is marked by the superiority of the hard sciences over the human sciences, by the hegemony of statistics and laboratory results, by a departure from the clinical diagnosis represented by the medical consultation and the "*colloque singulier*"[13] that protects medical confidentiality, as well as by mathematical modeling that can ignore field data.

In short, scientism has become a dogmatic value system that ultimately tends to distance itself from true knowledge of reality. As the philosopher Louis Jugnet (1913-1973) wrote, "Scientism is [...] the imperialism of laboratory science in all areas of human thought and consciousness."

Biopolitics: the common thread
In the course of my work, I came to realize that the irrational manner in which the COVID-19 crisis was managed could ultimately be explained by the concept of "biopolitics." This notion was conceived by the French philosopher Michel Foucault to explain how power is exercised over human populations, no longer solely within territorial limits, but on a global scale.

---

13. In medicine, the French expression "*colloque singulier*" refers to the primacy of the doctor-patient relationship, which underpins a large part of medical practice and protects medical confidentiality in particular.

Biopolitics originated with the industrial revolution, when populations came to be considered as sources of wealth for nations, hence requiring their control. In terms of health, this meant maintaining populations in a condition capable of producing and reproducing, to ensure their own productivity and the nation's prosperity. Vaccination developed around this time, ostensibly to control epidemics. Yet it is only in our era of globalized capitalism that vaccination has reached peak development.

The concept of biopolitics allows us to grasp the logic at work behind the formulation of health policies, the instrumentalization of science as a means of attaining other objectives, and the intrusive effects of biopower in our lives.

With the COVID-19 crisis, we have moved into a higher scheme of control, the control of bodies leading to the control of minds through a form of "terror by health." Biopower has understood that people consumed by fear are less likely to revolt and can continue to be exploited as productive bodies.

I will explain how biopolitics is now moving away from its original aim of keeping populations in a capacity to produce and reproduce: paradoxically, it is seriously deteriorating their health. In the third part of this book, I will present the undesirable effects of anti-COVID-19 vaccines and then in the final part, the risks of gene therapy. These therapies are billed as "revolutionary progress." We shall see that this is far from proven.

The pandemic has undoubtedly accelerated progress in immunology, virology and our understanding of virus evolution. It has also enabled those who were skeptical of the narrative from the outset to understand the biopolitical stakes involved, and to be better prepared in the future to react to decisions taken by the authorities, not only in the field of health.

Will the ecological and economic crises looming over us be tackled by means of the same logic, ostensibly to ensure safety yet in fact aimed at replicating the economic system and its biopolitical benchmarks to the detriment of people's health?

While remaining focused on my specialty, I hope with this book to nourish the vigilance of so-called "ordinary" people, non-specialists. For, indeed, biopolitics now extends its influence into many areas of our lives.

How is scientific knowledge formed?

Before getting to the heart of the matter, I would like to take a detour into the teeming world of scientific publication, to understand how "the current state of scientific knowledge," an expression which designates the scientific world's consensus on a subject, is elaborated. The essence of my work during the three years of the COVID-19 crisis was precisely to ascertain this state of knowledge, based on my reading of the literature and with the highest possible degree of intellectual integrity. My aim was to provide scientifically validated information on the origin of the pandemic, its evolution, our understanding of the disease and its treatment. As you will see throughout this book, this state of knowledge has little in common with the official narrative.

The long process of publication

The production of scientific knowledge obeys a rigorous and structured process. To begin with, researchers must obtain funding for their research projects. This involves responding to calls for tender, either public or private, and submitting detailed documentation on research protocols. In France, for example, researchers exert a great deal of their energy to filling out applications to the national research agency ANR (Agence nationale de la recherche), which funds project-based research.

Once the research has been carried out and the experiments conducted, their results need to be published. This involves finding a journal to which to submit an article for publication. The publication process is crucial, given that successful research funding and career advancement depend to a large extent on the number of publications and citations featuring in international journals.

Publication comes at a cost, however. The vast majority of publishers charge publication fees, which can be as high as €11,000 in prestigious journals such as *Nature*. That is the price that *Nature* charges for open-access articles.[14] Otherwise, readers have to buy the article(s) or subscribe to the journal. Consequently, a research team can only publish if its subject is part of a funded project. In passing, I would like to thank AIMSIB for financing the publication costs of my last article

---

14. *Open Access Comes to Selective Journal*, *Inside Higher Ed*, November 23, 2020.

in the *International Journal of Molecular Sciences*[15] and BonSens.org for my last article in *Current Issues in Molecular Biology*.

Peer-reviewed journals: the end of hegemony?
In the world of publishing, we need to distinguish between peer-reviewed journals and preprint journals, which are mostly websites.

Scientific journals operate on a *peer-review* basis. This means that when a researcher submits an article to a journal, it is analyzed by other experts in the same field (peers) to assess its quality, originality and relevance. The peers then give their assessment, make suggestions for improvement and, finally, decide whether or not to authorize publication of the article.

The aim of the peer-review process is to ensure that only high-quality work is published, and it is considered to be an essential element of rigorous scientific research. In reality, however, this criterion is vanishing: the majority of studies published appear to be false, according to Professor of Medicine John Ioannidis, in a 2005 article,[16] owing to study-design errors, selection bias and other methodological problems. You have all heard of *The Lancet* and the study that claimed that hydroxychloroquine was toxic and ineffective on COVID-19: those data were simply fabricated. Still, *The Lancet* continues to publish regardless, as though nothing had happened. The *NEJM (New England Journal of Medicine)* has also published dubious studies. The most prestigious scientific journals, often owned by large groups with close ties to the pharmaceutical industry, have become lucrative businesses, profiting from their publications. They are not immune to conflicts of interest,[17] which can influence their selection of articles, sometimes favoring less rigorous work or censoring other research. This has been my experience with these peer-reviewed journals.

In the second part of this book, I will recall the story of my article *Evolution of SARS-CoV-2* in 2021 in *Nephron*. In that instance, with

15.H. Banoun, *mRNA: Vaccine or Gene Therapy? The Safety Regulatory Issues, Int. J. Mol. Sci.* 2023, 24, 10514.
16. *Why most published research findings are false*, JP Ioannidis, PLoS Med. 2005 Aug.2(8): e124. doi: 10.1371/journal, Pmed.0020124. Epub 2005 Aug 30. Erratum in: PLoS Med. 2022 Aug 25;19(8):e1004085. PMID: 16060722; PMCID: PMC1182327.
17. *Justifying conflicts of interest in medical journals: a very bad idea, BMJ,* 2015.

the publication having been cited by other studies I received invitations to re-read articles on the same subject. I discovered that some articles of mediocre quality were ultimately published despite unfavorable reviews, even in prestigious journals. Clearly, these journals give in to the financial gain of publishing a large number of works, to the detriment of the rigorous selection that was once the hallmark of their reputation.

Among the exceptions, The *BMJ (British Medical Journal)* is one of the most honest, its editor Peter Doshi having criticized the management of the pandemic on many occasions. This journal publishes the work of doctors and scientists who do not publish elsewhere, and the articles are translated in a manner accessible to readers who don't master English.

Some publications that claim to be independent do not enjoy total freedom insofar as editors and reviewers are academics subject to the same public/private tenders for their research work. The Multidisciplinary Digital Publishing Institute (MDPI), a Swiss-based publisher of several journals, has based its business model on a more critical editorial line, open-access distribution and serious peer review. This is appreciated by researchers who do not adhere to the official "scientific consensus." This publisher has been accused by some scientists of being part of the "predatory journals," no doubt because he rocks the boat somewhat. Despite his denials to the contrary, these publications are also fee-based.

What is a "predatory journal"? A predatory journal is a scientific medium that exploits the open-access publication model for financial gain by charging publication fees. This type of journal does not respect peer-review standards and contributes to flooding scientific literature with low-quality work, undermining the credibility of open-access publication.

To conclude on peer-reviewed journals, it is important to know that all the studies they publish are listed on an international database called Pubmed. Though a must in the field of research, this database is not neutral insofar as it is an official service of the United States National Library of Medicine, controlled by the US National Institutes of Health. Only quality journals are indexed. Those considered too far outside the doxa are simply not referenced. In other words, you will not find everything on Pubmed, but it remains a valuable base from which to consult a large number of scientific references. Pubmed provides a search tool accessible to all, enabling you to find out more about the vast world of science.

The rise of preprints

Increasingly, researchers are choosing to submit their articles on preprint (or prepublication) sites, before peer review. The largest pre-publication sites make an initial selection, however, and reject articles that do not adhere to the dominant line. They are often associated with powerful groups. For example, MedRXiv and BioRxiv are sponsored by the Chan Zuckerberg Initiative, created in 2015 by Facebook boss Mark Zuckerberg and his wife, Priscilla Chan. The SSRN prepublication site is owned by Elsevier, whose main shareholders are BlackRock, Vanguard and major banks.[18]

This being the case, it is necessary to turn to independent, if less consulted, prepublication sites. Some are more open than others, such as Qeios and Research Square, while others are non-selective, such as OSF, a prepublication site that does not censor work. I would like to give special mention to Qeios, which seeks out top reviewers (and does so free of charge for the first article submitted).

These preprint sites should not be confused with scientific blogging platforms such as ResearchGate, where you can have a personal page and publish whatever you like. I have done this regularly in recent years to make my work more accessible.

With the development of the Internet, and especially since COVID-19, preprints have become more prevalent, with most articles available free of charge.

There are tens of thousands of specialist journals out there; if preprints are enjoying a certain boom period, it is also because peer-reviewed journals have reached their limits in terms of the credibility of the articles they publish... The COVID-19 crisis superbly illustrated how the major scientific journals have gone adrift. They used to be to science what the mass media are to the news. As for preprints, they give visibility to research with divergent or critical conclusions, which are key to scientific debate in any case even if, in the final analysis, the review process remains essential to validating any publication.

---

18. MarketScreener.com, Company Reed Elsevier plc.

Why is publishing in a peer-reviewed journal so grueling?

First of all, you need to posit the right question. It must be scientifically relevant and aptly constructed. Then you have to answer it by analyzing and synthesizing a large number of publications – not having a lab at my disposal, I can't conduct experiments. This phase, the crafting of a good question and a robust answer, is particularly stimulating. Next, it's time to present the arguments, justifying each word or assertion with previously published work. Ultimately, it comes time to find the right journal to which to submit your work, but that's not the end of the road: if the first draft isn't rejected, the text will be examined by reviewers selected by the publisher and experts in the field. On return of their reviews, a complete rewrite of the text is often required, both in terms of content and form, including the challenge of managing references to articles cited and sometimes requiring a second, if minor, revision. Working this process can take several months. I have found it best to submit the first draft on a prepublication site such as Qeios, which itself seeks critical review to greatly improve the draft. Incidentally, the proofreading work by reviewers is conducted entirely on a voluntary basis, to the sole financial benefit of the publication. The proofreading also benefits the authors, of course, who would not be able to publish without this service. This also explains why researchers accept this service free of charge; it's a "win-win" situation when it comes their turn to publish.

For my article *Evolution of SARS-CoV-2*, published in 2021 in Nephron, I have to admit that I struggled hard to draft my text in the decidedly distinctive style of scientific writing. Then I had to double up my efforts to respond to the criticisms of the two virologists appointed by the editor to proofread my work. Just before Christmas 2020, I even considered giving up, but the editor encouraged me to tread on. The truth is, I had promised myself I would never do this again. Since then, I have published a few more articles, the latest for *MDPI*, a journal also referenced in the Pubmed database. After this new article, however, on the sensitive subject of "mRNA regulation," I renewed my promise to myself to never again publish in peer-reviewed journals.

Guide to scientific references

You will find in this book a wealth of sources to substantiate my analyses. The job of referencing is particularly restrictive in the context of scientific publications, and it is much more flexible when it comes to personal publications. I have chosen to cite only essential or useful references. Readers seeking more details can refer to my published articles, all of which are referenced throughout the book.

"Further reading" inserts: each chapter of this book is based on one or more publications that I authored during the health crisis. You will find them with their title and publication date at the end of each chapter. They will help you to find all the scientific references.

Footnotes: these bring together other more recent or major references in the scientific log of the COVID-19 crisis. Many sources are from PubMed. Readers can easily access them by means of a PubMed identifier number (PMID), avoiding the need to recopy the title of the publication to access it. You can type "PMID study number" directly into the search engine.

To facilitate access to certain sources, I have used a function that shortens hypertext links ("Tiny URL"). These short links generally begin with "http://tiny.cc" followed by the topic. Example: the video of the conference on "The origin of the COVID-19 virus," presented at the International COVID-19 Summit 2022, is available at http://tiny.cc/ICS-origine.

You can also find all my publications, past and future, via:
https://www.researchgate.net/profile/Helene-Banoun
http://tiny.cc/HeleneBanoun.

Articles in French on the Aimsib.org site are also available there in English (see feature in the top left-hand corner).

A brief chronology

Select milestones in the biopolitical genesis of the health crisis:

1974: The World Health Organization (WHO) adopts its Expanded Program on Immunization (EPI), with the aim of extending access to all available vaccinations (there were six at the time) to every child on the planet by the year 2000.

1983: Ralph Baric, from the University of North Carolina (USA), begins work on coronaviruses. (No coronavirus dangerous to humans is known at the time).

1986: According to a law passed in the United States (H.R.5546 - National Childhood Vaccine Injury Act of 1986, https://www.congress.gov/bill/99th-congress/house-bill/5546), manufacturers are no longer liable for adverse reactions (ARs) to vaccines on the pediatric vaccine schedule and for pregnant women. The exoneration from liability also applies to ARs notified in package inserts. In Europe, manufacturers remain civilly liable for vaccine defects but may avoid paying compensation for "hidden defects." No further clarification has been given about the specific meaning or legal scope of a "hidden defect" in a vaccine.

1987: Baric obtains funding to study coronavirus-induced myocarditis in rabbits.

2001: Baric receives funding for reverse genetics on coronaviruses and a live attenuated vaccine candidate.

June 2009: The WHO declares the H1N1 pandemic.

September 2009: The EMA (European Medicines Agency) excludes gene vaccines (DNA and RNA) against infectious diseases from the regulation of gene therapy products (GTP).

2013: DARPA, the research agency of the US Department of Defense, awards $25 million to Moderna for mRNA vaccine research. The FDA (Food and Drug Administration) confirms that GTP regulation does not apply to infectious disease vaccines.

2015: Baric and Shi, chief virologist at the Wuhan laboratory, create a chimeric SARS virus adapted to humans.

2017: Eight new chimeras are published by Baric and Shi. A simulation is published of a lab-leaked coronavirus SARS pandemic.

January 10, 2020: Start of development of Pfizer's BNT162b2 vaccine.

January 11, 2020: Publication of the complete Wuhan SARS-CoV-2 sequence.

January 13, 2020: In France, hydroxychloroquine is classified as a poisonous substance, restricting dispensing to prescription only.

January 23, 2020: Containment in Wuhan and Hubei.

March 11, 2020: Declaration of COVID-19 pandemic by the WHO.

March 14, 2020: Decision on first containment measure in France. In California, on March 19, 2020.

October 22, 2020: FDA publishes list of adverse events to watch out for in future COVID-19 vaccines. December 2020: FDA approves Pfizer's COVID-19 vaccine (12/11/2020) and EMA (12/21/2020).

June 9, 2021: In France, a health pass is required to access certain areas.

August 5, 2021: COVID-19 vaccines are made mandatory in France for healthcare workers and professionals considered as such, as well as for civil and military security personnel. In the United States, COVID-19 vaccines become mandatory for federal employees, including military personnel, and certain private-sector employees.

January 24, 2022: In France, a vaccination pass becomes mandatory for access to certain places, to public transport and public activities, including to extracurricular school activities.

March 14, 2022: End of vaccination pass obligation in France and travel restrictions (to the UK and within the Schengen area).

May 5, 2023: The WHO declares the end of the COVID-19 pandemic emergency but continues to authorize emergency use COVID-19 vaccines.

PART I

THE ORIGINS OF THE PANDEMIC

Since 2020, the question of whether the origin of the COVID-19 virus was natural or unnatural has been the subject of bitter debate. Quite frankly, I think it impossible for a non-scientist to develop a clear idea of the origin of the pandemic. Scientists themselves have to spend a great deal of time gathering the material for their reflections, and a great deal of energy analyzing it. The virologists, the bolder among them, who have spoken out publicly have always done so half-heartedly, if at all. This didn't help the journalists who, although they were meant to provide for debate open to contradiction, limited themselves to relaying the official narrative. As for the general public, finding the right information obviously proved extremely difficult.

I was fortunate to benefit from the confidence of a virologist. From the very start of the pandemic, he was adamant that the origin of the virus was not natural. At the time, I was not ready to accept that idea. It took me quite a while to come round to the artificial-virus hypothesis. It has to be said that, in 2020, I knew next to nothing about the history of coronavirus research, rich though it was. I didn't know about the evolution of "reverse genetic" techniques. As a biologist and in the light of evolutionary theory I believed that such a "successful" virus, meaning one so well adapted to humans and so contagious, could not be produced in a laboratory. I was a long way from scientific reality.

I began to gather data from virology research, but also elements of the political context, which gradually led me to radically change my point of view. I soon realized that I had to look beyond the strictly scientific angle and integrate the concept of "biopolitics."

In autumn 2023, as I write these lines, there is still a great deal of confusion about the origin of the virus, fueled by the mainstream media, particularly in France. But the media aren't the only ones responsible: leading international scientists are playing a major hand in the misinformation.

A good summary of the state of the art was given in April 2023 by Adrian Gibbs,[19] an Australian professor emeritus of virology, retired and therefore... free to speak his mind. His article concludes that there is no evidence for the animal origin of the SARS-CoV-2 virus, the initial official hypothesis. No one has been able to demonstrate a natural passage from bats to humans involving intermediate animal hosts. The most likely cause to date is genetic manipulation.

Adrian Gibbs looks back on a landmark article: *The Proximal Origin of SARS-CoV-2,*[20] published in the prestigious journal *Nature*. In March 2020, this paper helped establish the hypothesis of the virus's natural origin. It spread like wildfire, being downloaded more than 5.7 million times, and cited in 2,650 scientific articles! Gibbs reveals that the first version asserted almost the opposite of the published conclusion. We learn that it was rewritten under political pressure at the highest level. Declassified emails attest to this, obtained thanks to a FOIA (Freedom of Information Act) request filed by the US Right to Know association. These emails contain exchanges between several scientists and high-ranking personalities: Jeremy Farrar, Director of the Wellcome Trust, a powerful British foundation dedicated to medical research, was since appointed WHO Chief Scientist in 2023; Anthony Fauci,[21] Director of the National Institute of Allergy and Infectious Diseases (NIAID) in the United States and White House advisor on the COVID-19 crisis; Francis Collins, Director of the National Institutes of Health (NIH).[22] All of them are said to have been very involved in these discussions with a view to influencing the study's authors.[23]

---

19. *How did SARS-CoV-2 get from bats to humans? Summary of a talk to the Australian National University Emeritus Faculty on 19 April 2023*, by Adrian Gibbs.
20. *The Proximal Origin of SARS-CoV-2*, K.G. Andersen, A. Rambaut, W.I.Lipkin, et al., *Nat Med*, 2020.
21. Director of the National institute of allergy and infectious diseases (NIAID) from 1984 to December 2022, Fauci had worked at the NIH since 1968. He retired at the age of 82.
22. From 2009 to December 2021. The National Institutes of Health (NIH) is a US government agency dedicated to medical and biomedical research. They are part of the US Department of Health and Human Services.
23. Kristian Andersen, author of *The Proximal Origin of SARS-CoV-2*, admitted that Fauci "incited" him to write the article in order to "disprove" the laboratory leak theory. Press release of June 23, 2023, from the Committee on Oversight and Reform (www.oversight.house.gov).

Declassified e-mails show that all the scientists involved in the exchanges were aware of a molecular peculiarity in the SARS-CoV-2 genome, the furin cleavage site. They all understood that this particularity favors infection and, above all, that it cannot be of natural origin. In the end, the authors chose to distort reality. Clearly, their position was influenced by a biopolitical logic embodied by Anthony Fauci, Francis Collins and Jeremy Farrar.

One month earlier, Jeremy Farrar condemned "conspiracy theories suggesting that COVID-19 has no natural origin" in a tribune published in *The Lancet* in February 2020, along with 26 other scientists. Here again, the scientists are not neutral: in September 2021, *The Telegraph*[24] revealed that all but one of the signatories had links with Wuhan researchers, including Jeremy Farrar...

Anthony Fauci's role in the genesis of the SARS-CoV-2 crisis soon became pivotal. In January 2022, US Senator Rand Paul made serious accusations against the Director of the NIAID during a public US Senate hearing on the management of the crisis.[25] According to Rand Paul, Fauci was aware of the gain-of-function experiments on coronaviruses by American NGO EcoHealth Alliance, funded by the NIH and conducted in partnership with the Wuhan Institute of Virology.

Fauci denies having played any role whatsoever in financing these controversial manipulations. Nonetheless, declassified documents show that these experiments were indeed conducted under the aegis of EcoHealth Alliance at the Wuhan laboratory and, above all, that they may have led to the creation of SARS-CoV-2... What did this research consist of? That's exactly what we're going to find out together here in Part 1.

---

24. *Revealed: How scientists who dismissed Wuhan lab theory are linked to Chinese researchers*, Sarah Knapton, September 10, 2021, Telegraph. co.uk.
25. *États-Unis : le sénateur Rand Paul charge le Dr. Fauci : « Il est une menace pour les Américains»*, FranceSoir.fr, January 12, 2022.

1.1 The surge of gain-of-function experimentation

In the same way that governments seek to anticipate economic crises with bank stress tests, governments are launching research programs to prevent emerging virus pandemics. Their aim is to protect populations by anticipating viral mutation phenomena on the one hand, and the health response on the other, in particular with medicines and vaccines. Sovereign states, in collaboration with supranational organizations and non-governmental organizations (NGOs), also conduct pandemic simulations. These scenarios are discussed at the end of this section.

As part of pandemic-prevention policy, the past two decades have seen the development of a particularly large number of virus research programs. They are carried out in the secrecy of high-security laboratories (often classified BSL-4).[26] Among the new genetic manipulation tools, gain-of-function technology in particular has been applied and developed, notably on coronaviruses. What does this involve?

Anticipating virus mutations

The term "gain of function" (GoF) was coined to describe experiments designed to explore how a pathogen can acquire an additional function to adapt to its environment, or even become pandemic, i.e. capable of infecting humans and spreading effectively across the globe.

Some scientists believe that they can anticipate the natural evolution of viruses, through various types of manipulation that reproduce what can happen in nature. In the laboratory, deliberate infection of humans is not allowed, of course, although a virus may accidentally be transferred from a cell culture or an animal to humans and thus adapt to them. On the other hand, human cell cultures can be infected for this purpose and, by that token, adaptation of a virus to humans can be studied or forced.

To obtain functional gains, we can traditionally:

– cultivate micro-organisms (bacteria or viruses) on animal or human cells and pass them from cell to cell

---

26. This is the highest level of security, but coronaviruses can be handled in BSL-3 or even BSL-2, https:/ /consteril.com/biosafety- level-guidance-COVID-19-research.

– infect animals and pass the micro-organism from animal to animal (*serial passage*).

These manipulations in the laboratory aim to increase transmissibility, pathogenicity and host tropism (which animal can be infected?) by exerting selection pressure on the micro-organism. Selection pressure consists in selecting mutant viruses that can adapt to a new host (cell or animal). Concretely, within a virus culture on cells or in an infected animal, there are always billions of *virions* (individual viruses) and among them mutants, some of which will spontaneously adapt to a host never before encountered by the virus. These mutations, capable of increasing pathogenicity or transmissibility, are then sought out and selected. With the development of molecular biology techniques, it is now possible to produce mutations at will, without waiting for them to appear spontaneously (reverse genetics). The latest of these techniques now even makes it possible to synthesize the complete genome of a virus.

Twenty years of research

Gain-of-function experiments began in the early 21st century. The fear that an avian flu virus could one day cause a human pandemic led two laboratories in the US to modify the H5N1 virus. The aim was to see whether the virus could evolve to be transmitted from birds to humans, using the ferret, a well-established experimental model for bird-to-human transmission. The two laboratories, using different approaches, succeeded in isolating viruses that could spread from ferret to ferret,[27] by aerosol, i.e. in the air.

Their attempts to publish these results in 2012 were ultimately successful and sparked the first major debate on so-called gain-of-function (GoF) experiments on pathogens with pandemic potential. Safety is obviously a key concern. The accidental release of a highly transmissible, highly pathogenic virus could lead to a potentially deadly global pandemic. Authorities also feared that publication of such an experiment would provide bioterrorists with an instruction manual for reproducing GoF and releasing dangerous biological agents. The results were finally published in 2012.

---

27. *Rethinking Gain-of-Function Experiments in the Context of the COVID-19 Pandemic*, M.J. Imperiale, A. Casadevall, mBio., 2020, PMID 32769091.

First moratorium

In 2014, several breaches of safety protocols in US laboratories were uncovered: vials of smallpox virus were left abandoned in a storeroom at the National Institutes of Health (NIH), dozens of Americans working at the Centers for Disease Control and Prevention (CDC) were potentially exposed to the anthrax bacillus, samples of ordinary flu virus were contaminated by the H5N1 virus mistakenly sent by the CDC... More than 200 scientists took up the cause and succeeded in stopping the experiments on functional gains.

A moratorium on GoF experiments on influenza, MERS and SARS viruses (the latter two diseases being caused by coronaviruses) was decided on October 17, 2014, across the Atlantic under Obama's mandate: "No new US government funding will be provided for gain-of-function research projects that can be reasonably thought to confer attributes to influenza, MERS, or SARS viruses such that the virus would have increased pathogenicity and/or transmissibility in mammals via the respiratory route. The pause in research funding does not apply to the characterization or testing of naturally occurring influenza, MERS (camel coronavirus) and SARS viruses, unless the tests are reasonably expected to increase transmissibility and/or pathogenicity."

GoF, a biopolitical issue

It could have all ended there, but GoF supporters weren't letting up. On December 19, 2017, under President Trump, NIH director Francis Collins lifted the moratorium,[28] and promised a safer framework: "GoF research is important to help us identify, understand and develop effective strategies and countermeasures against rapidly evolving pathogens that pose a threat to public health, he wrote in a press release (...). We have a responsibility to ensure that research into infectious agents is conducted in a responsible manner, and to consider the potential biosafety and biosecurity risks associated with such research.

This lifting of the moratorium came at a time when the Secretary of the Department of Health and Human Services was resigning. The position remained vacant until January 2018. The NIH and the extremely

---

28. *NIH Lifts Funding Pause on Gain-of-Function Research, Press release*, December 19, 2017.

powerful Anthony Fauci, previously mentioned in the introduction, took advantage of this context to occupy the vacant political space and, behind the scenes, relaunch GoF funding.

Anthony Fauci is a key figure in the US healthcare system. He has defended GoF research from the start, declaring in 2012 that "the risk-benefit ratio of this research is clearly in society's favor." On what grounds in favor – scientific argument or state interest in terms of health? For Fauci: "Nature itself is the most dangerous bioterrorist ..." A typically biopolitical statement justifying decision-making that could potentially be risky for public health.

Senators Ron Johnson and Rand Paul, who served on the Committee on Homeland Security and Governmental Affairs that contributed to the 2014 moratorium, were back at it again in 2020 and 2021. They accused Anthony Fauci of allowing GoF funding on coronaviruses.

A scientific illusion?
The research world was astonished to discover that the moratorium on gains in function had been lifted and appeared divided on the issue.[29] Supporters of these experiments argued that they could facilitate vaccine development and provide a better understanding of the molecular mechanisms of pandemic agents. Other researchers are more skeptical: "We can't even predict what current strains of seasonal flu will do from one season to the next," Ian Mackay from the University of Queensland in Australia explained. "Instead of focusing on understanding these viruses and improving vaccines, people prefer to worry about viruses that haven't yet become transmissible and may never do so."

In fact, isn't it presumptuous to try to anticipate the evolution of a virus through laboratory experiments? From my point of view, the attempt is doomed to failure insofar as it is impossible to reproduce *in vitro* the natural environment of a microorganism, with its multiple and complex interactions. This is also the opinion of Simon Wain-Hobson,[30] a professor at the Institut Pasteur. According to him, there are "a host of very detailed virological arguments" explaining why it is virtually

---

29. *Ban on gain-of-function studies ends*, Talha Burki, *The Lancet Infectious Diseases*. 2018. PMID 2941296.

30. *Gain-of-function research can't deliver pandemic predictions. Are there alternatives?*, Simon Wain-Hobson, *Bulletin of Atomic Scientists*, June 27, 2022.

impossible to predict pandemics: "Such experiments can identify mutations that may affect the characteristics of pathogens, but there is no guarantee that the next pandemic virus will follow one of the genetic roadmaps that gain-of-function research has mapped out."

Further reading
Origin of the COVID-19 virus, Hélène Banoun, update April 1, 2022.

What is meant by "natural" and "synthetic" origin?

Natural origin: in this case, the virus is a zoonotic (animal) virus capable of infecting humans and causing a pandemic, i.e. with the ability to be transmitted immediately and very efficiently from human to human. In the case of MERS (coronavirus camel "flu") and Ebola (hemorrhagic fever virus), sporadic spillover epidemics occur, but no pandemic. The SARS-CoV epidemic of 2003 may have begun with several repeated animal-to-human transmissions from a wild animal, the civet cat.

Artificial or synthetic origin: a bat virus that has been developed in the laboratory (on cell lines and in animals) and then escaped. This virus may have undergone deliberate modification (meaning human intervention to alter its sequence, or even total synthesis from a sequence modified from those known) or involuntary modification (by passages on cell cultures). In all cases, there is an obligatory passage on cultured cells. The origin of a virus is therefore never 100% synthetic, but rather it is the cells that enable it to "exist": if the genomic sequence of a virus is synthesized in the laboratory, this sequence must be injected into a cell to produce the first virus resulting from this manipulation.

1.2 Origin of the COVID-19 virus: a laboratory leak?

The first doubts about the natural origin of the virus emerged as of January 2020.

Following the publication of the complete SARS-CoV-2 genome sequence by the Chinese, virologists noticed some surprising molecular features in comparison with previously known coronaviruses. These are found on its Spike protein, enabling it to bind to human molecules. For the record, Spike proteins are located on the surface of coronavirus membranes, most prominently and in abundance. These new characteristics present in the SARSCoV-2 Spike make this virus particularly infectious.

In 2020, in France and in many other countries, media treatment of the origin of the virus was very much oriented to fit the "official" story, i.e. a natural origin via the pangolin, any other hypothesis being qualified as "conspiratorial." It should be noted, however, that among the mainstream media, as early as August 2020 the French newspaper *France Soir* published a series of scientific articles on the subject written by Valère Lounnas and Dr. Gérard Guillaume.[31]

The furin cleavage site

Located at the junction of the two subunits of the Spike protein, the furin cleavage site enables the coronavirus to infect humans and penetrate many organs. Furin is an enzyme located on many human cell types and can help the virus enter these cells. This furin cleavage site was mentioned as early as January 2020 by a Chinese team, who published in Chinese. Researchers from Aix-Marseille University, in France, the CNRS,[32] and Université de Montréal in Canada also

---

31. *L'histoire du Covid*, Valère Lounnas and Gérard Guillaume, Dossier France-Soir.fr, http://tiny.cc/dossierFranceSoir.
32. *The Spike glycoprotein of the new coronavirus 2019-nCoV contains a furin-like cleavage site absent in CoV of the same clade*, B. Coutard, C. Valle, X. de Lamballerie, B. Canard, N.G. Seidah, E. Decroly, *Antiviral Res.* 2020, PMID 32057769.
An article written by Étienne Decroly et al., CNRS research director of the Architecture and Function of Biological Macromolecules (AFMB) Laboratory, Aix-Marseille University.

identified the site in January 2020, highlighting its role in the emergence and pathogenicity of the virus. Indian researchers (the Pradhan team) also published on the furin cleavage site at the same time (see footnote 34).

The ACE2 receptor
Another feature of the SARS-CoV-2 Spike is its remarkable RBD (receptor binding domain) amino acid sequence, which has a strong affinity for ACE2, a molecule present on many human cell types. It enables the coronavirus to bind to human cells and spread throughout the body. ACE2, or angiotensin converting enzyme 2, is part of the renin-angiotensin system, a major regulator of blood pressure and many vital metabolic functions involving the lungs, heart and kidneys, among others. At the start of 2020, Jean-Marc Sabatier, a CNRS research director, explained the instrumental role of ACE2, and the inflammatory effects created by SARS-CoV-2's Spike protein (the virus's main surface protein). We will return to this in Part II, on the pathology of COVID-19.

Remarkably, whereas the furin cleavage site and the ACE2 receptor had already been detected in the coronavirus family, prior to SARS-CoV-2 they had never been concurrent in the same coronavirus.

What's more, the first official disclosure of the virus (and identification of its sequence) shows that the Spike's adaptation to human ACE2 is surprisingly advanced. Indeed, from the very emergence of SARS-CoV-2, the Spike appears to be much better adapted to human ACE2 than to any other animal ACE2. This would seem to contradict the fact that this coronavirus is the result of the virus evolving after many passages in an animal host.

HIV sequences
Another astonishing specificity of SARS-CoV-2 was detected by AIDS virus specialists, in particular Prof. Luc Montagnier,[33] namely, sequence homologies between SARS-CoV-2 and the HIV virus. The very first to note this phenomenon were Pradhan's Indian team. In January 2020, they published a paper on the subject. Hotly contested

---

33. *COVID-19, SARS and Bats Coronaviruses Genomes Unexpected Exogeneous RNA Sequences*, J.C. Perez & L. Montagnier, April 25, 2020.

soon thereafter, the authors finally decided to withdraw the article.[34] After verifying their work, they tried to republish, but unsuccessfully. Nonetheless, their work was subsequently confirmed by several studies.

Why HIV sequences?

The Spike contains three pieces of sequence similar to those of Gp 120, the HIV surface protein, which are capable of facilitating viral entry into immune cells. But these pieces of sequence may be too short to have any biological activity (according to Professor Jacques Fantini's comment following my presentation on the origin of the virus at the International COVID-19 Summit on March 30, 2022, at IHU Marseille).

In the case of the SARS-CoV-2 artificial origin hypothesis, these HIV sequences could have been used to facilitate penetration of the virus into immune cells (via DC-SIGN, a dendritic cell-specific receptor), perhaps in anticipation of the evolution of a pandemic virus where transmissibility via the ACE2 receptor would not be sufficient. It should be noted that SARS-CoV-1 was only mildly transmissible. Gain-of-function manipulators were able to try to increase transmissibility by this additional means.

The presence of HIV sequences could possibly be the result of research into an AIDS vaccine. Indeed, some experiments used a coronavirus as a vector in the search for an HIV vaccine.

---

34. *Uncanny similarity of unique inserts in the 2019-nCoV Spike protein to HIV-1 gp120 and Gag*, Prashant Pradhan et al., *bioRxiv*, 2020.

EcoHealth Alliance's dubious experiments

Astonishing as it may seem, all the mutations just mentioned can be found in a pre-pandemic research project dedicated to the creation of a new coronavirus, under the direction of American NGO EcoHealth Alliance. The project, called DEFUSE, aimed to anticipate a pandemic of bat-derived coronaviruses, first by constructing a virus transmissible to humans that could emerge from the wild virus, and second, to design a vaccine and therapeutics to combat it.

It is truly striking that the pandemic coronaviruses proposed in the DEFUSE project possess the specific molecular features of SARS-CoV-2: the furin cleavage site, the RBD receptor for adapting to ACE2 and HIV sequences.[35] It is hard to believe that this is a coincidence...

Project DEFUSE was originally drafted in response to a call for tenders from the US Army's research agency, DARPA (Defense Advanced Research Projects Agency). This call for tenders, issued in 2018, was part of the PREEMPT (PREventing EMerging Pathogenic Threats) epidemic-prevention program. It involved the development of models to anticipate the emergence of future coronaviruses with pandemic potential, the verification of the validity of these models through *in vivo* experiments on various animal species (assessing the ability of the modeled viruses to jump from one species to another) and, finally, ways to prevent the spread of these viruses from their animal reservoir, bats (by suppressing this virus).

In addition to Peter Daszak, director of EcoHealth Alliance, the researchers involved in the project included Ralph Baric, professor at the University of North Carolina, and Zhengli Shi, principal virologist at the Wuhan Institute of Virology. Daszak-Shi-Baric's DEFUSE project was ultimately rejected by DARPA because of the risks it presented. However, the agency did not rule out financing certain elements of the project if other funding were secured... So, DARPA's confidential participation in the project cannot be ruled out, since this type of project is funded by the NIH.

Long before this call for tenders, the Daszak-Shi-Baric team had already had the opportunity to collaborate closely on several gain-of-function research programs conducted at the Wuhan Virology Laboratory and

---

35. DEFUSE does not mention HIV sequences by name but refers to DC-SIGN receptors, which are sequences later identified as identical to HIV.

co-funded by the US National Institutes of Health through EcoHealth Alliance. This GoF research sought to enable the virus to bind to human ACE2, with a view to anticipating the emergence of a potentially pandemic virus and developing vaccine strategies in advance. We also know that numerous experiments involving the insertion of furin cleavage sites have been carried out since the 2000s to potentiate coronavirus infection.

To summarize, between 2004 and 2015, most of these experiments were conducted by teams led by Ralph Baric and Zhengli Shi. They concerned the furin cleavage site, binding to the ACE2 of coronaviruses, and binding to the DC-SIGN parts of immune cells (by the "HIV sequences," see box above).

A French-language article by three internationally renowned virologists from Marseille published in April 2021 in *Virologie*,[36] reviews the reasons leaning toward a non-natural origin. Research programs conducted at the Wuhan Institute of Virology (WIV) by EcoHealth Alliance and co-funded by the NIH are judged by the authors to be compatible with the hypothesis of a laboratory accident.

From North Carolina to Wuhan
These experiments began at the University of North Carolina, funded by the NIAID headed by Anthony Fauci, in collaboration with the Wuhan Virology Institute. In all likelihood they relocated to Wuhan after the US moratorium on GoF in 2014. Researchers Baric and Shi never ceased their collaboration, continuing their experiments to build a chimeric virus from a bat coronavirus.

In 2015, Baric and Shi distinguished themselves by building the first synthetic coronavirus using the reverse genetics technique and published their work.[37] Baric also raised the issue of the danger of this type of experiment: the risk of generating more dangerous pathogens was to be weighed against the benefit of anticipating future pandemics. He is in a good position to know.

---

36. *Le rapport de la mission OMS peine à retracer les origines de l'épidémie de SARS-CoV-2*, Étienne Decroly, Jean-Michel Claverie, Bruno Canard, viewpoint submitted to the journal *Virologie*, 2021.
37. *A SARS-like cluster of circulating bat coronaviruses shows potential for human emergence*, Menachery, Shi, Baric, *Nat Med*. 2015, PMID 26552008.

In 2017, Shi Zhengli and Peter Daszak's group published the creation of eight new chimeras from a virus collected from bats; these chimeras are close to the 2019 version of SARS-CoV-2...

Compromising statements

In an interview he gave in 2020,[38] Peter Daszak explained the experiments carried out by EcoHealth Alliance: "You can manipulate the virus in the laboratory, the Spike protein is responsible for the virus' ability to infect an animal, you can modify the sequence of the Spike protein (build a protein), that's what we're doing with Ralph Baric, we're inserting the sequence of this protein into another virus. We're trying to develop a vaccine against this new virus that we're building in anticipation of a pandemic." How can we ignore this information and this admission?

For his part, Ralph Baric declared in 2020 that if SARS-CoV 2 came from a laboratory, the answers were to be found in the archives of the Wuhan laboratory. "In the chimera we made in America in 2015 with the SARS virus, with Prof. Zhengli Shi of the Wuhan Institute of Virology, we had left signature mutations, so it was visible that it was the result of genetic engineering. Otherwise, there is no way of distinguishing a natural virus from one made in the laboratory." Unfortunately, Wuhan's Chinese databases disappeared, and the data was inaccessible as of September 12, 2019. Since June 2020, the entire page has been deleted from the web.

Ralph Baric's curriculum speaks volumes about his many manipulations of coronaviruses. This University of North Carolina professor received funding in 2005 for research into live attenuated SARS-CoV vaccine candidates (responsible for the 2003 epidemic in Asia) and, in 2008, for research into a mucosal,[39] HIV vaccine using a common cold coronavirus as vector. This could explain why the SARS-CoV-2 chimera contains HIV sequences.

SARS-CoV-2 could have been designed for an attenuated HIV vaccine, or, as described in the DEFUSE project, as a model virus with pandemic potential, or for an attenuated vaccine against all coronaviruses.

---

38. Granted to virologist Vincent Racaniello, TwiV podcast #615, May 19, 2020: https://www.microbe.tv/twiv/twiv-615/
39. Penetrates the mucous membranes, especially the nose.

Hide this site where I can't see it...

Another admission in favor of the laboratory leak hypothesis comes from Shi Zhengli. In February 2020, the Chinese virologist published the amino acid sequence alignments of the SARS-CoV-2 Spike against those of other coronaviruses. Surprisingly, the comparison stops at amino acid 675, just before the famous furin cleavage site, newly appeared at position 682-686. Shi claims that the only significant changes in the sequence of the new virus compared to other known coronaviruses lie elsewhere than at the furin cleavage site. She also fails to mention the new coronavirus's strong affinity for ACE2. This is somewhat like a police inspector being sent to a crime scene and overlooking the presence of a bloody knife.

Are these two "omissions" intentional on Shi Zhengli's part? Surely these features can't have escaped her notice, given that this is her specialty. We can't, however, expect her to publicly acknowledge to have inserted this furin cleavage site. For the record, as Director of the Wuhan Institute of Virology's Center for Emerging Infectious Diseases, Shi received over $1.2 million from the US government between 2014 and 2019.

From the point of view of evolutionary theory, the probability that these two characteristic mutations (human ACE2 binding and furin cleavage site) would have emerged in a virus by chance and at the same time is infinitesimal, if not zero. There is in fact no natural selection pressure for a virus perfectly adapted to a wild animal to mutate and jump to man with such efficiency. The same cannot be said of farm animal viruses, which go back and forth between animals and humans, adapting little by little. Furthermore, compared with previous natural viruses, the presence of the furin cleavage site is not accompanied by other point mutations in the sequence, as would be expected in natural evolution.

We can assume that this research into chimeric viruses was well advanced by 2017, since Anthony Fauci announced on January 10, 2017, that there would be a "surprise epidemic" during Donald Trump's term of office... Strange statement. And yet we will soon see other astonishing "anticipations" of pandemics before the COVID-19 crisis.

Moderna's collaboration with the NIH

Other US NIH collaborations are also likely to have played a role in this health crisis, so unusual in so many respects. For one, the partnership with Moderna on messenger RNAs (mRNAs), one of the components of the response to the pandemic.

In 2013, Moderna received $25 million in funding from DARPA to develop mRNAs capable of being rapidly deployed in the event of the emergence of a new pathogen. In particular, the collaboration concerns mRNA vaccines for Ebola, RSV and other viruses (unspecified). In 2017, Stéphane Bancel, Moderna's French CEO, decided to redirect the company's research towards vaccines against infectious diseases, after encountering toxicity problems with mRNA therapies in the case of rare diseases.

In June 2018, the NIH expanded its partnership with Moderna to include large-scale research for the purpose of finding a coronavirus vaccine. In 2019, the technology transfer and profit-sharing agreement between Fauci's NIAID (one of the NIH centers) and Moderna was amended. Moderna and NIAID had long been working on mRNA vaccines, but not on coronaviruses. In April 2019, mention was made of research into vaccines for MERS. And in June 2019, a new contract amendment mentioned the possibility of inserting a furin cleavage site on the Spike of a coronavirus. Why in spring 2019?

Researchers (Amabati et al.[40]) examined a Moderna patent from 2016, which concerns a search for cancer "vaccines." They found the same sequence of twelve nucleotides that make up the furin cleavage site of SARS-CoV-2! This sequence has not been "claimed," in other words it is not presented as Moderna property. In fact, it is common to that found in a bacterium and in a human DNA repair protein, which helps protect against cancer. It should be remembered that Moderna was originally working on anti-cancer mRNA drugs. None of this proves that Moderna had anticipated the exact sequence of this virus' furin cleavage site, but the coincidence is surprising. I mention this because it has been the subject of much discussion.

---

40. *MSH3 Homology and Potential Recombination Link to SARS-CoV-2 Furin Cleavage Site, Front. Virol*, 2022.

Viruses that have escaped from labs in the past

During my research for the articles on "The origin of the virus" and "Biopolitics in the 21st century," I discovered that other viral epidemics could be linked to laboratory viruses. These escapes have been documented in scientific literature. Here are a few examples:

– the Marburg virus was discovered in 1967, during a first epidemic; it apparently did not come from a GoF experiment (not practiced at the time), but from laboratory research on the polio virus in African monkeys

– the AIDS virus may have originated in a 1979 clinical trial of a hepatitis B vaccine on homosexuals; another hypothesis is that HIV may have come from experiments on polio vaccines in Africa, also on monkeys

– the 1977 H1N1 flu epidemic was due to a virus very close to those circulating in the 1950s, too close to appear natural, as if its evolution had been frozen... This could be explained by the escape from a virus kept in the laboratory. The 2021 Ebola epidemic could also be the result of a laboratory escape, for the same reasons, i.e. a low level of evolution of the virus compared to the previous epidemic.

– the H1N1 virus emerged from a laboratory in 2009 and could be the cause of the 2009/2010 pandemic. One hypothesis is that a poorly inactivated swine flu vaccine was then adapted and transmitted to humans (Gibbs et al., 2009, PMID: 19930669)

– for SARS-CoV in 2003, there are three documented cases of escape of this virus from P3 and P4 security laboratories (Singapore, Taiwan and China).

Source of this information: I recommend the Chemical and Biological Weapons Working Group's synthesis on laboratory incidents that have induced epidemics: *Laboratory Escapes and "Self-fulfilling prophecy" Epidemics,* Martin Furmanski MD. Scientists Working Group on Biological and Chemical Weapons Control. Center for Arms Control and Non-Proliferation.

https://armscontrolcenter.org or https://tinyurl.com/escaped-virus.

Wuhan or Fort Detrick?

All these factors point strongly to a laboratory origin of the virus. The other question now is, from which laboratory did SARS-CoV-2 emerge?

Could it have come from an American center involved in collaboration with China on gain-of-function research? This is a politically sensitive question, implicating as it would either the University of North Carolina (UNC), Fort Detrick (the US Army's BSL laboratory),[41] or both. The military laboratory holds patents jointly with Ralph Baric.

Anonymous scientists, gathered in the Milk Tea Alliance collective, signed a well-documented preprint article in December 2021,[42] which rekindled suspicion. The conclusion was unambiguous: on the basis of numerous arguments and blood sample tests taken before the pandemic, the United States was allegedly the first country to experience the COVID-19 epidemic! In August 2021, a senior Chinese diplomat also declared that Fort Detrick and UNC should be subject to a "transparent investigation with full access" as part of the search for the origins of the new coronavirus... This call is not without scientific substantiation, even if it remains politically inaudible for the USA.

In July 2019, a breach of safety procedures was reported at Fort Detrick, resulting in temporary closure of the laboratory following inspections by the CDC. The US government refused investigation by the WHO. After the laboratory closure, respiratory illnesses were reported in the lab vicinity. In July 2019, a mysterious epidemic of pneumonia, associated with the use of "electronic cigarettes" (sic!), was reported first in one, later in two nursing homes near Fort Detrick, causing many deaths. The symptoms bore a striking resemblance to those of COVID-19. Virological and bacteriological tests detected no known pathogens, and symptoms disappeared within a few days in residents treated for this atypical pneumonia.[43] This epidemic, which was attributed to vaping, spread across the country and, as of December 17, 2019, more than 2,500 hospitalizations were reported in 50 states.

41. From USAMRIID (United States Army Medical Research Institute of Infectious Diseases).
42. *Investigation Report on COVID-19 Transmission* (v1.0.0), Milk Tea Alliance, Zenodo, 2021, https://doi.org/10.5281/zenodo.5752000.
43. *Third person has died after respiratory illness outbreak at Greenspring Village, Fairfax officials say, Washington Post*, July 17, 2019, accessed June 20, 2023.

Highly active retroactive testing

In blood tests carried out on "pre-pandemic" sera (blood collected before the official emergence of the virus), it was discovered that some people in the US had specific anti-SARS-CoV-2 antibodies as early as December 2019. A study on this subject was published in November 2020.[44] The same phenomenon was subsequently confirmed in France for sera from November 2019,[45] and in Italy as early as September 2019.[46]

In the US, another article published in 2020 about an ultrasensitive and specific test for the detection of SARS-CoV-2 virus antigens showed that they were present as early as October 1, 2019 in American patients suffering from atypical pneumonia.[47] In this regard, it would have been interesting to test the sera of those affected by the vaping epidemic near Fort Detrick in July 2019. Although researchers were probably tempted to do so, they may have been discouraged since no studies on the subject have been published to date.

In any case, the concurrence between antibody and antigen detection prior to January 2020 provided evidence of an earlier presence of the virus. The question of whether the virus circulated before its official declaration was eventually raised in the *British Medical Journal*,[48] one of the world's most respected medical journals.

44. *Serologic Testing of US Blood Donations to Identify Severe Acute Respiratory Syndrome Coronavirus 2 (SARS-CoV- 2) Reactive Antibodies: December 2019-January 2020*, Sridhar V. Basavaraju et al., Clinical Infectious Diseases, June 15, 2021.
45. *Evidence of early circulation of SARS-CoV-2 in France: findings from the population-based "CONSTANCES" cohort*, F. Carrat et al., Eur J Epidemiol, 2021, PMID 33548003.
46. *Unexpected detection of SARS-CoV-2 antibodies in the prepandemic period in Italy*, Apolone et al., Tumori, 2021 Epub 2020 Nov. PMID 33176598.
Molecular evidence for SARS-CoV-2 in samples collected from patients with morbilliform eruptions since late 2019 in Lombardy, northern Italy, Antonella et al., Environmental Research, 2022.
Evidence of SARS-CoV-2 Antibodies and RNA on Autopsy Cases in the Pre-Pandemic Period in Milan (Italy), Lai et al., Front. Microbiol, 2022.
47. *Ultra-Sensitive Serial Profiling of SARS-CoV-2 Antigens and Antibodies in Plasma to Understand Disease Progression in COVID-19 Patients with Severe Disease*, Ogata et al., *Clin Chem*, 2020 Dec, PMID 32897389.
48. *Waiting for the truth: is reluctance in accepting an early origin hypothesis for SARS-CoV-2 delaying our understanding of viral emergence?*, Canuti et al., *BMJ Global Health*, 2022, PMID 35296465.

There appears to be a strong probability that the virus first escaped from an American laboratory, but there is no question of the US and its allies admitting this, of course.

UNC (University of North Carolina), where Baric practices, is not innocent either, considering that six accidents involving laboratory-created coronaviruses were reported[49] between 2015 and 2020....

The laboratory leakage hypothesis is becoming increasingly accepted officially. Indeed, the US Secret Service writes diplomatically that the origin of the virus is more likely linked to a laboratory leak than to a natural phenomenon.[50] Even in France, on April 20, 2023, *Le Point* magazine reported that "the Académie de Médecine is leaning towards a laboratory accident."[51] In June 2023, microbiologist and infectiologist Prof. Renaud Piarroux made the point very clearly during a debate at Sorbonne University.[52]

And yet, at the XVIth International Nidovirus Symposium, held in Montreux, Switzerland, in May 2023, focusing mainly on coronaviruses, no communication on artificial origin had been planned. The only scientist to raise questions on this subject was intimidated and censored.[53]

Were the congress organizers bribed? What were they afraid of?

What could be the purpose of these GoF experiments?
It is hard to say, but, to understand, we might look at Ralph Baric's CV (potentially the key figure). As early as 2005, he received funding to research candidate live attenuated vaccines against SARS-CoV and for a nasal vaccine (based on mucosal immunity) against HIV using a common cold coronavirus as vector. This could explain the SARS-CoV-2 chimera containing HIV sequences.

---

49. *Here Are Six Accidents UNC Researchers Had with Lab-Created Coronaviruses, ProPublica*, August 17, 2020.
50. *Declassified-Assessment-on-COVID-19-Origins*, National Intelligence Council, August 2021.
51. ANM, dedicated session : *De l'origine du SARS-CoV2 à la virologie/biologie dangereuse* (From the origin of SARS-CoV2 to dangerous virology/biology), April 18, 2023.
52. *Debate: Origines COVID-19*, Sorbonne University YouTube channel, June 20, 2023.
53. *The Great Raccoon Dog Mystery*, Jonathan Latham, PhD, *Independent Science News*, June 29, 2023.

In the case of a virus resulting from the DEFUSE project, i.e. with a view to anticipating the emergence of future coronaviruses with pandemic potential, the authors presented the realization of their modeling as if they had mastered "The Time Machine." In a twist of logic, the designers of the EcoHealth Alliance project were so certain that they had modeled future pandemic viruses that they planned to vaccinate bats against viruses that had yet to appear, using precisely these living synthetic viruses. They assumed that these viruses would appear naturally in bats, and that bats would need to be immunized to prevent them from transmitting these viruses to humans.

To verify the possibility of vaccinating bats against this future virus, EcoHealth Alliance proposed to use a live aerosolized virus; why not use a non-humanized or inactivated virus, or even a pseudo-virus incapable of replication? Not only did EcoHealth Alliance carry out forbidden GoF experiments, but it also planned to spread viruses with pandemic potential by aerosol: DARPA's caution was understandable.

New call for moratorium

In 2022, French virologists specializing in coronaviruses published a striking article entitled *Les apprentis sorciers du génome* (*The sorcerer's apprentices of the genome*). They called for a moratorium on GoF experiments involving viruses with pandemic potential, on genetic forcing projects and on self-disseminating vaccines.[54]

These positions deserve to be widely publicized, as should the international Biosafety Now initiative,[55] based in the US, which is also calling for a halt to GoF. Unfortunately, the authorities and the media continue to generate the greatest confusion on this subject in order to prevent the population from knowing the reality. Once again, biopower is at work against scientific observation.

In 2023, virologist Robert Redfield, CDC Director from 2018 to January 2021, also spoke out in favor of a moratorium on GoF research. As a member of the White House COVID-19 Task Force, he is one of the scientists who strongly disagree with Anthony Fauci on the "natural"

54. *Les apprentis sorciers du génome (Forçage génétique, vaccins autodisséminants, virus chimériques...)*, Bruno Canard, Etienne Decroly & Jacques Van Helden, *Le Monde Diplomatique*, February 2022.
55. https://biosafetynow.org/

origin of the virus. In an interview on the US network *The Hill*,[56] he warned that the next pandemic will once again be linked to research into functional gains, either through accidental leakage or an act of bioterrorism. A public and democratic debate is becoming urgent.

Despite three years of questioning the origin of SARS-CoV-2, the GoF debate is still not on the agenda. We will see in the final part of the book that GoF research continues, with impunity, on numerous viruses, and in the greatest media silence.[57]

The deforestation hypothesis as the origin of the pandemic?

This hypothesis is mainly supported by ecologists and critics of industrial agriculture, such as Rob Wallace. They had already highlighted the risks of intensive livestock farming in the apparition of influenza epidemics before the COVID-19 pandemic. According to Wallace, agribusiness brings together thousands of genetically similar domestic animals living under stressful conditions, making them susceptible to viruses to which their wild counterparts are resistant. For example, the wild ducks that transmit influenza viruses to chicken farms are highly resistant to them and are healthy carriers.[58]

With the emergence of COVID-19, criticism has extended from intensive pig and poultry farming to deforestation. The idea is that the destruction of natural habitats facilitates the passage of viruses from wild animals to humans. This explanation seems to be accepted by both supporters of the natural origin of the virus and ecologists. It is even taken up by evolutionists, such as those at the Muséum national d'histoire naturelle in Paris,[59] by scientists who, as early as 2020, raised the possibility of an artificial origin of the virus,[60] and by institutions such as UNESCO.

---

56. Robert Redfield, *On Rising: Gain- of- Function Research WILL Cause The ' NEXT GREAT PANDEMIC'*, https://youtu.be/3N676CD1rlw.
57. Author's note (update for the English version): Hulscher N, Leake J, Mc-Cullough PA (2024). *Proximal Origin of Epidemic Highly Pathogenic Avian Influenza H5N1 Clade 2.3.4.4b and Spread by Migratory Waterfowl. Poult Fish Wild Sci.* 12:286.
58. *Interspecies transmission and emergence of novel viruses: lessons from bats and birds*, J.F. Chan et al., *Trends Microbiol*, 2013, PMID: 23770275.
59. *L'émergence des zoonoses, une mécanique implacable*. Article on the Natural History Museum website. www.mnhn.fr. 2022.
60. *Retrouver les origines du SARS-CoV-2 dans les phylogénies de coronavirus*, Sallard et al., Medicine/science 2020. https://hal.science/hal-02891455

However, I take issue with this confusion between industrial farming and occasional encounters with wildlife. As the National Natural History Museum points out, a change of host from animal to human implies an evolutionary process. How, then, can we explain the fact that a virus perfectly adapted to an animal is transferred to humans and immediately causes a pandemic?

On the other hand, the back-and-forth of successive variants between humans and animals on a farm will enable progressive adaptation, which could lead to a pandemic. This is what regularly happens with avian or swine flu and is what occurred with the SARS-CoV-2 variant from mink.[61]

It is important to differentiate this process of gradual adaptation from the phenomenon of spillover. The latter allows a wild animal virus to infect a few humans exposed to a large quantity of viral particles, but this does not give rise to a pandemic, only to localized epidemics. This is, for example, what occurred in the Mojiang cave, where Zhengli Shi, from the Wuhan Institute of Virology, went looking for bats carrying the coronavirus that infected miners in 2012. Severely affected, some of them died, but did not transmit the virus to other humans. A similar phenomenon can be observed with Ebola epidemics, which affect people in contact with bats or bush monkeys.

Far be it from me to ignore the reality of the destruction of the natural environment by industrial agriculture, or to argue about climate change. We can see, however, that the deforestation hypothesis, in terms of an explanation of the origin of the virus, suits a lot of people: political ecologists, the heads of labs where GoF experiments are carried out, and organizations like the World Economic Forum, which are adorning ecological veneer at little cost. Deforestation contributes to modification of the atmosphere, since trees, like all vegetation, convert carbon dioxide into oxygen. The World Economic Forum could well be planning to use climate change as a biopolitical tool for population control.

By insisting on this aspect of the modification of the natural environment, these players can avoid addressing other damage to the biosphere. In France, there is even talk of regulating "treatment by

61. As Didier Raoult explained in an IHU Scientific Information Bulletin YouTube video on December 15, 2020.

the media of environmental issues," in other words limiting authorized publications to those that conform to the scientific "consensus."
Sound familiar?

Further reading

– *Origine du virus de la COVID-19 : update April 1, 2022*, Hélène
Banoun, 2022.

– A video presentation was made for the International COVID-19
Summit 2022 at IHU Marseille, March 30, 2022. It is available on the
Odysee platform, http://tiny.cc/ICS-origine.

– Origin of SARS-CoV-2: biopolitics, evolution, virology March 2024
update https://www.researchgate.net/publication/378877325_Origin_
of_SARS-CoV- 2_biopolitics_evolution_virology_March_2024_update

– *Que révèle la gestion de la Covid-19 sur la biopolitique au XXIᵉ
siècle : Comment le concept de biopolitique peut nous aider à com-
prendre la politique sanitaire mondialisée*, Banoun, Hélène, 2023.

1.3 Biopolitics, the key to understanding globalized health policy

As we have seen, the COVID-19 epidemic originated from increasingly risky laboratory experiments. Such experiments are part and parcel of a broader biopolitical context. The concept of biopolitics was formulated by French philosopher Michel Foucault in the late 1970s to designate a novel approach to the exercise of power, focused more on controlling the lives of populations than on controlling territory.

Biopolitics explains many of the inconsistencies that were so striking in the management of the COVID-19 crisis. Clearly, some decisions were motivated more by ideological and political imperatives than on scientific grounds.

Shifting from territorial control to population control

In late medieval Western Europe, from the 15th century onwards, modern states began to emerge from feudal institutions. In the newly formed states, it gradually became apparent that the prosperity of a nation depended above all on its population and not on size of territory, however vast and rich it might be, for without manpower, the earth's riches could not be extracted.

With this in mind, power began to rule over bodies. Indeed, the health of a population and its reproductive capacities condition its efficiency in exploiting the earth's wealth and, later, in producing manufactured goods. It is no coincidence that biopolitics really took off with the industrial age, the aim being to ensure productive and reproductive capacities that meet new productivist imperatives.

Health as a matter of State interest

With the advent of the industrial era grew awareness of the importance of hygiene. The "health revolution" was no doubt the first major articulation of the biopolitical era. Along with measures such as sanitation and urban planning, vaccination was privileged.

Even earlier, variolation, the first mass vaccination campaign, was promoted and imposed with the aim of improving productivity, with benefits shown to outweigh the known risks, as Swiss physicist and mathematician Daniel Bernoulli explained in 1760,[62] using mathematical modeling:[63] "If inoculation is adopted, the result will be a gain of several thousand people for civil society; even if it is murderous, as it kills children in the cradle, it is preferable to smallpox, which kills adults who have become useful to society..." Bernoulli concludes that, consideration of the individual aside, "it will always be geometrically true that the interest of Princes is to favor inoculation." From the outset, vaccination was justified in the name of health as a matter of State interest. As such, any objection in terms of risk to individuals is not tolerated, no more today than in the past.

Biopolitics quickly focused on widespread, compulsory vaccination, first against smallpox, later against other diseases. Since the 2000s, this propensity for mass vaccination has been reinforced under the aegis of the WHO and its programs.[64] As soon as a vaccine becomes available, it must be used. The WHO is not bothered about whether the disease is dangerous, for whom, nor about whether a treatment exists. Vaccination against a growing number of diseases is promoted intensely, even made mandatory, in virtually every country in the world.[65]

---

62. *Essai de l'analyse de la mortalité causée par la petite pérole et des avantages de l'inoculation pour la prévenir*, Histoires et Mémoires de l'Académie des Sciences, 2, 1766, Anne Marie Moulin, doctoral thesis in medicine, 1979, quoted by Michel Foucault.
63. *Un exemple de modélisation*, Annette Leroy, Institut de Recherche sur l'Enseignement des Mathématiques.
https://www.apmep.fr/Bulletin-459.
64. In Resolution WHA42/32-1989, the WHO outlines its immunization program against measles, poliomyelitis, neonatal tetanus and pertussis: the aim is to achieve complete population coverage with these vaccines. It was also decided to incorporate new vaccines into national immunization programs as and when they became available. World Health Assembly, 42 (1989). Forty-second World Health Assembly, Geneva, 8-19 May 1989: resolutions and decisions, annexes, World Health Organization, p.33. https://apps.who. int/iris/handle/10665/171211.
65. In France, the last two episodes in this intensification of vaccine immunization concern compulsory infant vaccinations, which rose from three to eleven in 2018, and HPV vaccination, which has been intensely promoted in secondary schools since the start of the 2023 school year.

Vaccination, "foundation of the primary healthcare system"

The WHO thus supports the Immunization Agenda 2030, aka IA2030, promoted by a number of partners (Gavi,[66] the Bill and Melinda Gates Foundation, UNICEF, the US CDC). The IA2030 site's home page states: "Immunization is the foundation of the primary healthcare system and an indisputable human right. It's also one of the best health investments money can buy. IA 2030 envisions a world where everyone, everywhere, at every age, fully benefits from vaccines to improve health and well-being."[67]

In this "vaccinist" context, the speed with which the new COVID-19 vaccines were granted authorization to market is not so surprising. It is also easy to see why counter opinion has proved impossible. The vaccine ideology is all the more difficult to counterargument because the financial stakes for the pharmaceutical industry are enormous. Vaccines have become more profitable than most conventional medicines, whose patents lapse after the maximum twenty-year validity period. For example, the HPV vaccine Gardasil, the most expensive of all vaccines, is sold at around €130 a dose and earns Merck $2 billion a year.[68] In 2020, global coverage with two doses of the HPV vaccine was 13%. The WHO has declared that it seeks to eradicate cervical cancer through a global vaccine coverage rate of 90% by 2030.[69] This raises the question, is this global organization still genuinely neutral? To date, there is indeed no formal proof that this vaccine reduces the incidence of cervical cancer, but serious adverse reactions to Gardasil do occur and are the subject of controversy in scientific and medical circles.

Even supporters of vaccination are concerned about the influence of the pharmaceutical industry on global health policy,[70] its degree now constituting a danger to health.[71]

66. Gavi, the Vaccine Alliance. A public-private global health partnership to increase access to immunization.

67. https://www.immunizationagenda2030.org/, accessed June 29, 2023.

68. *Vaccins : les raisons de la méfance,* Arte, March 2017.

69. *Immunization coverage,* April 22, 2022, WHO, https://www.who.int/fr/newsroom/fact-sheets/detail/immunization- coverage

70. *A proper 'pandemic treaty' would value universal access over profit,* Human Rights Watch, A. Kayum Ahmed, April 19, 2023.

71. *The pharmaceutical industry is dangerous to health. Further proof with COVID-19,* Fabien Deruelle, *Surg Neurol Int*, 2022 Oct, PMID 36324959.

The authoritarian manner of vaccine ideology is likely rooted in French statesman Léon Bourgeois' doctrine of Solidarism,[72] which influences contemporary liberal socialism. This radical politician of the Third French Republic drew his inspiration for social protection from the work of Louis Pasteur. Solidarism served as the philosophical and moral underpinning of the social protection system drafted under the Third Republic, from which Social Security, established in 1945, was derived. Solidarism was a middle ground seeking to stabilize the Republic and guarantee social peace. The source of social obligation is what solidarists call the "quasi-contract," i.e. a contract that is "retroactively consented to," since it is clear that no individual can choose freely at birth whether or not to participate in social life. The contemporary political left is still influenced by this doctrine and the work of Pasteur: this may explain its "vaccinalist" stance.

In fact, biopolitics today are moving away from their original aim; they are leading to a serious deterioration in health, not least through the introduction of insufficiently tested therapeutics, which are sources of significant harmful effects.

Forbidden debate
During the coronavirus crisis, we all noticed the disappearance of counter debate.[73] The authorities sought to discredit any views opposed to their biopolitics by systematically equating them with conspiracy theories. Originally, the terms "conspiracy theory" and "conspiracy/conspiracism" surfaced to refer to the non-official explanations of President Kennedy's assassination. Since the health crisis, these terms have enjoyed great success and posterity, with the support of all subsidized media.

It has to be said that since March 2020, there has been no shortage of criticism of biopolitics on alternative media channels, less accessible to censorship by biopower. For example, the European Commission has noted an upsurge in conspiracy theories linked to the coronavirus pandemic and is equipping itself with an arsenal of communication tools to counter these "excesses." Among these theories is the claim

72. *Le solidarisme de Léon Bourgeois, un socialisme libéral ?* by Nicolas Delalande, *La vie des idées*, January 30, 2008.
73. See *Le Débat interdit – Langage, COVID-19 et totalitarisme*, Ariane Bilheran and Vincent Pavan, ed. Trédaniel, March 2022.

that the virus was artificially engineered. Presumably, this will soon be removed from the blacklist.

In my view, the genuine sense of the word "conspiracy" is aptly illustrated in references to current health policy in terms of a programmed plan to reduce the world population. This is the result of a misunderstanding and imputes any disruption of the social system to malicious intent on the part of the powers that be.

I stand against this, because the powers that be use the term to discredit all scientifically grounded counterargument, smearing it as "conspiratorial." I make a point of sticking to the facts. My aim is to highlight the contradictions proffered by biopower, its scientistic ideology and its manifest errors in the light of state-of-the-art literature. I believe that the concept of biopolitics fittingly explains the underpinnings of how the COVID-19 crisis was managed, without any reason to infer planned depopulation by those involved.

Instrumentalizing the pandemic

The COVID-19 pandemic has enabled biopower advancement on several fronts: GoF research, marketing of vaccine gene therapies, generalized vaccination and the notion of digital identification,[74] linked namely to generalized vaccination.

Identification of individuals through vaccination was initially projected in November 2017 by Seth Berkley, then head of Geneva-based global organization Gavi, the Vaccine Alliance. At the time, he stated that it was necessary to improve the means of tracing the vaccination coverage rate of children around the world; to do this, the United Nations was considering a 2030 digital identity plan, via cell phones, to keep data collected on children in remote areas up to date.

For their part, G20 leaders issued a joint declaration in Bali on November 16, 2022, to promote a global standard for proof of vaccination for international travel purposes, inspired by the COVID-19 vaccine passports. This initiative was based on an international agreement signed under the aegis of the WHO in 2005: International Health Regulations 2005. It is precisely this Pandemic Treaty that was due to be revised between May 21 and 30, 2023, in Geneva at the WHO World Assem-

74. See CSI n°102, April 27, 2023: Fréderic Boutet – *Identité numérique* – with Emmanuelle Darles and Dr. Eric Ménat, on Crowdbunker.com.

bly. As yet, nothing has been signed. Initially postponed to September 2023, the discussion has apparently been postponed sine die.

In June 2023, the EU and the WHO laid the foundation for a global health pass and announced a partnership,[75] to set up a global certification system, along the lines of the EU's digital COVID-19 certificate. "In June 2023, WHO will adopt the EU's COVID-19 digital certification system to establish a global system that will help facilitate global mobility and protect citizens worldwide from current and future health threats. This is the first building block of the WHO Global Digital Health Certification Network, which will develop a wide range of digital products to improve health for all [...]. This partnership will work to technically develop the WHO system in a phased approach to cover additional use cases, which may include, for example, the digitization of the international certificate of vaccination or prophylaxis." In short, a global health passport that would include many mandatory vaccinations.

WHO and EU pandemic treaties

In 2023, the future WHO treaty on pandemics caused a stir on social networks. According to US law Prof. Francis Boyle, it will establish a medical and scientific police state,[76] allowing the WHO to dictate the primary care to be provided by doctors, and order confinements, masks and vaccines.

Nothing has been reported in the press about what has already been established at the European level. A new European regulation came into force on the sly in November 2022,[77] on "serious cross-border health threats." It institutionalizes everything that was done during the COVID-19 pandemic for future pandemics. It should be noted that an emerging disease with no severity criteria is now considered a serious cross-border threat... Digital monitoring of populations, pandemic simulation exercises, group purchase of "medical countermeasures,"

---

75. European Commission press release of June 5, 2023: "*Santé numérique: La Commission et l'OMS lancent une initiative historique dans le domaine de la santé numérique pour renforcer la sécurité sanitaire mondiale*".
76. Video Debriefings on FranceSoir.fr, *Le traité sur les pandémies*, February 23, 2023.
77. *Regulation EU 2022/2371 of the European Parliament and of the Council of November 23, 2022*, on serious cross-border health threats and repealing Decision n°1082/2013/EU.

i.e. medicines and vaccines, are thus already legally provided for, long term, in Europe.

A control agenda reaching beyond health

For the World Economic Forum, founded and chaired by German-born Klaus Schwab, vaccine passports will open the gateway to digital identity. The idea is to identify people primarily on the basis of their vaccination status, and to open up certain rights to them, or not: "Digital identity determines which products, services and information we can access, and conversely those that are inaccessible to us." Does the World Economic Forum, an unelected entity, have the power to enforce its decisions through the WHO?

In *The Great Reset*, authored by Klaus Schwab and Thierry Malleret, we read that the pandemic presents a "window of opportunity" to restructure and reset the global economy according to an outline drafted by the World Economic Forum.[78] For the authors, there will be a before and an after the COVID-19 crisis, and not only for those industries that will have benefited greatly from the management of the pandemic, such as big tech and the healthcare industries. In their view, a return to pre-pandemic conditions is inconceivable for the entertainment, travel, hotel and other economic sectors, all of which will have to adapt... Time will tell whether these gurus of the great reset succeed, but their intentions are certainly clearly stated.

New crisis-management programs

As operated, management of the COVID-19 pandemic stems logically from the recent history of biopolitics. What is decided for the future remains along the same lines. States and supranational organizations will continue to promote pandemic-prevention programs, which include, on the one hand, simulation exercises (see next chapter) and, on the other, research into pathogens (GoF) and new vaccine technologies, particularly mRNA.

In October 2022, with the aim of "creating a world free of catastrophic biological incidents," the White House launched an $88 billion national biodefense strategy. In the event of a pandemic, the US aims to test

---

78. *The Great Reset*, Klaus Schwab and Thierry Malleret, World Economic Forum publication, July 2020.

new pathogens within twelve hours, make rapid tests available to the public within 90 days, reprogram existing drugs within 90 days, and ultimately develop new vaccines within 100 days.

Another "100 Days Mission" is being promoted by non-elected organizations supporting vaccine biopolitics. The highly pro-vax Coalition for Epidemic Preparedness Innovations (CEPI), sponsored by the Bill and Melinda Gates Foundation among others, is aiming to get ahead of the next viruses with the leaders of the G7 and G20 nations in: "an ambitious plan – the 100-Day Mission – that will dramatically reduce the time it takes to develop new vaccines against emerging viral threats. ... These viral families include coronaviruses, which produced SARS and MERS before COVID-19; the filoviruses, including Ebola and its Sudan strain now spreading in Uganda; and orthopoxviruses, to which both smallpox and monkeypox belong."[79]

The trend is for certain "classic" vaccines to be replaced by mRNA vaccines, starting with flu vaccines. I will come back to these vaccines of the future and the status of gene therapies in the final section on the future of biopolitics. These products and their formulation pose major safety and efficacy problems. It is therefore urgent to launch a real debate about them.

One thing is certain: biopower has not yet finished taking care of us.

---

79. *We must stop being one step behind whichever virus comes for us next,* op-ed by Richard Hatchett, Director of CEPI, *The Financial Times*, October 24, 2022.

1.4 Pandemic simulation

How are we to understand the simultaneous adoption of quasi-identical health measures around the world? Was a global strategy already at work? The reality is that, before the 2019 crisis, governments had had the opportunity to prepare themselves by means of pandemic simulations organized by supranational organizations. Hence they were aware of several hypothetical scenarios designed to help them in the complex management of a global pandemic, including institutional communication (particularly against "disinformation" on social networks), the development and distribution of medicines (vaccines, new and/or experimental therapies) and other sanitary measures (containment, masks, tests).

Scenario producers included the WHO, the World Economic Forum, CEPI[80] (the Coalition for Epidemic Preparedness Innovations) and think-tank NGOs such as the Johns Hopkins Center for Health Security (CHS).[81] People like Bill Gates, a major funder of the WHO, and Klaus Schwab, head of the World Economic Forum, also played a key role. If these players have been warning us, for years, about the risk of a pandemic, it could likely be because they are well placed to know the danger of the experiments on functional gains being conducted across the entire planet... Experiments about which they make little or no mention in their official communications. Some interpret these simulations as proof that the SARS-CoV-2 pandemic was organized upstream by these same organizations. We should not, however, confuse anticipation (the aim of these scenarios) with the programming of an epidemic.

By way of comparison, the film industry also excels in anticipatory fiction. In 2011, for example, nine years after the SARS outbreak and two years after H1N1, Steven Soderbergh's film *Contagion* staged

80. A coalition launched at the 2017 World Economic Forum Annual Meeting in Davos, Switzerland.
81. Independent non-profit organization of the Johns Hopkins Bloomberg School of Public Health. The Center strives to protect the health of populations from epidemics and pandemics. It also focuses on biological weapons and the biosecurity implications of emerging biotechnologies. It advises the US government, the World Health Organization and the United Nations.

the emergence of a mysterious, highly deadly virus, MEV-1, featuring maximum contagiousness, quarantines, social distancing, all based on the famous transmissibility measure "R0" (R-naught or the average number of cases generated by one case). Many of these features bear striking resemblance to what we in fact experienced in 2020-2021. Fortunately, and contrary to the very real, dramatic epidemiological forecasts of Imperial College London,[82] the pandemic was far less severe.

The authors of disaster scenarios are not necessarily their programmers. Still, they can in effect prepare us psychologically to anticipate the possibility of deadly pandemics, and thus "program" us to accept certain confiscation of freedoms.

I will now spotlight five major simulations conducted since 2009, concentrating on their political and health characteristics. In that year, the H1N1 flu pandemic, which turned out to be much less severe than predicted,[83] provided the Centers for Diseases Control and Prevention in the US with an opportunity to refine their methods for monitoring pandemics and accelerating the availability of vaccines. That epidemic episode also ultimately generated a growing number of pandemic simulations. A chronological review of these fictitious scenarios since 2010 reveals a progressive refinement and an increasing resemblance to the COVID-19 crisis.

First foresight by the Rockefeller Foundation

In 2010, in the wake of the H1N1 epidemic, the Rockefeller Foundation published a pandemic scenario occurring in 2012.[84] It was described as highly deadly (8 million deaths in a few months), with poor countries more seriously affected than wealthier ones. Containment and authoritarian measures were applied everywhere; people easily give up their freedoms, but then began to rebel.

---

82. Imperial College London used a mathematical model assuming an R0 of 2.4, motivating the British government to impose containment. Neil Ferguson and his team had predicted 510,000 deaths in the UK and over 2.2 million in the US in the absence of health measures.
83. It is particularly damaging among the obese: 477 deaths in the United States between April and August 2009.
84. *Scenarios for the Future of Technology and International Development*, May 2010, https://www.fichier- pdf.fr/2020/04/13/rockefeller/

Second simulation (2017): The Spars Pandemic

This forecast is the subject of a 90-page publication,[85] by the Johns Hopkins Bloomberg School of Public Health. It features a coronavirus pandemic originating in Asia and leaked from a laboratory... The sequence of events, depicting a crisis management fiasco, is edifying in its similarity to the COVID-19 crisis. In this instance, the design is presumably to anticipate the worst possible scenario so as not to repeat it in a future epidemic crisis.

The simulation focuses in particular on the communication errors to be avoided and how to counter fake news about the inefficiency and toxicity of the treatment proposed by the authorities.

The coronavirus is identified using diagnostic tests based on the now famous RT-PCR technology (Reverse transcription polymerase chain reaction). Patients are infectious before the onset of symptoms, making their isolation difficult and facilitating the spread of the disease. Children are affected more than adults, and mortality is higher among them. An antiviral developed against SARS in 2003 (responsible for the first known coronavirus pandemic) is approved as a treatment, although not without adverse effects. It is soon proven that this drug does not reduce transmission. Official communication is characterized by contradictions about the antiviral's efficacy.

The pandemic rages most severely in poor countries with weak health systems. The CDC finally acknowledge that the death rate is much lower than predicted. The public is beginning to lose interest in the disease. Health agencies prepare a worldwide communication campaign to counter this disinterest until the vaccine is available: celebrities and scientists take part in the campaign. Shortly afterwards, the US FDA publishes the results of a clinical study showing that antivirals are ultimately ineffective against the virus.

The vaccine is due to arrive soon, and governments can't afford to miss out on communication. The first vaccines will be scarce, so priority must be given to children, adolescents and pregnant women. Adverse reactions to the vaccine are reportedly emerging in proportion to the number of Americans receiving it. Parents claim their children are experiencing neurological symptoms. In May 2027, parents begin suing and demanding the revocation of the protection from liability granted to the pharmaceutical companies that developed the

---

85. http://tiny.cc/spars-pandemic.

"Corovax" vaccine. The simulation reports that "conspiracy theories also proliferated on social networks, suggesting that the virus had been created and intentionally introduced into the population by pharmaceutical companies, or that it had escaped from a government laboratory secretly testing biological weapons."

I leave it to you to appreciate the striking similarities with the SARS-CoV-2 pandemic. It is worth recalling the chronology of GoF experiments in this regard: as early as 2015, reverse genetics were used to create chimeric viruses by Ralph Baric and his teams. In 2017, Shi Zhengli and EcoHealth Alliance published eight chimeras highly similar to the future SARS-CoV-2.

Have governments learned anything from this simulation? Yes and no ... We can already see that the authors of this scenario, *The Spars Pandemic* 2025-2028, are aware of the dangers of new treatments, particularly vaccines. Neurological risk is commonly associated with many vaccinations. The Johns Hopkins Bloomberg School of Public Health harbours no illusions about the efficacy of future remedies proposed by the pharmaceutical industry to counter emerging viruses.

The scenario anticipates competition between countries to position their antivirals despite the low efficacy of these. In reality, we have seen how the company Gilead Sciences tried to place its antiviral Remdesivir in good position worldwide, despite its known toxicity and lack of efficacy.

Inflated estimation of the pandemic's death rate is also forecast. When this becomes obvious enough, the public begins to lose interest in the pandemic risk. Official communication must counter this indifference until the vaccine arrives. On this point, the lesson seems to have been learned, since interest in COVID-19 did not wane until 2022: restrictive stop-and-go measures and uninterrupted communication about the severity of the disease kept people in a state of continuous fear, awaiting the vaccine and accepting inoculation.

"A world at risk," the WHO scenario for 2019
A World at Risk was published in September 2019, a first report by the Global Preparedness Monitoring Board (GPMB), which defines itself as an "independent oversight and accountability body responsible for ensuring preparedness for global health crises." Jointly founded by

the WHO Director-General and the President of the World Bank, the GPMB comprises leaders and experts from a wide range of sectors.[86]

Their scenario features a respiratory pandemic originating from a virus possibly manufactured in a laboratory and proving more dangerous than a natural virus, capable of killing millions of people and wiping out 5% of the world economy, creating widespread devastation, instability and insecurity. Here are a few extracts :

"The world is under-prepared particularly with regard to the development and manufacture of innovative vaccines, broadspectrum antivirals, appropriate non-pharmaceutical interventions *[such as masking, containment, A/N]*, targeted therapies (including monoclonal antibodies), systems for sharing the sequences of any new pathogens, and means to equitably share limited medial countermeasures between countries."

"New therapies and broad-spectrum antivirals are widely available to treat and reduce mortality from a range of viruses; new pathogens are systematically identified and sequenced, and the sequences are shared on a globally accessible website *[this is what actually happened with the creation of GISAID, which registers virus sequences deposited by scientists, A/N]*. Decentralized vaccine manufacturing *[including nucleic acid vaccine types, although the term mRNA is not used, A/N]* begins within days of obtaining the new sequences, and effective vaccines are pre-tested and approved for use within weeks *[this is what happened with the start of manufacturing in January and February 2020 for Pfizer and Moderna, A/N]*.

"It is necessary to coordinate the response on a planetary level with a clearly identified direction."

"In addition to the increased risk of pandemics due to natural pathogens, scientific progress has made it possible to design or recreate pathogenic micro-organisms in the laboratory. If countries, terrorist groups or scientifically advanced individuals create or obtain and then use biological weapons with the characteristics of a new high-impact respiratory pathogen, the consequences could be as serious as, or even more serious than, those of a natural epidemic, as could an accidental release of micro- organisms capable of causing an epidemic."

---

86. In 2020, the GPMB published *A World in Disorder,* which builds on its first *A World at Risk* report and the lessons learned from COVID-19. Press release on *A World in Disorder*, GPMB 2020 report, September 14, 2020.

Event 201 Pandemic Exercise (October 2019)

This scenario was the most talked-about on social networks during the health crisis, so close was it to reality and in terms of timing. This simulation is all the more disturbing insofar as certain elements, mentioned in the chapter on the origins of the virus, show that the virus was already circulating at the time of the simulation.

Event 201 was an exercise that took place in October 2019 in New York, organized by the Johns Hopkins Center for Health Security, the Bill and Melinda Gates Foundation and the World Economic Forum. A video was released in October 2019 on the Johns Hopkins Youtube channel.[87] It simulates an outbreak of a new coronavirus transmitted from bats to pigs and humans, leading to a serious pandemic.

The pathogen and the disease it causes are largely inspired by the SARS of 2003, although with increased transmissibility in the community setting by people with mild symptoms. No vaccine is available for the first year. There is a fictitious antiviral drug (sic!) that can help sufferers, but it does not significantly limit the spread of the disease. As the number of cases and deaths rise, the economic and societal consequences become increasingly serious. The scenario ends after 18 months, with 65 million deaths. The pandemic begins to recede as the number of susceptible people declines. It continues at a certain pace, until an effective vaccine is available or 80-90% of the world population has been exposed. At that point, it is likely to become an endemic childhood disease.

The following recommendations are made for the next pandemic:

- reinforce stocks of medical countermeasures (masks, gloves, gowns, etc.)

- support the accelerated development and manufacture of vaccines, therapeutics and diagnostics

– give priority to reducing the economic impact of epidemics and pandemics

– fight disinformation ...

It should be noted that Event 201 makes no mention of confinement. Were discussions held on the economic impact of confinement? Why

87. *Event 201 Pandemic Exercise: Segment 1, Intro and Medical Countermeasures (MCM) Discussion*, Center for health security, Youtube channel, 1,600,260 views (accessed June 30, 2023).

was confinement introduced in March 2020, when all the scientific studies had already demonstrated its futility and harmful effects?[88] The cost of confinement was enormous and exacerbated the economic crisis, but biopower thus demonstrated that it could impose its biopolitical logic on the world's economic authorities for a time.

It is also worth noting that, in this scenario, natural immunization through infection is ultimately pronounced to be as effective as the vaccine in bringing the crisis to an end. Yet during the actual epidemic in 2020, the efficacy of natural immunization was denied by the powers-that-be. Recall Melinda Gates' words at the start of 2021 with the roll-out of the vaccine campaign: "Normal life cannot resume until the entire world population has been vaccinated."

The World Economic Forum simulation (November 2019)
In addition to global economic policy, the World Economic Forum is also concerned with the risks associated with pandemics. In a November 2019 report (no longer available online but saved on Web Archives),[89] it expresses concern about the progresssive ease with which synthetic viruses can be made from DNA strands. These strands can be ordered from commercial companies. The Forum calls for close monitoring of DNA strand orders to prevent the manufacture of dangerous biological agents.

Here again, the scenario focuses on a laboratory-derived virus. In 2019, not only was it impossible for scenario drafters to ignore that chimeric coronaviruses had already been fabricated, but they may also have been fully aware of the Fort Detrick laboratory accident in July 2019.

---

88. See the work of Jean-Dominique Michel in particular, his books and talks at the Conseil Scientifique Indépendant in 2021: https://www.anthropologiques. ch. In 2020, it still seemed possible to raise the subject, since the *Tribune de Genève* published an article by J.-D. Michel criticizing these "non-pharmaceutical" measures: *COVID-19: un immense virologiste partage mes analyses*, May 12, 2020.
89. http://web.archive.org/web/20200124051000/https%3A//www.weforum. org/projects/managing-the-risk-and-impact-of-future-epidemics

What can we deduce from these scenarios?

Over time, these simulations have become increasingly explicit. As early as 2017, there was talk of a coronavirus pandemic. The risks associated with synthetic viruses were also highlighted. Clearly, these organizations have been keeping abreast of research developments and published work since 2017, particularly on functional gains. In the two simulations conducted in 2019, it could well be that national authorities took seriously the unusual pneumopathy that began in the summer of 2019, in the close vicinity of the largest military laboratory in the USA... They would then have tried to prepare the States to manage the epidemic spread to come.

These simulations are not infallible, of course, especially considering that they come from institutions known for their conflicts of interest. Consequently, they are not neutral in their projection of events. In fact, the scenarios display a number of weaknesses in terms of scientific and medical analysis, probably linked to a certain dogmatic cecity. For example, simulations always predict highly severe pandemics, no doubt because their calculations are based on unreliable mathematical models of epidemic propagation, worthy of Hollywood scenarios. But these models have already demonstrated their limitations many times in the past. Furthermore, these forecasts do not consider the fact that developed countries may be more affected than emerging countries, that Western populations may, paradoxically, be in poorer health (obesity, diabetes, developmental disorders, cancers...), nor do they imagine that part of the population may be more susceptible to a respiratory virus. The 2009 H1N1 flu pandemic, which mainly affected children and young adults, proved particularly severe for obese people.

Strangely enough, the scenario designers also fail to factor in the conditions prevailing in the healthcare systems of the so-called affluent countries: overcrowded emergency units in hospitals, shortages of staff and equipment, unsustainable workloads, state control of healthcare decisions to the detriment of the skills of practitioners in the field... The medical world is in crisis and this is nothing new, but the pandemic forecasters display no insights for any improvement.

More scenarios to come

Pandemic exercises are as topical as ever. In fact, Bill Gates has proposed that a pandemic exercise be conducted every five years. Gavi, the Vaccine Alliance, embodiment of the "solution component," has set itself the task of compiling a listing of all emerging viruses to better orient research funding towards new vaccines: Rift Valley fever virus, hanta virus, other coronaviruses, Crimean-Congo hemorrhagic fever, Lassa fever, Marburg virus, yellow fever, H1N1 and H7N9 flu, Chikun-gunya, Ebola, Nipah.

The WHO faithfully replicated this list of priority pathogens in November 2022.[90] "It has become a reference point for the research community on where to focus energies to manage the next threat," according to Dr. Soumya Swaminathan, former WHO Chief Scientist.

Vaccines, tests and new treatments... In the end, if there is one big issue missing from institutional epidemic forecasting, it is preventive healthcare, as an individual means of improving immunity through healthy eating, regular exercise and stress management. A healthy immune system can help resist a large number of pathogens (see chapter on Natural immunity to COVID-19, p. 77). This scientifically documented solution is apparently not a priority. Could it be because it is less profitable than the development of multiple disease-specific vaccines?

Further reading

– *Simulations de pandémies depuis 2010 : ce qu'elles nous apprennent de très déplaisant sur la COVID-19, February 21, 2021*, aimsib. org.

– *Influence et pandémies* (Ed. Marco Pietteur, 2022). This book by Michel Cucchi is a valuable reference. A doctor of sociology and medicine, and hospital civil service executive, Cucchi is interested in the influence of financial powers on health decisions.

"Since the late 1990s, the United States has been conducting regular exercises involving leading politicians of all nationalities, to test homeland security scenarios revolving around population control. The

---

90. *UN Info : L'OMS recense les agents pathogènes susceptibles de provoquer de futures pandémies*, November 21, 2022,
https://news.un.org/ en/story/2022/11/1130032.

pandemic is seen as a means of triggering a form of control over the population that would otherwise be difficult to achieve: a convenient way of stupefying and conditioning a population thus placed in a state of anxiety and dependence on instructions from higher authorities rendered inaccessible to any criticism."

PART II

COVID-19: THE DISEASE

I have to admit that at the start of the pandemic, in March 2020, I felt a certain apprehension about the virus: the shock of the first confinement made me anxious for a few hours. After meeting with friends who had contracted a moderate form of COVID-19, I had a slight cough, which quickly disappeared without a trace, so I came to my senses just as quickly. This "incident" had no influence whatsoever on my subsequent investigations into the disease. With the epicenter of the pandemic in China, I naturally turned to that country for my initial research.

On March 28, 2020, an *Asia Times* article with an unflattering headline reminded the French that, as of January 13, 2020, hydroxychloroquine had been classified as a toxic substance by the Minister of Health: *Why is France hiding an inexpensive treatment that has been tested against the virus?* On March 1, 2020, a consensus of experts,[91] was published in Shanghai, presenting the epidemiology of the disease, the clinical aspects, diagnostic criteria and treatments. Hydroxychloroquine and high doses of vitamin C were suggested as initial treatments. Antibiotics and high-dose corticosteroids, on the other hand, were not recommended. Close attention was already being paid to protecting the intestinal microbiota.

It is important to note that in a later version of these recommendations published in the *Chinese Medical Journal*,[92] hydroxychloroquine was still featured but downgraded to the bottom of the list, and antibiotics were still considered unsound treatment. These changes reflected the global homogenization of biology as the pandemic progressed.

Later, I had the opportunity to meet Jean-Marc Sabatier, director of

---

91. *Consensus and Guide to New Corona Virus Infections*, Expert Group on Clinical Treatment of New Corona Virus Disease in Shanghai, *China Journal of Infectious Diseases*, March 2020, https://COVID-19evidence.paho.org/ handle/20.500.12663/1098/ http://tiny.cc/shanghai-consensus.
92. *Guidance for the management of adult patients with coronavirus disease*, Chinese Thoracic Society and Chinese Association of Chest Physicians, 2019. Chin Med J (Eng), July 5, 2020.

research at the CNRS and a protein specialist. He had published an article,[93] in early 2020 predicting and explaining all the pathologies associated with COVID-19, based on the binding of Spike to the human ACE2 receptor. These pathologies stem from the disruption of the "renin-angiotensin system," which coordinates many vital body functions.

In my information-gathering work, I focus mainly on virology and immunology, as well as on antigenic testing and PCR, seeking to understand how the immune system reacts to this virus, and how this reaction can be detected in the laboratory.

The aim of this book is not to provide an exhaustive clinical presentation of the disease, nor to list its symptoms, such as respiratory failure or loss of taste and smell. These aspects are largely covered by doctors, who are experts in these fields. Rather, my aim is to share with you the results of my personal research, to offer you deeper insight into the health crisis.

My efforts to understand immune-pathological phenomena, such as the immune storm characteristic of severe cases of COVID-19, leads me to wonder why some people are spared this severe reaction. In 2020, I first interpreted this protection as "cross-immunity" with common cold coronaviruses. In other words, having been in contact with viruses close to SARS-CoV-2 would have trained the immune system of a large number of people to respond effectively to this new aggressor. At that time, we believed that children were spared from COVID-19 thanks to this cross-reaction.

In 2022, however, when I delved once again into studies on the subject, I observed that the absence of the disease in children (with the exception of those suffering from severe chronic pathologies) was explained by their rather more naive immune system, pre-activated to react to viruses, rather than by cross-trained immunity. The protective role of the intestinal microbiota was also highlighted. Adults who escaped the symptoms of COVID-19 may have preserved this "young" immune system and healthy microbiota.

Delving still further, I tried to understand why certain antibodies play a harmful role, in contrast to the classical view of immunology, which

93. Cao Z, Wu Y, Faucon E, Sabatier JM, *SARS-CoV-2 & COVID-19: Key-Roles of the 'Renin-Angiotensin' System / Vitamin D Impacting Drug and Vaccine Developments*, JM. *Infect Disord Drug Targets*. 2020. PMID 32370727.

considers them as "protectors." Indeed, a correlation had been established between severe COVID-19 and a high level of circulating antibodies. How can this be explained?

My article on this subject is largely inspired by the groundbreaking work of Pierre Sonigo, who worked at the Pasteur Institute in the 1980s and 1990s on HIV and the unsuccessful search for an HIV vaccine. Based on evolutionary theory, Pierre Sonigo challenged the finalistic view of the immune system, which holds that its cells are made to protect us. Instead, we should think of them as microscopic primitive animals that seek food above all else. In this sense, antibodies become "fishhooks," capturing nutrients whether or not they benefit the host organism.

This potentially detrimental role is recognized for both natural (infection-induced) and vaccine antibodies. I investigated this in vaccinations against dengue fever, influenza, measles and, of course, COVID-19 and anti-COVID-19 vaccines.

At the same time, I was interested in the evolution of the COVID-19 virus on the immune system, and in 2021 published an article on this subject covering the first phase of the pandemic (2020).

Evolutionary theory also helped me to understand the "competition" between the influenza virus and the COVID-19 virus at the start of the pandemic, which may explain why the influenza virus was less prevalent.

When it comes to the practical diagnosis of disease, I am critical of the excessive tests that have replaced human diagnosis. As a biologist, I have always held that the clinic comes first and foremost. If laboratory results are at odds with clinical examination, then the clinical diagnosis ultimately has the final word. The difference between a COVID-19 case and a sick person is fundamental from a scientific point of view, but biopolitics has fueled confusion between cases and actual patients. Epidemiologist Laurent Toubiana, who contributed to developing France's world-renowned Sentinelles infectious disease surveillance system, has also widely emphasized this distinction as fundamental to the assessment of influenza epidemics.[94]

---

94. Epidemiologist and researcher at the Institut national de la santé et de la recherche médicale (INSERM). See his website : http ://recherche.irsan.fr/ and his book COVID-19 *Une autre vision de l'épidémie : Les vérités d'un épidémiologiste*, Ed. L'artilleur, April 20, 2022.

We will revisit at length the role of biopolitics in the treatment of this disease. Political decisions continue to play a decisive role in the development of therapeutic strategies against this disease, at times devoid of any scientific evidence. The example of India is significant: in the state of Uttar Pradesh, ivermectin is the preferred treatment, while in Kerala, the treatment strategy is vaccination-based. Uttar Pradesh has significantly lower mortality rates and has rapidly knocked out the Omicron variant.[95] Biopolitics does not always serve public health well.

Natural immunity: a term with two meanings

The word "immunity" signifies two aspects, designating both a process and the result of that process (protection against a pathogen).

Natural immunity, therefore, refers to both the active process of defending the body and to the protection acquired as the result of natural infection. The expression "natural immunity" is used in contrast to "vaccine immunity", which refers to both the body's response to a vaccine and to the protection it affords.

---

95. *Retour en Inde*, Gérard Maudrux, June 9, 2023, www.COVID-19-factuel.fr and *Tour du monde des traitements – Inde*, interview with Dr. Anil Chaurasia : "l'l2.vermectine, ça marche", March 24, 2021, Francesoir.fr.

2.1 Natural immunity to COVID-19

Understanding immunity or immunization and its duration against COVID-19 has not been an easy task. Much of the research dedicated to this issue tends to confuse markers of immunity, such as antibodies or immune cells, with genuine protection, measured by the absence of symptom reappearance upon a new encounter with the virus.

Studies based on clinical observations and not on biological tests alone are rare. Moreover, they do not specify the nature of the protection against reinfection: is it against a mild form of the disease or a more severe form? Such lack of precision often results in ambiguous conclusions. It is therefore difficult to form an accurate opinion on natural immunity to COVID-19 in light of the scientific literature.

Can you be infected with SARS-CoV-2 more than once?

What main elements of our natural immunity are involved in the response to this new virus?

Why aren't children affected by COVID-19?

These questions are all significant in determining natural immunity to COVID-19 and, subsequently, to assessing the efficacy of vaccination. In fact, the vaccines were produced in record time, even before the immune system's natural response to infection was fully understood, and their efficacy was established on the basis of traditional markers of vaccine immunization, the famous antibodies, without asking whether they were relevant to this new pathology. As we shall see below, these antibodies are not a panacea for immunity.

The natural immunity ecosystem

Our immune system is like a wise gardener, working on two main fronts to maintain good terrain: innate immunity and acquired immunity.

Innate immunity acts as the natural fence of the immune garden, providing the first barrier of defense against any type of infectious agent. It is located in our mucous membranes, notably via the intestinal microbiota, as well as in respiratory and cutaneous tissues. Innate immunity cells are non-specific, recognizing viruses through protein and nucleic acid patterns that trigger a response (phagocytosis and secretion of a large number of antiviral and pro-inflammatory molecules, cytokines and interferons).

In the case of SARS-CoV-2, recognition by immune cells in the mucous membranes of the airways and lungs initiates a local immune response, leading to the recruitment of other immune cells from the bloodstream: neutrophils, macrophages, killer cells (NK), etc.

Acquired immunity refers to the abilities of the experienced gardener who has learned to analyze his environment and distinguish the elements to be eliminated. It is specific (capable of targeting a particular agent) and has a memory. This immunity plays a part in eliminating pathogens via two pathways: humoral immunity and cellular immunity.

Humoral immunity produces antibodies thanks to B cells, which neutralize pathogens, marking them for destruction, or activating a system called "complement" to eliminate them.

Cellular immunity, orchestrated by T cells, directly detects and eliminates infected cells. Cellular immunity is crucial to controlling infections that occur inside cells, such as viral infections.

The cells of these two types of immunity work together continuously. Our immune system is always interacting with its environment, constantly learning how to identify visitors, both known and new. It maintains its natural barriers and adapts to many external aggressors. It contributes to maintaining our health, which is why we need to take good care of it.

What is a cytokine storm?
This is one of the main causes of disease severity in COVID-19 patients. It refers to an immune overreaction to SARS-CoV-2, probably due to disturbance in immune function caused by the virus itself. It can be compared to a devastating storm in our immune garden, where over-activation of the immune system massively frees pro-inflammatory cytokines, the substances that signal the arrival of an invader.

This phenomenon, also known as a cytokine storm, starts as a local squall, but can quickly spread to all organs, recruiting more immune cells to infected tissues.

The controlled release of cytokines usually plays a key role in the resolution of infection. However, an imbalance in the levels of these pro-inflammatory and antiviral mediators can be accompanied by acute respiratory distress syndrome and multi-visceral failure.

A word about neutralizing antibodies

A semantic clarification is needed to distinguish inconsistencies between the results of various scientific studies and real-life observations. We are talking here about the neutralization of a virus and the expression neutralizing antibodies. It is essential to distinguish between two concepts: on the one hand, virus neutralization in vivo, or what occurs in an infected person who responds well to the virus and shows few or no symptoms; and, on the other, the *in vitro* study of the neutralizing capacity of antibodies in a laboratory environment.

The Plaque Reduction Neutralization Test (PRNT) is recognized as the gold standard for measuring neutralizing antibodies against SARS-CoV-2. This test involves taking serum from recovered (or vaccinated) individuals and assessing its capacity to block the entry of a virus (or pseudo-virus) into susceptible cells grown in the laboratory.

Without going into the technical details, it remains important to stress that laboratory conditions fail to accurately reproduce what occurs *in vivo* on a mucous membrane or in the blood. This disconnect could explain why we sometimes find large quantities of neutralizing antibodies in a severely ill COVID-19 patient, who has clearly failed to neutralize the virus *in vivo*.

It should be added that the *in vitro* test often serves to assess vaccine efficacy: if the antibodies it inserts are sufficiently neutralizing *in vitro*, the vaccine is considered to be effective.

Natural immunity to COVID-19: a complex assessment

To promote vaccine immunity, many studies suggest that natural immunity does not protect against reinfection. In most cases, however, these studies are based on PCR tests that may indicate repeated contact with the virus, but in no case on genuine reinfection, i.e. based on symptoms. This is something we have all seen for ourselves during the testing mania.

Take, for example, this Danish study,[96] published in *The Lancet* in March 2021, which claims that almost half of people over age 65 can be reinfected by the virus. The study is based solely on PCR tests, which are used as the marker of reinfection, as is the case in the vast majority of studies. The authors acknowledge the limitation of their study: "Our data set includes test results from people with few or no symptoms." In other words, they readily admit that the people tested are not really sick. Nevertheless, researchers consider them as cases of reinfected people. Above all, the *asymptomatic reinfection* scam reflects the fragile state of knowledge about immunity. And yet, the authors conclude: "Our data indicate that vaccination of previously infected individuals should be performed, since there can be no claim to natural protection."

The vast majority of these reinfections are not actually reinfections, since they are asymptomatic: they are simply nasal carriage of the virus, or parts of the virus, without systemic infection. This is not surprising for a cold virus. It is often located in the nose, as blood antibodies do not circulate there, the nose being an "immune sanctuary," as French biologist Pierre Sonigo reminds us.[97] "Infection produces a simple cold, more or less symptomatic, sometimes accompanied by a mild flu syndrome, and the immunity protecting the mucous membranes is neither as effective nor as long-lasting as in the lungs."

In practice, in many people the virus invades without penetrating the mucosal barrier or generating the slightest symptoms. The widespread use of PCR tests uncorrelated with the patient's clinical condition overestimates the rates of real (pulmonary) infection and

---

96. *COVID-19: 47% reinfections in the over-65s, in a Danish study, Medscape,* April 8, 2021.

97. *Faut-il vacciner contre la détection par PCR ou contre la maladie COVID-19?* Pierre Sonigo, Caroline Petit, Nathalie Jane Arhel, John Libbey Eurotext, September 21, 2021.

reinfection, and downplays the real protection provided by the immutability acquired after infection.

The use of PCR tests as a marker of reinfection is all the more flawed in that this diagnostic tool was not properly calibrated from the outset and has not been regularly checked for sensitivity or specificity. We will return to this later in the section on the political influence over the disease.

Honorable studies have shown that genuine reinfections are extremely rare,[98] (at least that was the case before vaccination became widespread). They also conclude that natural immunity is superior to the protection conferred by the vaccine.

What about serological tests?

I addressed in detail the problem of the reliability of these tests in another survey published at the end of October 2021 on the AIM-SIBwebsite, *Évaluer l'immunité naturelle anti-COVID-19: sérologie, immunité cellulaire (Assessing natural immunity to COVID-19: serology and cellular immunity)*. Like PCR tests, serological tests present many weaknesses. Their performance varies considerably, with some tests falling far short of the sensitivity and efficacy criteria proposed by the FDA. On the other hand, they were designed using antigens from the reference strain isolated in Wuhan in 2019. Secondly, the virus has mutated tremendously, and certain antigens of the variants circulating subsequently could induce the synthesis of antibodies not recognized by these serological tests. This possibility was highlighted by the FDA at an early stage.

A final problem with serologies that assess antibody levels is that they tend to underestimate population immunity, since many people do not need to secrete antibodies and can rely on cellular (cross-) or innate immunity to defend themselves against disease. We will also see later that nobody really knows what antibody level corresponds to immunity, and we don't even know if any antibody level correlates with protection against reinfection.

---

98. *COVID-19, immunité naturelle versus immunité vaccinale*, Hélène Banoun, October 3, 2021, Aimsib.org.

Antibodies unsuitable for assessing immunity

In the French series *Info ou intox*, the media focus on questions such as "Does contracting COVID-19 protect you more than the vaccine?"[99] The answers given are always in favor of vaccination, with plenty of expert opinion. For example, a member of the French National Academy of Medicine told France Info: "A benign infection in a child or young person will not produce an immune response or, at best, very little. Reinfection is therefore possible. As far as antibody levels are concerned, the vaccine offers more guarantees."

Some people who have COVID-19 may not have detectable antibodies. In fact, protection against reinfection by SARS-CoV-2 is the result of the reaction of the various branches of the immune system. Non-specific innate immunity (that of the mucous membranes) plays a major role and is not measurable. Specific adaptive immunity (cellular and humoral) then comes into play. Often, individuals can be protected by cross-reactivity to similar viruses they have previously encountered: this is enough to protect them before they develop antibodies (or T cells) specific to the new virus. In this case, specific immunity to SARS-CoV-2 cannot be detected, even though these individuals are well protected. Ultimately, antibodies (or specific T cells) will only be detected in those who have failed to eliminate the virus rapidly. This is, of course, schematic, and there may well be exceptions: for example, people who have never had COVID-19 symptoms but have specific antibodies to SARS-CoV-2.

The immune responses of people who have been exposed to the virus are highly heterogeneous, and some may not produce antibodies against any of the virus' antigens. What's more, the virus mutates frequently. Depending on which variant the patient has encountered, the antibodies produced may not be detected by certain serological tests.

In short, antibodies have amply demonstrated their limitations as markers of immunity, whether natural or vaccine induced. According to a French study,[100] from the University Hospital of Strasbourg, cited by the US CDC, use of serology to detect SARS-CoV-2 infection is unreliable in the sense that we observe an absence of antibodies

---

99. www.francetvinfo.fr, on 23/11/2021.
100. *Intrafamilial Exposure to SARS-CoV-2 Associated with Cellular Immune Response without Seroconversion*, France, F Gallais, A Velay, C Nazon, M Wendling, M Partisani, J Sibilia, et al., Emerg Infect Dis, 2021.

yet solid cellular immunity in people with few symptoms or who are asymptomatic. This is also exactly what another study published in 2020 showed:[101] seronegative individuals may have very good cellular immunity,[102] with B and T lymphocytes. I have addressed this issue at length in my articles.[103]

Finally, while some people deplore the drop in circulating antibodies in the months following vaccination or infection, it should be noted that this drop is completely normal: it occurs in all infections, otherwise the blood would be thickened by all the antibodies that accumulate throughout life. At the same time, the immune memory is built up and refined.

For all these reasons, a significant percentage of the infected population may present negative serology in the months following infection. The search for markers of cellular immunity is more precise, but these tests are not routinely applicable, and expensive.

What causes the onset of a second COVID-19 infection?

Natural infection with coronaviruses does not generally offer complete and lasting protection: with each exposure to a common cold virus, the virus may develop in the nose but will not give cold symptoms in most people.[104] Why do some people develop COVID-19 symptoms again with each new exposure to SARS-CoV-2? From my understanding of the scientific literature, this is most likely due to an inappropriate immune system response. Upon reinfection in a person who was not properly cared for during a previous infection, the immune system overwhelms its protective effect and causes excessive inflammation responsible for the symptoms of reinfection. This occurs with every re-exposure to viral antigens (Spike in particular), whether due to infection or vaccination.

---

101. Cox RJ, Brokstad KA. *Not just antibodies: B cells and T cells mediate immunity to COVID-19. Nat Rev Immunol.* 2020 Oct. 20(10):581-582. doi: 10.1038/s41577-020-00436-4. PMID: 32839569; PMCID: PMC7443809.
102. Banoun, 2021, *Covid-19 : Natural immunity versus vaccine immunity,* https://medwinpublishers.com/All/covid-19-natural-immunity-versus-vaccine-immunity-abstract.pdf
103. See also: Banoun, 2021, *Assessing Natural Anti-Covid Immunity: Serology, Cellular Immunity,* https://medwinpublishers.com/All/assessing-natural-anti-covid-immunity-serology-cellular-immunity.pdf
104. See *Vaccins anti-COVID-19 et immunité de groupe, c'est non et encore non,* Aimsib.org, May 3, 2020.

During a second exposure to the virus, these phenomena can develop even in some people who reacted well the first time: the famous furin cleavage site is a "superantigen" capable of provoking serious immunopathological phenomena.[105] The more the immune system is stimulated by the virus (or by the vaccine which induces the production of the Spike protein carrying this superantigen), the greater the risk of triggering these harmful phenomena. What's more, as Jean-Marc Sabatier,[106] director of research at the CNRS, has shown, the binding of the virus to ACE2 deregulates the renin-angiotensin system and, by domino effect, the immune system. It is therefore important to treat COVID-19 as soon as symptoms of systemic infection appear. If the virus is not eliminated from the upper respiratory tract, it spreads throughout the body.

Long COVID-19: when symptoms persist
The persistence of COVID-19 symptoms on a chronic or recurrent basis is a distinctive feature of SARS-CoV-2 compared with other coronaviruses. This can be explained in several ways. There may be reinfections, as described here, with renewed exacerbation of immunopathological phenomena. We will also see that the virus genome is capable of integrating into the genome of patients, thereby expressing the virus's toxic Spike protein and thereby sustaining the pathologies associated with SARS-CoV-2. The role of "anti-idiotypic" antibodies in mimicking Spike toxicity in the absence of virus or Spike will be discussed later. Long COVID-19 does exist and has come to be recognized by the authorities. As we shall see, vaccine Spike can be as toxic, or even more so, than the viral protein, so that the vaccine's effects reproduce the pathology of the virus. It will therefore be difficult to distinguish a vaccine side effect from a long-lasting COVID-19. The authorities take full advantage of this proximity to pass off adverse vaccine reactions as long COVID-19.

---

105. *Superantigenic character of an insert unique to SARS-CoV-2 Spike supported by skewed TCR repertoire in patients with hyperinflammation,* M.H. Cheng et al., *Proc Natl Acad Sci* USA. October 2020, PMID 32989130.
106. *COVID-19. Jean-Marc Sabatier's censored articles 2020 – 2021 – 2022,* January 19, 2023, IDJ.

What the immune response of children tells us

Over the past few months, we have gradually been refining our understanding of how our immune system reacts to COVID-19. Part of this understanding comes from observing children and some adults who, surprisingly, are not affected by the disease.

In 2022, I investigated this matter further in an article[107] that explores why some people rapidly eliminate the virus, thus preventing an over-reaction of the immune system that could lead to moderate or severe forms of COVID-19.

In that text, I compare the immune response of children with that of adults. I also review the scientific literature concerning the difference between the response of symptom-free adults or those with a mild form of the disease, and those who develop a severe form of COVID-19.

Morbidity and mortality data show that, on the whole, children are little affected by COVID-19. They are often asymptomatic, and serious cases are rare, except in those with pre-existing health problems. In adults, around 40% of cases are asymptomatic.

Several factors have been put forth to explain why some people are less affected by COVID-19, but none of these seems to be an overriding factor. For example, the quantity of virus receptors (ACE2) in the body does not appear to be a determining factor. What's more, infected children and adults have similar viral loads[108], with little difference in the quantities of virus present in their bodies. Finally, pre-existing immunity to cold viruses (coronaviruses close to SARS-CoV-2) does not seem to explain why children are less affected either, as it is not specific to them.

Clearly, the innate immune response, our first line of defense against infection, plays a crucial role. It seems that the key to resistance to COVID-19 in children and most adults lies in their basic state of

---

107. *Why are children and many adults not affected by COVID-19? Role of the host immune response, Infectious Diseases Research*, 2022. https://www.tmrjournals.com/public/articlePDF/20220819/a4960afc38dcc4a651d-f7a085e0a1064.pdf

108. Viral load: quantity of virions produced by the infected person. The quantity of virions that infects an individual during contagion is called the "inoculum." It is this viral load that is estimated by Rt-PCR.

inflammation:[109] the lower this level of inflammation, the less likely a person is to develop the disease.

Other important factors are potential co-infections and the state of the microbiota – the microorganisms that live in our body – in the respiratory and digestive tracts. Several studies have shown that the health of our microbiota is a crucial factor in the prevention of COVID-19.

These observations help us to understand why age has rapidly been identified as a determining factor. As we age, our immune system changes, often becoming more inflammatory ("inflamm-aging"). This chronic inflammation, combined with deficient innate immunity and age-related disruption of adaptive immunity, could be the main cause of severe forms of COVID-19.

On the other hand, children and adults with a low incidence of COVID-19 have an early and effective immune response, particularly in the mucous membranes. This response is linked to the presence of mucosal IgA, a type of antibody found in our secretions, and to a controlled production of interferons and cytokines, key proteins in the early response of our innate cellular immunity.

Interferon, part of our first line of immune defense, helps eliminate the virus. However, if this innate immunity fails to rid the body of the virus, it multiplies, leading to excessive interferon production. This excess production can have harmful effects. As such, interferon plays an ambiguous role: it can be protective, but it can also contribute to a severe form of COVID-19. The timing of interferon manifestation is crucial: it must be produced before the first signs of disease symptoms appear. If interferon manifestation occurs during the symptomatic phase, it can accentuate the "cytokine storm," an excessive inflammatory reaction responsible for severe forms of the disease. Note that the amount of viruses (or viral load) present in the nose is directly related to the amount of interferon circulating in the body.

In the final analysis, the adaptive immunity that is specific to the COVID-19 virus seems to play little or no role. It could even be harmful

---

109. Inflammation is the immune system's response to injury, infection or irritation. It is a complex process involving many different types of cells and molecules in the body. Unlike acute inflammation, which is often localized and accompanied by visible symptoms, chronic inflammation can be more diffuse, manifesting itself in a variety of chronic symptoms. Biologically, it can be assessed by blood tests: erythrocyte sedimentation rate, C-reactive protein (CRP) levels, pro-inflammatory cytokines and white blood cells.

On the other hand, the microbiota of the respiratory tract (and intestinal tract), which comes into play first, plays a significant role in protection against COVID-19. Microbiota imbalance (dysbiosis) is often observed in severe forms of the disease and often associated with the presence of coinfections. The latter overload our immune system, preventing it from fighting COVID-19 as effectively as it should, and promote growth of the virus.[110]

What does this imply for treatment?
These observations indicate the way to therapeutic solutions. First, to prevent COVID-19, it is essential to contain the basic inflammatory state that contributes to the aging of the immune system. This inflamm-aging is aggravated by obesity, lack of physical exercise, chronic stress and microbiota imbalance. The first step that everyone can take is to pay particular attention to the health of their oral and intestinal flora, notably through the use of probiotics.

From a medical point of view, drugs that modulate the immune response, such as hydroxychloroquine and ivermectin, can be effective. However, these two remedies have given rise to intense controversy about their efficacy and safety. This controversy is more political than scientific, as will be discussed below.

Other possible remedies include corticosteroids, which act as anti-inflammatories, to be used only with medical guidance. Antihistamines, which are generally used to treat allergies, also have a role to play in the treatment of COVID-19: they have demonstrated antiviral action against several viruses and can inhibit the production of certain inflammatory substances. And, of course, antibiotics which, contrary to popular belief, can have an antiviral effect and also combat coinfections.

In a nutshell
Clearly, vaccine science relies far too heavily on antibodies as the main indicator of efficacy. As we have just seen, the reality is far more intricate.

---

110. See the work of Dr. Claude Escarguel : *La fin d'un mythe : "Si c'est un virus, pas d'antibiotique ?"*, (*The end of a myth: if it's a virus, no antibiotic – seriously?*) Francesoir.fr, November 14, 2022.

Cellular immunity, one of the mainstays of our disease defense system via acquired immunity, has been neglected since the early days of immunology. This discipline has developed by focusing primarily on the study of antibodies, notably in the service of emerging vaccine science. The study of cellular immunity was neglected in favor of the study of interactions between anti-genes and antibodies. Today, the emphasis is still too often on serology, which looks for circulating antibody levels, because it is more easily automated and better integrated into industrial processes. Conversely, this is not yet the case for the individualized study of cellular immunity in patients.

A worrying new trend in vaccine research is the substitution of full clinical trials by immuno-bridging tests. The latter measure only antibody levels, supposedly THE correlate of protection. This assumption is nevertheless far from proven in scientific literature...

Further reading

– *COVID-19: Natural immunity versus vaccine immunity,* October 2021 https://www.researchgate.net/publication/354985096_Covid- 19_ Natural_immunity_versus_vaccine_immunity DOI:10.32388/DP264J

– https://www.qeios.com/read/DP264J

– *Assessing natural anti-Covid immunity:* serology, cellular immunity https://www.researchgate.net/publication/355671266_Assessing_ natural_anti-Covid_immunity_serology_cellular_immunity

October 2021 https://www.qeios.com/read/STSOHC

– *COVID-19: cross-immunity with other coronaviruses, immunopathological phenomena-update* - August 2020 https://www.researchgate.net/publication/343828049_Covid19_ cross-immunity_with_other_coronaviruses_immunopathological_ phenomena-update-august20

– *Why are children and many adults unaffected by COVID-19? Role of the host immune response,* Infect Dis Res, 2022.

– https://hal.science/hal-03754848v1/document

– htps://web.archive.org/web/20220820133628/

– htps://www.tmrjournals.com/public/artclePDF/20220819/ a4960af-c38dcc4a651df7a085e0a1064.pdf

2.2 The antibodies that can potentially facilitate infection

Antibodies are often perceived as protectors. Yet, in reality, some of our immune system's responses involving antibodies can have harmful consequences for the organism by facilitating viral infections.

In this chapter we will take a close look at two antibody-related phenomena which, although related, should not be confused:

– First, the immune or antigenic imprint, originally described under the surprising name «Original Antigenic Sin" (OAS);

– Second, antibody-mediated infection facilitation (ADE, Anti-body-Dependent Enhancement).

In the course of my research, I have spent a lot of time trying to grasp these immune processes. We will explore how these two phenomena can combine to lead to increased vulnerability to certain infections, COVID-19 included. They also offer insight into how certain vaccines, including traditional ones, can sometimes have the opposite effect to that intended by promoting infection.

We will see that *the facilitation of infections by antibodies* goes a considerable way towards explaining the severity of certain COVID-19 diseases and the excess of post-vaccinal COVID-19s.

Immune imprinting, for its part, could be implicated in the inefficacy of vaccines on successive variants.

This chapter is one of the most challenging in this book, as it is difficult to simplify the observations that show that the immune system does not always play a beneficial role, and the theory that explains this phenomenon. This will be an opportunity to demonstrate the relevance of Theodosius Dobzhansky's aphorism, all too frequently overlooked: "Nothing in biology makes sense except in the light of evolution."

Before probing into the details, let's summarize these two complex concepts:

– Immune imprinting (OAS), features a partial or total blockage of the production of antibodies specific to a new virus, matched to a virus (natural or contained in a vaccine) already encountered. OAS prevents the production of antibodies specific to the "new" virus encountered by the organism.

– In antibody-mediated infection (ADE), initial contact with the virus, whether through a vaccine or natural infection, can produce antibodies that are not perfectly adapted to fighting the various versions of the virus. Subsequent contact, when these imperfect antibodies bind with the virus, can help it to enter our cells and multiply.

The "original sin" of primary infection

The concept of *immune imprinting* was developed less than a century ago. In the 1940s, US physician and epidemiologist Dr. Thomas Francis Jr made a surprising observation during a clinical trial of a flu vaccine: vaccinees had lower antibody levels than non-vaccinees during a subsequent infection. This infection was caused by a circulating virus close to the inactivated virus used in the vaccine, but which had evolved (a variant, in other words). Dr. Francis also observed this phenomenon in successive natural infections.

In 1960, he described and named this paradoxical phenomenon the "original antigenic sin."[111] Dr. Francis was the son of a pastor... There is no reason to be critical of researchers who adhere to a religious tradition, whatever it may be, but shouldn't they always keep their faith, and their scientific work separate?

Original antigenic sin describes the tendency of the immune system to rely on its memory of a previous infection when it encounters the same or a slightly modified version of the infectious agent. This "imprinting" leads to a rapid but ill-adapted response. Paradoxically, it can also limit the immune system, rendering it incapable of developing more effective responses to subsequent infections by a slightly different agent. Later, this phenomenon was renamed "antigenic impregnation" or "immune impregnation" to discard the religious connotation.

Thomas Francis suggests a solution to the immune imprint: vaccinate children at an early age against all strains of influenza that have circulated in the past. "In this way," he said, "the original sin of infection could be compensated by the initial blessing of vaccination. And so, the ideology of vaccination began to replace the science of immunology. Researchers continued to recommend vaccinations with higher doses or more frequent booster doses to avoid the famous original antigenic sin of a primary infection or vaccination.

---

111. *On the Doctrine of Original Antigenic Sin*, Thomas Francis, *Proceedings of the American Philosophical Society*, vol. 104, no. 6, 1960.

Deciphering the biological mechanism of immune imprinting

There are many unconvincing interpretations of "antigenic imprinting" in scientific literature. I eventually found a coherent explanation compatible with evolutionary theory in some studies (PMID: 19648276 and PMID: 26497532). The imprinting could possibly stem from competition between two subtypes of B cells, antibody-producing lymphocytes: "memory" lymphocytes and naive lymphocytes. Memory lymphocytes, which have already been exposed to the natural or vaccinal virus, recognize it on subsequent contact, owing to their antibodies, which are not perfectly adapted, but sufficiently able to bind to it; naive lymphocytes, intended to produce specific antibodies, i.e. adapted to the new version of the virus, do not have time to come into contact with the virus: memory lymphocytes, which are faster, seize the viral antigens, thus preventing naive lymphocytes from encountering them and producing the necessary specific antibodies. Naive lymphocytes are thus unable to undergo the maturation stages that would enable them to produce specific antibodies, better adapted to successive variants.

An unexpected obstacle to vaccine efficacy

The phenomenon of antigenic imprinting could possibly explain the now well-documented low efficacy of the flu vaccine.[112]

Research on mice immunized with inactivated influenza viruses showed that the viral load (number of virus particles) in the lungs of vaccinated mice was much higher than in unvaccinated mice.[113] Vaccinated mice probably failed to produce antibodies specific to the new virus, due to the phenomenon of immune imprinting, which favors memory lymphocytes at the expense of naive lymphocytes.

We can conclude from this that, in the case of flu vaccination, if the vaccine is based on a version of the virus that is too different from the circulating strain, then the antibodies produced by the vaccine will not

---

112. A case study published by the CDC shows 0% effectiveness in 2021: *Influenza A (H3N2) Outbreak on a University Campus Michigan*, October-November 2021, https://www.cdc.gov/mmwr/volumes/70/wr/pdfs/ mm7049e1-H. pdf. See also the metanalysis on Cochrane.org: *Vaccines to prevent influenza in healthy adults*, V Demicheli, T Jefferson, E Ferroni, A Rivetti, C Di Pietrantonj, February 1, 2018.
113. J.H. Kim et al., 2009.

effectively recognize the virus. This means that the vaccine will not be effective in preventing infection.

If it is based on a version that is antigenically very close to the circulating virus, then the antibodies produced by the vaccine will prevent naive lymphocytes from producing antibodies specific to this new virus and reduce the vaccine's efficacy. So, in both cases, we have a biologically plausible explanation for the overall low efficacy of flu vaccines.

The reaction of immune cells is unpredictable and heavily dependent on individual immunity. It's a little like playing Russian roulette.

The concept of antigenic imprinting has been documented in the scientific literature mainly for flu viruses, but it could also apply to other seasonal viruses such as coronaviruses, which frequently mutate and cause successive natural infections in humans. We still have a lot to learn about OAS, including the specific conditions that trigger this phenomenon and how it influences the immune system's response, particularly to vaccination.

Discovery of dengue-facilitating antibodies

Leaving aside the notion of antigenic imprinting, let's return to the discovery of facilitator antibodies, which date back to the 1960s. This will help us to understand why some people contracted COVID-19 just after being vaccinated... a phenomenon that caught the general public's attention.

In the 1960s, Thai doctors noticed that people previously infected with a dengue virus showed more severe forms of the disease when reinfected with a slightly antigenically different version. Based on this, US physician Scott Halstead, who participated in initial observations of this,[114] proposed an explanation involving *facilitating antibodies*: the presence of antibodies linked to a previous infection can facilitate the virus' entry into host cells and amplify the disease.

One characteristic of this facilitation of infection is that it generally occurs on the second exposure to an infectious agent, the first

---

114. See this study which traces the references of Halstead's early observations and publication: E.E. Nakayama, T. Shioda, *SARS- CoV-2 Related Antibody-Dependent Enhancement Phenomena In Vitro and In Vivo, Microorganisms*, 2023.

triggering no particular reaction or, at most, a normal one. The coronavirus crisis, however, shows us that this is not always the case: in the case of COVID-19, the ADE phenomenon is identified as early as the first infection. This is a major difference from what has previously been documented!

I spent many hours scouring the scientific literature throughout the health crisis to understand this phenomenon of facilitating antibodies. Quite often, researchers focus on complex molecular interactions, sometimes excessively so. Even for a scientist, this becomes indigestible. Still, underneath the complexity an underlying logic greatly simplifies our understanding: the theory of evolution. At the end of this chapter, we will discover the biological processes by which antibodies can facilitate virus entry into cells. Without getting bogged down in details, we will highlight this evolutionary logic at work. It should be remembered that this phenomenon is a major issue in vaccine development since vaccines are not immune to this paradoxical effect: instead of preventing disease, when a vaccine encounters the targeted virus, it can facilitate disease and even make it worse through the harmful effect of ADE.

The tragic experience of the Philippines
The French pharmaceutical company Sanofi came up against this phenomenon in the course of a mass vaccination campaign against dengue fever in the Philippines. The risk of facilitating antibodies had already been documented for decades when Sanofi set about creating a new vaccine. The laboratory sought to assess this risk during clinical trials. And indeed, in 2015, Sanofi observed a higher occurrence of severe dengue fever in the vaccinated, particularly in children aged two to five years of age. Despite these preliminary observations and expert warnings, a massive vaccination campaign was launched in the Philippines in 2016, widely advertised by the government. What followed was tragic: more than 100 children died (officially, according to the local press) from severe dengue fever after receiving the vaccine. The president of Sanofi and several senior executives were charged with homicide by the Philippine justice system.

This disaster is due to the presence of vaccine antibodies with low affinity to the circulating virus and, above all, produced in quantities too minimal in young, vaccinated children. When there are many anti-bodies, they bind *en masse* around the virus and block it. When there are too few, they are insufficient to block the virus, especially if they are poorly adapted to the circulating viral subtype. In unvaccinated children aged between six and twelve months, but whose mothers had been vaccinated, the weakness of maternal antibodies transmitted to babies also caused a large number of cases of severe dengue fever in infants.

ADE confirmed with measles

Since the first findings on dengue fever, research has discovered that the phenomenon of facilitating antibodies is also at work in other infections.[115] My focus here is on measles, which I have studied at length. Measles is an emblematic case, but also a particularly controversial one, since the vaccine is highly recommended by the WHO and is compulsory in France for infants since 1918.

Measles is an infection which, once contracted, offers life-long protection against reinfection. A single encounter with the wild-type virus seems sufficient to produce this robust immunity, without the need for repeated exposure to the virus. The situation is quite different with vaccination, which can act as an initial silent infection, subsequently leading to so-called "atypical" measles, or even severe measles.

Atypical measles occurs in people partially immunized against the virus, as can occur after vaccination with a vaccine virus not quite identical to the circulating wild-type virus. Symptoms of atypical measles may differ from those of conventional measles. This form of measles is much less common than the conventional version.

This has been published since 1965 with the first inactivated virus vaccines. It is recognized that they are likely to cause atypical measles,

---

115. Notably Flaviviruses: dengue virus (DENV), Zika virus (ZIKV), Japanese encephalitis virus (JEV), yellow fever virus (YFV), West Nile virus (WNV), Murray Valley encephalitis virus (MVEV);coronaviruses: - severe acute respiratory syndrome coronavirus (SARS-CoV), Middle East respiratory syndrome coronavirus (MERS-CoV), feline infectious peritonitis virus (FIPV); retroviruses: equine infectious anemia virus (EIAV), HIV; arteriviruses: porcine reproductive and respiratory syndrome virus (PRRSV); pneumoviruses: respiratory syncytial virus (RSV). Yang et al., *Antibody-Dependent Enhancement: "Evil" Antibodies Favorable for Viral Infections, Viruses*, 2022.

probably ADE-related, involving certain types of antibodies induced by vaccine immunization. This is why researchers have been trying to produce a new type of vaccine and have moved towards a live attenuated (able to replicate) rather than inactivated (dead) vaccine.

In 1970, however, with the live attenuated vaccine, similar to that used today, cases of atypical measles and a worsening of the disease were reported. In a 2006 publication from the Mayo Clinic,[116] the authors show in vitro, on human and mouse cells, that antibodies induced by the live attenuated measles vaccine are capable of inducing ADE. When infection with circulating wild virus occurs after vaccination (with attenuated virus), the induced antibodies may facilitate disease by helping the virus to enter cells, rather than preventing it. This phenomenon is attributed to an imbalance between two types of antibodies produced by the vaccine: facilitating antibodies and neutralizing antibodies, which target different virus antigens.

ADE has clearly been proposed as a mechanism that could explain cases of "atypical" measles following a live attenuated MMR vaccine (combined measles-mumps-rubella vaccine). I have investigated this question in greater depth and elaborated on it in an article specifically addressing the issue of facilitating antibodies in the case of post-vaccination measles.[117]

Cases of "severe" measles could also be explained by the phenomenon of infection being facilitated by vaccinal antibodies, whose levels decrease over time and which have less affinity with circulating wild-type strains: the vaccine was designed against a viral strain isolated in the 1960s. Wild-type viruses are still circulating and are antigenically distant from the original vaccine virus: circulating strains of wild-type measles virus may therefore prove partially resistant to the antibodies induced by the live attenuated vaccine.

116. *Immunoglobulin g antibody-mediated enhancement of measles virus infection can bypass the protective antiviral immune response*, Iankov et al., J. Virol, 2006. PMID 16912303.

117. *Measles and Antibody-Dependent Enhancement (ADE): History and Mechanisms, Exploratory Research and Hypothesis in Medicine*, 2022. https://web.archive.org/web/20220429084325/https://www.xiahepublishing.com/2472-0712/ERHM-2022-00018

Epidemic outbreak after vaccination in Samoa

Could the phenomenon of amplified infection through vaccination explain the disastrous 2019 epidemic in Samoa? The WHO and UNICEF decided to vaccinate the entire population of this small island state, which was then suffering from a measles epidemic. Epidemiological data show that the real outbreak occurred from the start of the vaccination campaign, as I explained in my first article on the subject for the AIMSIB website.

Out of a population of 200,000, over 5,000 cases of measles and 79 deaths were registered, mainly among children under four years of age. It is possible that low levels of maternal antibodies in infants (linked to the vaccine or to a previous infection) aggravated the infection by the live vaccine virus, again through the ADE phenomenon. What was observed for dengue with maternal antibodies could therefore be reproduced with measles.

It is also possible that recombination transpired between the (live) vaccine virus and the circulating wild-type virus, giving rise to a more pathogenic virus. All these hypotheses could dispute the use of vaccines during epidemics.

Facilitating antibodies and severe COVID-19

Now to the main topic of this book. I addressed the hypothesis of antibody-mediated infection in the case of COVID-19 as early as 2020, during a review of the literature on the subject.[118] First, a link was established and confirmed between the severity of the COVID-19 disease and the quantity of antibodies in the blood: the presence of antibodies does not protect against severe COVID-19. Although it cannot be asserted that the quantity of antibodies is the cause of disease severity, here is how we can interpret this observation, in the light of the knowledge available to us in 2023.

People exposed to the virus (who encounter it) but have few or no symptoms of COVID-19 react with their innate immunity and cross-immunity (cellular and antibody) to the SARS-CoV-2 virus. In fact, they

118. *Covid19: cross-immunity with other coronaviruses*, immunopathological phenomena-update-august20
https://www.researchgate.net/publication/343828049_Covid19_cross-immunity_with_other_coronaviruses_immunopathological_phenomena-update-august20

benefit from their previous exposure to common coronaviruses, those responsible for colds. In healthy people, innate immunity is sometimes able to strongly limit virus multiplication and avoid the second stage of the disease (the inflammatory stage). This innate immunity is produced by cells that are non-specific to a particular antigen, before the antibody-producing adaptive response kicks in. In this case, people remain seronegative, i.e. they have no detectable antibodies in their blood. They are nonetheless well protected since they do not fall ill.

This has been demonstrated by studies of contact cases who had been in proximity with severely ill COVID-19 sufferers.

People with severe COVID-19 have a weakened immune system — for example, the elderly, people with reduced immunity, diabetics, those overweight and so on. In such cases in particular, the innate response is unable to control the virus, which invades the whole body, leading to the production of large quantities of the virus's antibodies specific to SARS-CoV-2. This is where ADE comes in. Certain antibodies have a facilitating role in infection: they help the virus to penetrate cells and contribute to an excessive inflammatory reaction, the cytokine storm. Several publications,[119] provide evidence of the deleterious effect of facilitating antibodies in severe COVID-19.

Antibodies to previous common cold coronavirus infections have not been shown to play a role. Previous cold infections do not play a facilitating role in SARS-CoV-2 infection. Here, the facilitating antibodies are those produced during infection with SARS-CoV-2, and this phenomenon occurs from the very first contact. This is the first time that this has been observed. Previously, facilitation had been observed for reinfection or post-vaccination infection.

---

119. *High titers and low fucosylation of early human antiSARS-CoV-2 IgG promote inflammation by alveolar macrophages*, W. Hoepel et al., Sci Transl Med. 2021. PMID 33979301.
At the Intersection Between SARS-CoV-2, Macrophages and the Adaptive Immune Response: A Key Role for Antibody-Dependent Pathogenesis but Not Enhancement of Infection in COVID-19, K. Jennifer et al., *bioRxiv*, 2021.
Antibody-Dependent Enhancement of SARSCoV-2 Infection Is Mediated by the IgG Receptors FcγRIIA and FcγRIIIA but Does Not Contribute to Aberrant Cytokine Production by Macrophages, T. Maemura et al., mBio, 2021, PMID 34579572.
COVID-19 Severity Is Associated with Differential Antibody FcMediated Innate Immune Functions, O.S. Adeniji et al., mBio, 2021, PMID 33879594.

Facilitating antibodies after COVID-19 vaccination?

"When immunologists talk about vaccine research against coronaviruses, the spectre of so-called "facilitating antibodies" immediately arouses a shiver of anxiety. [...] Facilitating antibodies have been identified in dengue fever, influenza, HIV/AIDS infection, Ebola and... SARS, among others. In SARS, it was only eight years after the 2003 episode that these antibodies were identified," reported Stéphane Korsia-Meffre in 2020, on the Vidal.fr website, in an article[120] devoted to the search for the anti-COVID-19 vaccine. At the end of 2020, it was still possible to talk about post-vaccination ADE...

These fears were well-founded, as we shall see. An entire chapter will cover this subject. As with influenza and measles, COVID-19 vaccines can induce this facilitation phenomenon through the antibodies they enable. It is easy to see why so many people contracted COVID-19 immediately after vaccination.

We couldn't anticipate OAS, the antigenic imprint mentioned above, because before the vaccines were launched, no one could have known that we were heading for endless booster shots... This accumulation of antigenic stimuli against Spike, the Wuhan strain, and then successive variants when vaccines were adapted to "Omicron" variants, may have led to the immune system being hamstrung and unable to respond to new viruses.

Do maternal antibodies facilitate COVID-19 in infants?

We have seen that maternal antibodies may be responsible for facilitating dengue fever and influenza. Could this be the case for COVID-19? Theoretically, yes, but studies dedicated to COVID-19 show that babies are refractory to the disease and that maternal antibodies transmitted via milk do not cause facilitation. This is probably because they are associated with other protective factors not found in milk: cellular immunity, non-specific protective factors? The question remains open. In fact, transmission of SARS-CoV-2 from mother to newborn is rare.

---

120. *Vers un vaccin COVID-19 : les leçons du SRAS, du MERS et des données récentes sur la réponse immunitaire au SARS-CoV-2*, April 14, 2020.

When evolutionary theory sheds light on easy antibodies

The action of facilitating antibodies seems at odds with immunological theory, which asserts that the "role" of antibodies is to protect organisms against pathogens, including viruses. Evolutionary theory can guide us to understanding this phenomenon.

Following in the footsteps of Pierre Sonigo and his evolutionary vision of immunology, which he developed alongside Jean-Jacques Kupiec in *Ni Dieu ni gène* (*Neither God nor gene*), I tried to understand the role of antibodies. In 2021, I published the results of this research in a scientific journal.[121] This is a particularly technical subject, so I offer a summary here.

The cells in our body, including immune cells, should be seen as microscopic, autonomous entities seeking above all to feed themselves. It is far more coherent to think of our immune cells as primitive animals in search of food, with no particular intention of protecting us.

Antigens on the surface of viruses, bacteria or proteins are perceived by immune cells as sources of food and are phagocytized (swallowed). The cells then regurgitate *metabolites*, the products of their digestion. Classical immunology calls these metabolites, or waste products, "signals." In fact, they constitute a new food source for other cells. This metabolic chain illustrates the cooperation operating between cells, another constant in biological evolution that Darwin insisted on.

What role do antibodies play in this context? We can think of them as hooks that immune cells use to capture their food. B lymphocytes release antibodies into the extracellular environment, while T lymphocytes carry them on their surface. In the latter case, they are called T-cell receptors, but they are exactly the same molecules as circulating antibodies. So far, we understand that hooks have a beneficial role, since they enable lymphocytes to phagocytize pathogens: specific antibodies attach themselves to viruses, bacteria, cells, etc., and enable lymphophocytes to feed on them.

---

121. *The role of antibodies in the light of the theory of evolution, African Journal of Biological Sciences*, July 2021. https://web.archive.org/web/20240326191624/ https://www.afjbs.com/uploads/paper/3c3c463c8451c7c9 191bc41603d19fe8.pdf

How antibodies facilitate virus entry

When antibodies bind to the antigens of a pathogen, they do so via their variable part, which is able to recognize and bind to particular motifs present on the antigens. However, at the other end of the antibody molecule is a portion called the Fc *fragment*. It can bind to hooks (Fc receptors) present on the surface of many cell types. These cells have the capacity to engulf both the antibody attached to the antigen and the antigen itself. When the antigen is a virus, the cell also ingests the (very small) virus. However, if the cell is unable to destroy the virus, it can multiply inside and destroy the cell. This is how certain antibodies can facilitate infections rather than fight them.

This reality invites us to abandon the idea that antibodies always have a protective role. In some cases, they may simply reflect the encounter between the immune system and a pathogen. It is important to integrate this duality into our understanding of immunology. An approach informed by evolutionary theory could possibly even lead us into new directions of immunology research and teaching.

Further reading

– *Flambée de rougeole aux Samoa, prévenez l'OMS et l'UNICEF*, Aimsib.org, January 5, 2020.
– *Vaccin anti-COVID-19 et immunité de groupe, c'est non… et encore non*, Aimsib.org, May 3, 2020.
– *Covid19: cross-immunity with other coronaviruses, immunopathological phenomena-update-* august20, https://www.researchgate.net/publication/343828049_Covid19_cross-immunity_with_other_coronaviruses_immunopathological_phenomena-update-august20
– *Vaccin anti-grippal et facilitation de l'infection par les anticorps*, Aimsib.org, September 27, 2020.
– *Covid graves, admettre l'existence des anticorps facilitateurs*, Aimsib.org, August 23, 2020.
– *Facilitation par les anticorps : la Dengue et le Dengvaxia*, Aimsib.org, August 27, 2021.
– *Rougeole et facilitation par les anticorps*, Aimsib.org, February 6, 2022.
– *Comment expliquer biologiquement l'excès de COVID-19 post-vaccinaux*, Aimsib.org, July 30, 2021.
– *The role of antibodies in the light of evolutionary theory*, AFJBS, 2021.

Tailor-made antibodies: the adaptive power of the immune system

How do lymphocytes produce the right antibodies to recognize a new, never-before encountered pathogen?

Niels Jerne's clonal selection theory, proposed in 1955, explains this phenomenon. According to this Danish immunologist, lymphocytes produce a wide range of antibodies in small quantities, even in the absence of infection. A specific region of the immune cell genome presents a high capability for recombination. This recombination enables a small number of genes to generate a large number of variable antibody parts. So, even before being exposed to a specific antigen, these cells are constantly producing new antibodies with a wide range of specificities.

When a new antigen appears, it doesn't trigger the formation of antibodies from scratch. Instead, cells appear (always at random) that carry antibodies capable of binding to the new antigen. These cells are then selected, and the process continues, eventually leading to a large number of cells producing high-affinity antibodies to a particular antigen. Why are cells that just happen to carry the right antibody selected? Quite simply because they can take up this new nutrient and reproduce more easily.

Thanks to genetic recombination and a process of selection, lymphocytes are able to generate an immune response adapted to unforeseen threats.

2.3 Evolution of the virus during the pandemic

Beginning in early 2020, the University Hospital Institute (IHU) in Marseille and then director Prof. Didier Raoult began to evoke the evolution of SARS-CoV-2, and the emergence of mutants or variants. Before a Senate committee hearing in September 2020, Raoult reaffirmed a common trait among viruses, particularly RNA viruses: "Everything mutates all the time."

Yet public health authorities and the mainstream media persisted in convincing the public of the contrary, assuring us that the virus did not mutate, as repeatedly echoed by a string of media experts. But why? It would seem that the mainstream press had been instructed to hound Prof. Raoult for his prescribed treatment of COVID-19 and his criticism of health policy. Many of these media "experts" were not experts at all and knew nothing about microbiology. Somewhat later, this narrative of the virus's immutability served to evade any debate on the efficacy of a future vaccine against a virus that mutates continuously... Nor was the general public to imagine that the epidemic could become progressively less dangerous as variants emerged, for this would make mass vaccination less necessary, especially given the availability of effective treatments.

Mutation = evolution
One fine example of failed oversimplification of science was epitomized by the radio program *La Question du Jour* (*Question of the Day*), aired on France Culture on September 25, 2020,[122] which purported to correct Raoult's conclusions. In combined in one all the hapless misinformation that we have been subjected to for three years: the incompetence of so-called experts, arrogant journalists, denigration of insightful scientific voices, accusation of extremism and even anti-Semitism ...

The journalist, a self-proclaimed expert, stated peremptorily that Prof. Raoult was mistaken in asserting that the SARS-CoV-2 virus mutates. "It's not true to say that today, the version of the virus that is circulating and infecting us is less virulent than the one we had in March. In principle, it's strictly one and the same."

---

122. *Radiographie du coronavirus : le SARS-CoV2 a-t-il muté ?*, France Culture, September 25, 2020.

According to this journalist, everything Didier Raoult says is "either completely false, or very approximate." Even while admitting that coronaviruses mutate, they are, according to him, very stable and mutate much less than those of influenza. It is comical to hear in the same sentence that SARS-CoV-2 is both very stable thanks to an "error correction tool» yet presents "perennial mutations about once or twice a month" — an obvious paradox. In fact, if these mutations did not stabilize, we wouldn't be able to detect them. At this point, the journalist's total lack of understanding of the subject was clear.

Among his many other arbitrary assertions, "Mutation does not mean evolution," a perfectly nonsensical statement. Even synonymous mutations,[123] those which appear to change the genome only slightly, can influence the expression of the virus genome and as such play a part in its evolution. If these mutations are conserved and, above all, correlated with other, non-synonymous mutations, this indicates that they are not neutral but interact epistatically, in other words, producing cumulative effects.

The journalist tends to downplay the role of the D614G mutation, which appeared on the SARS-CoV-2 Spike protein at the start of the virus' global spread. He claims that this mutation would have given the virus an evolutionary advantage *in vitro*, but this could not be confirmed *in vivo*. So, according to this gentleman, there could be an evolutionary advantage in laboratory cultures, but not in real life. Is the virus mutating just to please researchers? In reality, this D614G mutation probably played a key role in enabling the variant to spread across the planet, notably by amplifying infectiousness.[124] In fact, it gave the virus an evolutionary advantage.

At the end of the interview, the journalist turns to ideology in an attempt to discredit Didier Raoult. He insinuates that the researcher is more or less a racist, based on a statement made in late summer 2020, in which Raoult attributed the increase in COVID-19 cases to a virus imported from North Africa. Not only is this insinuation meaning-

---

123. A synonymous mutation, also known as a "silent mutation," does not change the amino acid produced when RNA is translated into protein. These mutations were once considered to have no effect, hence the term "silent," but research has since shown that they can in fact affect the final structure of the protein.

124. *Tracking Changes in SARS-CoV-2 Spike: Evidence that D614G Increases Infectivity of the COVID-19 Virus*, Korber et al., Cell, 2020, PMID 32697968.

less, but it also contradicts Didier Raoult's esteem for Africa, which is reciprocated.

In fact, Prof. Raoult stated quite the contrary: this variant did not spread, as it was probably less contagious and less competitive than the virus already circulating Marseille. According to Raoult, the severe variant originated from intensive mink farming,[125] in France, an observation that has since been confirmed by international coronavirus experts in the Netherlands.[126]

The long road to publication

The intense polemics around virus mutations and my keen interest in evolutionary theory prompted me to write an article on *the evolution of the virus*, published in April 2021, and on which I started work in June 2020. It took a full year to navigate the publishing process, which is particularly long for international peer-reviewed journals. *Evolution of SARS-CoV-2: Review of Mutations, Role of the Host Immune System featured in Nephron,*[127] a Pubmed-referenced journal that is part of the Karger catalogue in Basel (Switzerland). Founded in Berlin (Germany) in 1890, this reputable publishing house specializes in biology.

The hypothesis of my article was that the virus evolves not randomly, but under the influence of its environment, i.e. our own immune system. This may seem obvious, but so few publications have focused on this subject. In the case of SARS-CoV-2, many researchers have noted a decline in the virus' virulence, but few have sought to put this observation into perspective within a biological framework. The purpose of my article was to explain why the decline is consistent with evolutionary theory, my chosen frame of reference for the analysis.

The general public would benefit from understanding this phenomenon, in the event of a future epidemic crisis. We saw how the media tried to convince us that the virus doesn't mutate. As the months went by, however, faced with the evidence of emerging new variants, a new opportunity was seized to sustain fear: each new mutant was declared potentially more dangerous than the last. This does not make sense from an evolutionary point of view; on the contrary, we should have been reassured by such development.

---

125. Video IHU Scientific Newsletter, December 15, 2020.
126. *Transmission of SARS-CoV-2 on mink farms between humans and mink and back to humans*, Bas B. Oude Munnink et al., *Science*, 2021.
127. PMID 33910211.

Viral evolution: between random mutations and natural selection

When a virus is transmitted from a sick to a healthy person, it has to overcome several obstacles to survive and reproduce. The first of these is our immune system's first line of defense. It consists of surface cells on the mucous membranes in the nose and bronchi, which contain cilia capable of eliminating viruses. The respiratory mucus secreted by these cells also fights viruses and bacteria. In addition, there are cells, such as the macrophages, which act like "garbage collectors," phagocytizing foreign elements and eliminating waste from destroyed virus. Soluble molecules such as interferons are also part of this innate immunity.

If the virus manages to resist this initial barrier it multiplies, and the host's specific adaptive immunity kicks in. It generally takes from five to 15 days for lymphocytes to come into play, cells that specifically attack and destroy virus-infected cells. They also cooperate with other cells to produce virus-specific antibodies.

It is in this context that viruses such as SARS-CoV-2 mutate. Each replication cycle of the virus and its RNA genome introduces potential "copy error". If not corrected, the errors result in mutations. Occurring randomly rather than by intention, the mutations are then pressure selected by the environment, that is, by the host immune system. To survive, the virus must be contagious and escape the immune system. Consequently, it is the best-adapted variants, evolving from random mutation, that survive owing to natural selection.

It is in this context that viruses such as SARS-CoV-2 mutate. Each replication cycle of the virus and its RNA genome introduces potential "copy error." If not corrected, the errors result in mutations. Occurring randomly rather than by intention, the mutations are then pressure selected by the environment, that is, by the host immune system. To survive, the virus must be contagious and escape the immune system. Consequently, it is the best-adapted variants, evolving from random mutation, that survive owing to natural selection.

In June 2020, I wrote and sent the first version of my article to 10 Italian medical professors who had treated patients for COVID-19 since March. They had documented an attenuation of the virus. In their view, the crisis was practically resolved by June 2020, but that information, shared with the media,[128] sparked a controversy not unlike the outcry surrounding *Fin de partie*, the video in which Didier Raoult flagged the end of the pandemic with his initial results on hydroxychloroquine.

In September 2020, I updated and returned my manuscript to one of these professors, nephrologist Giuseppe Remuzzi, Director of the Mario Negri Institute of Pharmacology in Milan and, incidentally, Editor-in-Chief of *Nephron*. In response, he offered to publish the article, waiving publication charges, in my capacity as guest author of a literature "review." In this sense, the term "review" refers to a type of article in which the aim is to probe a scientific issue, drawing on all the studies previously carried out in the field.

Progressively less dangerous variants
I began that article by reporting the observations of doctors treating COVID-19 patients who had noticed a decline in the virus. Using the figures available in summer 2020, I showed that it was real: at IHU Marseille, where the testing and care strategy had not changed since early March 2020, patient mortality was lower in June 2020 than in March-April. The same was also observed in Philadelphia (USA), and a published article (references in my paper) also calculates a general drop in the virus fatality rate. The declining nature of RNA viruses has been known for a long time.

At the heart of my study is an overview of the mutations detected in the virus since its "official" emergence. I use the term "official" because, in the article, I highlight a series of indicators suggesting an earlier manifestation of the virus, as early as summer 2019. At the time, I postulated that it must have originated in China, in the absence of evidence pointing to an American or other origin. In any case, we have no trace of the genetic code of an early version of the virus in the summer of 2019. We must therefore rely on the publication of the first sequence in December 2019, and on those that follow, through its various mutations.

---

128. *The ten intrepid scientists: "Clinical evidence. The crisis is over"*, Il Giornale, June 24, 2020. No longer available!

It takes only one small change in the virus's genetic code to cause a big change in one of the proteins it produces. This is what happened with the D614G mutation in the virus' Spike protein. This mutation spread throughout the world at the start of the pandemic and became the most common. It increases the transmissibility of the virus from one person to another but does not cause more serious illness. This mutation of the Spike protein is always associated with another mutation in another part of the virus called polymerase (RdRp323). Polymerase is like the engine of the virus: it enables it to co-pierce its genetic code and thus multiply in host cells. Thanks to this mutation, the polymerase operates faster. These two mutations give the virus an advantage, enabling it to infect cells more easily (D614G) and reproduce more rapidly (RdRp323). However, there is a downside: when the polymerase works faster, it makes more errors and consequently creates more mutations.

The host immune system forces the virus to mutate
The key point of my article concerns mutations in relation to the immune system of the host, i.e. the human population. A good example is the defense mechanism that forces the virus to mutate, making it less aggressive. This is the Apobec system. What does this involve?

The virus is unable to replicate on its own; it needs our cellular apparatus. This forces the virus to mutate to a less stable position, from base C (cytosine) to base T (thymidine): known as the Apobec mechanism. The virus reacts to the Apobec by mutating in the opposite direction, from T to C. This race against time between the virus and its host substantiates the Red Queen hypothesis in *Alice in Wonderland*, proposed in 1973 by US evolutionary biologist Leigh Van Valen. To remain effective, living organisms must always evolve as quickly as those with whom they interact. In Wonderland, you have to run as fast as you can to stay in the same place.

It is difficult to associate greater transmissibility or pathogenicity with a single mutation: the virus phenotype (its contagiousness and pathogenicity) is not defined by a single mutation, but by the aggregate of all mutations. I have insisted on the epistasis, the interaction existing between several mutations. The variants that emerge, i.e. the virus lines that take over from the others, always possess several fixed mutations, and we need to consider the association of mutations with each other: studying mutations in isolation by testing pseudoviruses with a single mutation is illogical. I criticized this in an article published in a preprint on *Qeios*.[129]

The state of knowledge in 2021, when my article was published, tended to show an evolution of the virus along two axes:

– greater contagiousness (through mutations on the Spike);

– reduction (probably through loss of genes encoding aggressive proteines).

There are two distinct selection pressures. One is transmissibility: the fastest viruses with the greatest affinity for cellular receptors will be selected; the other is interaction with the host immune system and, in particular, pre-existing innate and adaptive immunity. Here is what I wrote:

> Severely ill people fought the virus ineffectively, while those exposed to it but not ill destroyed most of the infecting virus and were able to select less virulent (less efficiently replicating) forms unaffected by the innate immune system. In fact, immunopathological phenomena seem to be responsible for the severity of the disease... Viruses that stimulate these phenomena less, by interacting less with innate immunity, would be selected, and the virus would evolve towards a benign phenotype.

> In asymptomatic patients (the majority of infected individuals), few complete sequences are isolated, so little is known about the mutations responsible for this attenuation. But it is safe to assume that these "less aggressive" viruses are ultimately the ones that circulate most widely in the general population today, to the point of completely supplanting the "more aggressive" ones.

> The accumulation of mutations could potentially have caused the epidemic's decline.

Herein lies the explanation for a common observation in biology: the more contagious a virus is, the less dangerous it is. Conversely, the more dangerous a virus is, the less contagious it is.

All this has since been confirmed, although I have not been able to keep up with the literature on the subject (I now have to study vaccines). Among the confirmations, Prof. Raoult suggests that a viral

---

129. *Review of: Neutralization of Spike carrying the SARS-CoV-2 69/70 deletion, E484K and N501Y variants by BNT162b2 vaccine-induced sera*, Hélène Banoun, Qeios, 2021, https://www.qeios.com/ read/HGI4LE.

line loses efficacy as it accumulates mutations and is replaced by a new variant after a few weeks.

To sum up, in 2023 it was confirmed that the SARS-CoV-2 virus had indeed evolved towards ever greater contagiousness and attenuation of its pathogenic effect.

Has COVID-19 made the flu disappear?

By considering viruses as micro-organisms that continuously evolve to adapt to their environment, in line with evolutionary theory, I was able to decode certain mysterious observations, such as the sudden disappearance of several respiratory viruses, starting with influenza. It was with this in mind that I wrote an article asking *Has COVID-19 caused the disappearance of other respiratory viruses in 2020?*, published in November 2020 on the AIMSIB website. Messages circulating on social networks claimed that COVID-19 was really just the 2019-2020 seasonal flu under a different name... The doubt raised was shared widely among the general public. The aim of my article was not to discuss the symptoms of the disease, which doctors had clearly identified as different from those of the flu, but to attempt to explain a statistical disappearance.

Indeed, as of March 2020, influenza had disappeared from official WHO charts. The question is whether this disappearance was real, or merely the result of a lack of interest in what is considered a commonplace virus and resulting in a lack of data collection. After all, if you do not seek, you do not find. This may seem the most obvious explanation, but the study of biology has often shown me that reality is far more complex.

The hypotheses that I put forward in November 2020 regarding this phenomenon include: the higher contagiousness of SARS-CoV-2 (as estimated in spring 2020) could be explained by the competition between the two viruses for the same ecological niche, making way for the more efficient. In addition, the physical distancing measures imposed from mid-March onwards virtually worldwide would have enabled the dominance of the more contagious virus. It is also possible that the influenza virus had not disappeared (like other less famous and less sought-after respiratory viruses), but that the focus of all virological surveillance on SARS-CoV-2 since March 2020 had left it unattended. The two hypotheses are not mutually exclusive.

According to official bulletins from the French national public health agency (Santé publique France), influenza had indeed been around since October 2019, and the flu virus was found in half of all samples tested for ARI (acute respiratory infection) up to March 15, 2020. Thereafter, the percentage falls rapidly, and the influenza virus disappears as of March 30, 2020. No influenza virus is found until May 18, when surveillance ceases. Monitoring resumed on September 14, 2020, and by autumn 2020, no influenza virus had been detected.

At the start of autumn 2020 (according to the Sentinelles network https://www.sentiweb.fr), many more cases of rhinovirus than SARS-CoV-2 were found in primary care. According to university hospital data for this period (source wishing to remain anonymous), influenza was not really circulating among patients presenting to hospital either: both SARS-CoV-2 and rhinovirus cases were found. According to the US Centers for Disease Control (CDC), the percentage of influenza viruses found in acute respiratory infection (ARI) samples began to decline before confinement (and this at a time when the influenza epidemic generally declined sharply in the US in previous years). With regard to WHO data, the same can be said: the influenza epidemic died out at the start of the pandemic, as usual, with a clear break in March 2020. I should also mention that, in a country where COVID-19 had not yet penetrated (Cambodia), influenza was raging in 2020.

Looking back over those three years, I would say that a number of factors came together: SARS-CoV-2 must really have had an advantage in terms of transmissibility over the influenza virus, thanks to all its synthetic molecular characteristics specified above. It was already well adapted to humans from the outset. During its silent circulation between summer 2019 and February-March 2020, it was able to increase its capacity to infect the upper respiratory tract. What's more, disinterest in influenza led to a significant drop in specific research: any positive test or suspicion of COVID-19 outweighed the mundane flu.

Further reading
– *Evolution of SARS-CoV-2: Review of Mutations, Role of the Host Immune System, Nephron,* April 2021. PMID 33910211.

– *La COVID-19 fait-elle disparaître les autres virus ?* Aimsib.org, November 8, 2020.

"Surfers" and "locksmiths"

The metaphor of lock and key is often used to explain molecular interactions, and in particular the means by which viruses enter host cells. The virus (the key) binds to a specific receptor on the host cell (the lock) to enter the cell. If the key doesn't match the lock, it can't get in. This vision is easy enough to grasp, but it doesn't reflect the complexity of biological interactions.

Marseille-based biochemist Jacques Fantini and his team offer a more refined description of the infection process. In an article published in 2023, the researchers compare the mode of action of HIV and SARS-CoV-2. These viruses first recognize the lipid rafts on the host cell surface, "micro-domains" composed mainly of cholesterol. These act as a landing strip for viral particles, enabling them to surf on the cell surface. The viruses then use these "rafts" to search for a receptor capable of triggering the process of entry into the cell. In the case of SARS-CoV-2, the ACE2 receptor is targeted.

So, it is not just a matter of finding the right lock, but also of surfing the cell surface correctly to find that lock. Viral envelope proteins must be both geometrically and electrically compatible with the cell surface.

By targeting the interaction with lipid rafts, this description makes it possible to envisage drugs that are active against all viruses, rather than ones sought by "locksmiths," specific to each virus.

Ecological niches and viruses

An ecological niche refers to a set of environmental conditions in which a species is able to survive and reproduce. In the context of viruses, an ecological niche could be defined by the host they infect, the type of cells they target, their mode of transmission, and other environmental factors that may influence their survival and reproduction. For example, some viruses may have a specific ecological niche in certain populations, such as humans, animals or plants, and be unable to survive or reproduce outside these hosts.

Two species cannot coexist indefinitely in the same niche, according to the concept of "competitive exclusion". In the context of viruses, two viruses that target exactly the same cell type in the same host cannot coexist for long. One virus will eventually dominate the other, either by infecting cells more efficiently, or by reproducing more rapidly.

2.4 Political treatment of the disease

In chapter 2.1, we looked at natural immunity to COVID-19, high-lighting the complexity of its assessment, which goes far beyond antibodies alone. In particular, we noted that the WHO itself has set aside the notion of natural immunity in favor of vaccine immunity, deemed by it to be more reliable on the basis of antibodies, more easily quantifiable, driving, as such, an official narrative and a vacci-nation-oriented policy.

We then turned to the phenomenon of facilitating antibodies and immune imprinting, which can impede vaccination efficacy, or even render it harmful by promoting infection. It is clear from all this that the scientistic prism of the political authorities has resulted in the deliber-ate disregard of the risks described in the scientific literature, in favor of decisions based on a biopolitical logic that is far from what a public health policy should be.

Laboratory instruments amplified the scale of the epidemic and un-dermined natural immunity: PCR or antigenic tests tended to inflate the number of cases to the detriment of the number of sick people, to the point where patients suffering from other pathologies but with positive PCR test results were counted as "COVID-19 patients." On the other hand, serology tests largely underestimated the number of people who were naturally immune. Benefiting from innate or cross immunity, they did not need to develop specific antibodies. This sit-uation generated widespread fear, resulting in wider acceptance of isolation and confinement measures.

We also saw how the media and health authorities concealed the phenomenon of virus mutation and the emergence of new variants, despite the scientific evidence. This omission, at least in the initial stage of the pandemic, served the purposes of the official discourse about the severity of the epidemic and the absolute need for collec-tive vaccination.

All these contradictions are rooted in a biopolitical logic seeking to control populations through health considerations.

This is the main theme of this book, in an effort to make sense of the scientific nonsense that we have come up against in recent years.

All things considered, clearly, the biopolitical objective was to magnify the severity of the epidemic to maintain the population in a state of anxiety and hopeful for a vaccine. This design corresponds to the "pandemic simulations" described earlier. And yet those at the highest levels of government who propelled such rhetoric could not have ignored certain data on hospital activity, to which they had access in real time. Generally speaking, the supposed threat posed by the virus was inflated by governments. Pierre Chaillot, a statistician, demonstrated this in his analyses of actual morbidity and fatality rates of the virus on the basis of official French statistics.[130] This information, made public in France by the Technical Agency of Information on Hospital Care (ATIH, Agence technique de l'information sur l'hospitalisation), confirmed that, on the whole, hospitals were never overloaded. There were a few exceptions, notably Paris hospitals or hospital units reserved solely for COVID-19 treatment, but the majority of the rest registered a drop in activity. At the height of the crisis, in April 2020, COVID-19 represented a mere 7.5% of hospital activity. This being so, it was incorrect to claim that hospitals were overwhelmed, and that the elderly could not be admitted...

One particularly blatant example of the exaggeration concerned the risk of stroke after suffering COVID-19 disease. The French International Journal of Medicine (*Journal International de Médecine* or JIM, on the Medscape network), generally aligned with official doctrine, noted a significant overestimation: initial estimates, often based on biased observational studies, put the post-COVID-19 stroke rate at 1% to 5%. In reality, this figure was less than 0.2%.[131] This example illustrates the need for a critical analysis of official data.

I would now like to turn to the madness of testing, which has been a major instrument of dramatization. I had the opportunity to explore this subject in greater depth during my contributions to the Conseil Scientifique Indépendant (CSI), so I am going to focus particularly on this point. We will then take a look at other areas where disease management has been subverted by biopolitics. In each case, we will see how scientism has supplanted real science. I will be more succinct on

130. *COVID-19, ce que révèlent les chiffres officiels*, L'artilleur, 2023.
131. *L'incidence des AVC dans la COVID-19 a certainement été surestimée*, JIM.fr, December 6, 2022; *Incidence of Stroke in Randomized Trials of COVID-19 Therapeutics: A Systematic Review and MetaAnalysis*, S. Nagraj et al., *Stroke*, 2022.

subjects that I haven't personally dealt with but will draw on the work and research of the contributors to the CSI, who have always endeavored to find the most reliable sources.

This overview will give us a clearer appreciation of the biopolitical deviation at work, and how the concept of biopolitics helps us to understand what actually occurred during the pandemic. Biopolitics has proven to be particularly detrimental to the health of populations, leading to a rise in general mortality through a variety of mechanisms, starting with inadequate healthcare.

Testing mania

Never before have populations been subjected to such mass screening and such media concentration on the number of cases. Prior to COVID-19, clinical observation had always taken precedence over laboratory testing. It was firmly established that only the number of people actually ill should be considered during an epidemic. That authentic measure must remain firmly anchored in our minds. The confusion reigning between the simple status of "case" and that of "patient" was the crux of how the health crisis was managed.

At the start of the epidemic, testing was reserved exclusively for symptomatic individuals, in line with standard practice. Subsequently, testing of the population was generalized by political decision. This gave rise to statistical irregularities, with the counting of cases replacing the counting of patients. The anomaly soon became a major source of concern for the CSI. I explored the subject in depth, presenting my findings on the April 15, 2021, in a CSI edition, and again on May 20, 2021. The first edition in April was censored on YouTube, presumably because of my demonstration of the artificial inflation of epidemic figures by the health authorities.

From the outset of the epidemic, we have had access to reliable official data. In France, weekly data on acute respiratory infections (ARI) of all causes are collected by the Sentinelles network, based on consultations in general practice. At the same time, the French Public Health Agency (Santé Publique France) gathers data on hospitalizations, intensive care units and emergency departments. In Belgium, Sciensano statistics can be consulted, and we have access to those of the Robert Koch Institute in Germany.

In April 2021, the Sentinelles network[132] published estimates of the number of COVID sufferers that differed significantly from the "case" figures reported by the French Public Health Agency. Based on consultations with general practitioners, the Sentinelles estimate indicated a number of sufferers 100 times lower than that of "cases" (based on figures derived from PCR and antigenic tests carried out nationwide). German and Belgian data confirm the Sentinelles estimates, indicating that we were no longer in an epidemic phase. At this point, SARS-CoV-2 had been surpassed by other viruses responsible for the majority of acute respiratory infections, such as rhinoviruses, commonly associated with the common cold.

As a pharmacist-biologist, I know that the clinical evidence takes precedence over biology: if a biological test (such as a PCR) yields a result that is not consistent with clinical observation, the validity of the laboratory test must be called into question. A clinical test is designed to help the doctor establish a diagnosis for a patient presenting symptoms. It is not intended for inclusion in public health statistics, quite simply because it cannot reflect the reality of an epidemic.

When I spoke again at the Conseil Scientifique Indépendant in May 2021, the Public Health Agency was totaling 20 times more "cases" than there were COVID-19 patients, according to Sentinelles data. Since mid-2020, we have been confronted with political manipulation of the disease. Most of the cases tested positive by PCR (or antigenic tests) presented no symptoms and should therefore not have been taken into account.

For a thorough analysis of this subject, the work of French epidemiologist Laurent Toubiana is a good reference. Research Director at Inserm, author of *COVID-19, une autre vision de l'épidémie*,[133] (*COVID-19, A Different Take on the Epidemic*), this specialist in the epidemiology of respiratory diseases is one of the foremost architects behind the development of monitoring systems for seasonal epidemics. As such, he knows perfectly well how to assess the magnitude of a seasonal epidemic and its evolution. On March 11, 2020,[134] he predicted that the coronavirus epidemic would probably end in late April 2020. In fact, it ended a week earlier.

132. www.sentiweb.fr.
133. Published April 19, 2022, Ed. L'Artilleur.
134. In an article on the website of his research institute: *COVID-19: Une épidémie déconcertante*, COVID-19.irsan.eu.

Laurent Toubiana identified this confusion very early on, owing to his knowledge of the Sentinelles network's flu epidemic count. On December 23, 2021, on Cnews,[135] he mentioned 40 cases per week per 100,000 inhabitants, according to the network of general practitioners, while the race for testing in the run-up to Christmas pushed the official count up to 90,000 positive cases per... day.

An epidemic of false positives?

Tests on the market are of variable quality, and interpretation can vary from one laboratory to another according to criteria that are not always transparent and uniform. What's more, the reagents used in these tests have not evolved much, whereas the virus itself has mutated considerably. Although brandished as the holy grail of diagnosis, the PCR test is likely to give both false positives and false negatives, with no connection to the disease. Pierre Chaillot raised this point in his book *COVID-19, Decoding Official Data*.[136] This contributed to distorting the reality of the epidemic, particularly in hospitals, where a positive test alone was enough to register a death (or illness) as COVID-19-related.

The PCR (polymerase chain reaction) test aims to identify a portion of the genetic material of an organism or virus. To do this, it uses amplification with specific DNA probes that search for these sequences in a biological sample (in this case, a nasopharyngeal sample). The minute quantity of genetic material present must actually be amplified before it can be visualized.

Incredible though it may seem, the French Society for Microbiology disclosed that the specificity of the commercial tests had not been assessed.[137] Furthermore, to estimate the quantity of virus present in a sample, it would have been necessary first to "calibrate" PCR results according to the number of cycles required to obtain a positive result. In the case of SARS-CoV-2, for example, it has been shown that after 24 to 30 cycles (depending on the reagents used and the teams involved), there is no longer any viable virus, i.e. no virus that can be cultured on cells. Yet, without the slightest scientific justification, the French authorities recommended up to 40 cycles! Such

---

135. Popular 90-minute morning show on French television.
136. Ed. L'Artilleur, January 2023. UK Prof. Norman Fenton, identified the same bias in https://www.normanfenton.com
137. *COVID-19 Réactifs/Evaluations*, sfm-microbiologie.org.

amplification considerably multiplies the risk of false positives, thus increasing the number of cases and thereby intensifying the fear factor of the public in a seemingly endless bout with the epidemic. It could even be said that, with this system, it is possible to provoke an epidemic on demand, at any time: it would suffice to test millions of people for any known pathogen with 40 or more cycles of amplification. The false-positive rate (generally 1 to 4%) would automatically produce hundreds of thousands of "cases," enabling coercive measures to be put into place (masks, physical distancing, confinement, health pass, vaccination, and so on). In France alone, no fewer than 18 million people underwent the unpleasant ordeal of swabbing between March and October 2020, the newspaper *Les Echos* recalls.[138] Testing 18 million people can thus generate 180,000 to 720,000 false positives. It is easy to see why it is costly and pointless to test asymptomatic people in the general population.

Clearly, we have witnessed the perversion of this analytical tool, which was used to pressure the population into getting vaccinated to avoid having to take repeated tests. This policy also cost the public purse a great deal of money: no less than one billion euros for December 2022 alone.[139]

Abuse of swabs

Why did we opt for nasopharyngeal swabbing with an 18 cm-long swab? According to the data available at the beginning of 2020, salivary tests were just as sensitive, if not more so.[140] Spitting into a cup is far less constraining and humiliating than nasal cavity friction, and it is also less dangerous. The risks and potential complications of deep swabbing were underscored by the French Academy of Medicine in a press release in April 2021.[141] It also recommended that saliva testing be preferred for children.

---

138. *COVID-19 : le nombre de tests PCR en nette accélération en France*, *Les Échos*, October 23, 2020.
139. *COVID-19 : la ruée sur les tests a coûté 1 milliard d'euros en décembre*, *Les Échos*, January 4, 2022.
140. *Vaccine Breakthrough Infections with SARS-CoV-2 Variants*, *The New England Journal of Medicine*, 2021.
Just 2% of SARS-CoV-2-positive individuals carry 90% of the virus circulating in communities, Yang and al., PNAS, 2021.
141. *Les prélèvements nasopharyngés ne sont pas sans risque*, *press release of the Académie nationale de médecine*, April 8, 2021.

In fact, nasopharyngeal sampling has never been the subject of scientific consensus. Shallow nasal swabs could have been used just as well. A good summary of the state of knowledge on the efficacy of different types of sampling is provided by the Canadian National Institute of Excellence in Health and Social Services (INESS, Institut national d'excellence en santé et en services sociaux).[142] Study data are mixed, and no single type of sampling has been shown to be superior.

Although imposed under psychological pressure, the possibility of having a less invasive sample taken remained open in many countries, even in France (on strong insistence...) since the French National Authority for Health (Haute Autorité de santé. or HAS) issued a favorable opinion on September 20, 2020:[143] "Saliva samples represent an alternative, but only for symptomatic patients. Today, the HAS validates the use of oropharyngeal swabs for RT-PCR testing of asymptomatic individuals for whom nasopharyngeal swabs are contraindicated." The HAS should at least have protected the children, needlessly martyred with the swab.

Denial of treatment
As early as March 2020, the health authorities firmly declared that COVID-19 could not be treated. This instruction not only contradicted the usual practice of general practitioners, who are the first line of defense against epidemics of respiratory viral diseases, but neither did it make sense: the SARS-CoV-2 virus responsible for COVID-19 is very similar to SARS-CoV-1, which was treatable despite being more dangerous. It was therefore disconcerting that COVID-19 was presented as an untreatable disease. The medical establishment should have been alerted by this, and in turn, it should have alerted the general public.

---

142. *COVID-19 et pénurie d'écouvillons*, May 27, 2020, www.inesss.qc.ca. "Two American studies, Kojima et al. (2020) and Tu et al. (2020), tested a different approach: self-sampling. They concluded that positivity rates obtained from oral (saliva) and nasal swabs taken by patients themselves were similar to positivity rates obtained from nasopharyngeal swabs taken by healthcare professionals."
143. *Covid-19: avis favorable au prélèvementoropharyngé en cas de contre-indication a un asopharyngé*, press release of Sept. 25, 2020 on www.has-sante.fr.

According to guidelines issued by the French Ministry of Health in March 2020,[144] in the event of COVID-19 symptoms such as cough and fever, patients were advised to isolate themselves at home and take symptomatic treatment, usually paracetamol. They were also encouraged to make use of teleconsultation and, in case of worsening respiratory discomfort, contact the Samu (Urgent medical aid service) to be transferred to a hospital.

Primary care management was updated in May 2022 by the HAS, with some minor therapeutic developments.[145] COVID-19 patients were to continue to be isolated at home and take paracetamol to relieve symptoms. Antibiotics were still not recommended, except in cases of confirmed bacterial infection. Corticosteroids were also not advised, and an anticoagulant was recommended for bedridden patients. Home oxygen therapy could be considered in exceptional cases. For immunocompromised patients, Paxlovid was recommended. At no point did health authorities acknowledge that patients could be effectively cared for.

Vaccination before treatment
This approach can be explained by a biopolitical objective: had an effective treatment been officially recognized, emergency-use authorization of vaccines before completion of clinical trials would have been impossible. In fact, the preamble to all emergency-use authorizations for COVID-19 vaccines granted by health agencies (European and American) includes the following justification: the authorization is granted "in the absence of any treatment for the disease." It is easy to see why biopower, known for its support of vaccination, had to deny the existence of any potential treatment. It should also be borne in mind that conflicts of interest were omnipresent at the highest political level, and that the vaccines generated far superior revenues than older treatments that had fallen into the public domain (generic drugs).

---

144. *Lignes directrices pour la prise en charge en ville des patients symptomatiques en phase épidémiques de COVID-19*, sante.gouv.fr, March 20, 2020.
145. 143 http://tiny.cc/HAS-MAI2022.

The hydroxychloroquine affair

The most controversial molecule, at least in France, was hydroxychloroquine. It was already on the radar of the health authorities even before the crisis began, since on January 13, 2020, a decree issued by the French Minister of Health placed it on List II of poisonous substances.[146] Many people were astonished by this sudden change of category for this old remedy, especially as the change occurred so shortly before the start of the epidemic.

The most striking example of misinformation concerning hydroxychloroquine is the famous fraudulent study published in *The Lancet* on May 22, 2020. It claimed to demonstrate the toxicity of this remedy and its inefficacy against COVID-19. Critical observers were quick to point out that the study in question was based on falsified data, which sent shock waves through the research establishment and tarnished *The Lancet's* reputation. The study was quickly withdrawn by its authors on June 5, 2020. With the media actively ignoring this affair, the French Minister of Health issued a decree banning the use of this old drug, despite its well-known safety record.[147] The decree appeared in the *Journal Officiel* (French official gazette) on Wednesday May 27, 2020, repealing the derogations that authorized the prescription of hydroxychloroquine against COVID-19 in hospitals in France, outside clinical trials.[148] Despite the withdrawal of the study, hydroxychloroquine is still strongly discouraged.[149]

Disregarding the obstacles, the IHU Marseille, under the leadership of Prof. Didier Raoult at the time, continued to administer hydroxychloroquine within the framework of a strict protocol (associated with azythromycin and zinc, as a minimum). This perseverance enabled the institute to publish an entire series of studies as early as 2020 that demonstrated both the safety and efficacy of this remedy. Over time, these studies have involved an ever-increasing number of patients. The most recent study, in 2023, involved more than 30,000 patients, whose medical files were checked by the judiciary. This study, the

146. Decree of January 13, 2020, concerning classification on the lists of poisonous substances.
147. *De l'hydroxychloroquine à la Spike, les controverses sur la toxicité des médicaments*, Jean-Paul Bourdineaud (Université de Bordeaux), International COVID-19 Summit 2022, IHU Marseille, March 31, 2022.
148. Press release of May 27, 2020, Sante.gouv.fr.
149. ANSM press release of April 5, 2023, Ansm.sante.fr

validity of which is difficult to contest, was nevertheless withdrawn owing to government pressure on one of the cosignatories.[150] The political executive prefers to ignore the facts rather than acknowledge them.

However, the IHU Marseille was not alone in using this drug and publishing on the subject, quite the contrary! The COVID-19 early treatment website lists almost 500 related studies (c19early.org). After meta-analysis, the results are largely in favor of this treatment, particularly in terms of reducing mortality and severe forms of the disease, provided it is administered at the right time and in the right dosage.[151]

The COVID-19 early treatment website offers a goldmine of information. It provides a real-time summary of all the studies carried out on treatments used to combat COVID-19. Browsing through it, one realizes that numerous medical teams around the world worked tirelessly to treat, with positive outcomes. This makes the official claim that there is no cure all the more incongruous. Clearly, tangible action has made it possible to treat patients effectively. This is in fact what many doctors in France have done, going against the rigid grain of the health authorities.

The vendetta against ivermectin

Ivermectin was another treatment studied.[152] Conducted by 54 different teams in 24 countries, the studies demonstrated ivermectin's efficacy in both the prevention (prophylaxis) and treatment of COVID-19, with significant improvement in terms of mortality, need for ventilation, admission to intensive care, hospitalization, cure, cases and elimination of the virus. More than 20 countries use ivermectin to treat COVID-19.

Yet ivermectin's journey was not without pitfalls. Initially prescribed to treat scabies in the West, the drug proved very useful in the treatment of COVID-19. In January 2021, French attorney Jean-Charles Teissedre, with the support of the BonSens.org association, applied to the ANSM (French National Agency for the Safety of Medicines and

---

150. *Early Treatment with Hydroxychloroquine and Azithromycin: A 'Real-Life' Monocentric Retrospective Cohort Study of 30,423 COVID-19 Patients*, medRxiv, 2023.
151. https://c19hcq.org.
152. https://c19ivm.org.

Health Products) on behalf of doctors and doctors' associations for a temporary recommendation of use (RTU) of ivermectin as a treatment for COVID-19.[153] Following the agency's refusal, the association filed a criminal case for fraud against ivermectin.

A researcher commissioned by the WHO to assess the efficacy of ivermectin on COVID-19 completely changed his position under pressure, ultimately concluding that it was ineffective, despite having expressed the opposite view a few days earlier. Via his blog, COVID-19 Factuel,[154] Dr. Gérard Maudrux put the spotlight on this large-scale biopolitical operation.

Gérard Maudrux plays an important role in France in the defense of ivermectin. He penned an interesting article on the differences in results between Uttar Pradesh, one of the pro-ivermectin states, with the lowest vaccination rate, and Kerala, India's poorest state with the highest vaccination rate. In Kerala, vaccination has yielded disastrous results, whereas ivermectin stopped the COVID-19 epidemic in India's most populous state in a matter of days. Even the WHO recognizes this.[155]

And many other remedies...

In one of my previously quoted articles on children's immunity, I touched briefly on treatments for COVID-19, which manifests itself as an excessive inflammatory reaction. It is only logical that immunomodulators such as hydroxychloroquine and ivermectin, as well as antihistamines and glucocorticoids, should prove effective.

Incidentally, microbiota imbalance is an exacerbating factor in the disease, given that the intestinal microbiota directly influences the lung microbiota. Early on in the pandemic, Chinese researchers recommended restoring microbiota balance with probiotics. Meanwhile, Western researchers were successfully testing a molecule capable of reducing intestinal permeability.

---

153. *L'ivermectine enfin examinée par l'ANSM comme traitement contre la COVID-19*, Bonsens.info, January 27, 2021.
154. *Ivermectin/Andrew Hill: the biggest health scandal in history*, February 24, 2023. For the history of FDA opposition see *Ivermectin, FDA's surreal mea culpa*, August 2023, covid-factuel.fr.
155. *Uttar Pradesh Going the last mile to stop COVID-19*, May 7, 2020, www.who.int.

Currently, trials are underway to explore treatments capable of slowing down the aging of the immune system and stimulating innate immunity. In terms of prevention, it would be wise to maintain a low degree of basic inflammation. To achieve this, it is recommended to combat inflamm-aging, a phenomenon favored by obesity, lack of physical exercise and an unbalanced microbiota.

Among other solutions and remedies that have been ignored, vitamin D should be mentioned first and foremost. It would have been extremely useful, particularly in the pre-spawning period, especially as the health crisis lasted for many months. It is never too late to supplement, as this vitamin/hormone plays an important role in regulating immune system response. Beginning in 2020, CNRS director of research Dr. Jean-Marc Sabatier has recommended vitamin D supplements for COVID-19 patients. Large numbers of publications have since confirmed his vitamin D supplementation recommendations as sound preventive and therapeutic measures against COVID-19.[156]

Studies, confirmed by meta-analyses, are rapidly showing that death and severe forms of COVID-19 are linked to vitamin D deficiency.[157] In fact, the populations most at risk of this type of deficiency (the elderly, obese, diabetic or hypertensic) are also those who are most at risk of contracting severe forms of COVID-19. As early as May 2020, the French Academy of Medicine published a press release recommending "rapid measurement of 25(OH)D levels in people over age 60 with COVID-19, and, in the event of deficiency, a loading dose of 50,000 to 100,000 IU, which could help limit respiratory complications."[158] It also recommended "vitamin D supplementation of 800 to 1,000 IU/day in people under 60 as soon as the diagnosis of COVID-19 is confirmed."

Internationally, in December 2020, a collective of 210 renowned persons, including 127 health professionals, joined forces under the #VitaminD4All (Vitamin D for All) initiative to recommend to the general population a daily supplementation of 10,000 IU (250 µg) of vitamin D for two to three weeks, to reach a blood level of 30 ng/mL. Meanwhile,

---

156. https://pubmed.ncbi.nlm.nih.gov/32972631/.
157. *Therapeutic and prognostic role of vitamin D for COVID-19 infection: A systematic review and meta-analysis of 43 observational studies*, Fausto Petrelli et al., The Journal of Steroid Biochemistry and Molecular Biology, 2021.
158. *Vitamine D et COVID-19 : la supplémentation présente-t-elle un intéret ?* Vidal.fr.

in France, an article was published on January 8, 2021, in *La Revue du Praticien* (*The Practioner's Review*).[159] Regardless of these powerful appeals, and of recommendations by international experts of such supplementation, the reaction of the French health authorities was marked by a silence beyond astonishing.

Vitamin C, known for its antioxidant properties and role in strengthening the immune system, is being considered by researchers and physicians as a potential complementary treatment. The Chinese were the first to include high-dose vitamin C infusions in a treatment protocol for COVID-19.[160] Subsequently, groups of doctors in France,[161] and the United States,[162] also incorporated vitamin C into their treatment protocols, both as a preventive and a curative measure. These health professionals advocated the use of a trio of natural supplements – vitamin D, vitamin C and zinc – as a complement to medication. To be perfectly honest, to my knowledge, there have been no publications on the efficacy of vitamin C against COVID-19.

Elderly abuse

Management of elderly care during the health crisis raised serious ethical concerns. In particular, the "no treatment exists" hypothesis had particularly dire consequences for the elderly, which some even likened to euthanasia. Palliative care protocols were implemented all too excessively, often to the detriment of more conventional treatments (such as classic antibiotics), causing increased mortality in this vulnerable group. This was enabled by the "Rivotril" decree, issued in March 2020,[163] which authorized use of an anti-epileptic drug,

---

159. This platform is signed by the Association française de lutte antirhumatismale (AFLAR), the Société française d'endocrinologie (SFE), the Société française de gériatrie et gérontologie (SFGG), the Société française de pédiatrie (SFP), the Société française d'endocrinologie et diabétologie pédiatrique (SFEDP) and the Société francophone de néphrologie dialyse et transplantation (SFNDT) ; *Effet bénéfique de la vitamine D dans la COVID-19 : quelles sont les données ?*, Larevuedupraticien.fr.
160. See the introduction to chapter 2, http://tiny.cc/shanghai-consensus.
161. https://stopCovid19.today/coordination-sante-libre/.
162. Front Line COVID-19 Critical Care Alliance (FLCCC). https://Covid19criticalcare.com/treatment-protocols/.
163. Decree no. 2020-360 of March 28, 2020, supplementing decree no. 2020-293 of March 23, 2020, prescribing the general measures necessary to deal with the COVID-19 epidemic as part of the state of health emergency.

normally contraindicated in cases of severe respiratory insufficiency in the patient, which was a common condition in COVID-19 patients.

Statistician Pierre Chaillot explained that the Greater Paris University Hospitals (Assistance publique-Hôpitaux de Paris, APHP) set up rapid intervention groups (GIR) to administer Rivotril, not to rescue patients in distress, but for palliative care purposes, to prevent hospital overflow. We know that French hospitals were never overwhelmed in 2020, but rather disorganized, especially their intensive care units.

In France, Pierre Chaillot highlighted the under-use of antibiotics and the over-use of Rivotril and Valium in spring 2020 and again in late 2020, periods of high mortality attributed to COVID-19. In the UK (and Sweden), benzodiazepines and morphine were also recommended for patients at the end of life, despite the fact that these substances are not normally administered to people with respiratory difficulties. Here, too, the use of these drugs is correlated with peaks in COVID-19 mortality.[164]

This raises questions as to how many deaths were actually due to COVID-19 and how many were iatrogenic, that is, caused by the medical treatment itself. It is legitimate to question the impact of the therapeutic choices for the elderly, which potentially have made COVID-19 more lethal than it actually is, and how these mortality statistics, possibly overestimated, may have influenced national political decisions.

The harmful effects of intubation
In France, at the start of the COVID-19 pandemic, Dr. Louis Fouché, an anesthesiologist at the Hôpital de la Conception-Marseille, observed as early as with his second patient that intubation of people with COVID-19 could worsen their condition. Intubation is an invasive procedure that requires artificial coma and can cause further damage. Resuscitators around the world are rapidly discussing this issue and concluding that it is preferable to provide patients with a large amount of oxygene rather than intubate them.

Thus, as early as March 2020, Italian and German doctors and researchers confirmed this recommendation, highlighting the atypical

---

164. Video by Dr. John Campbell (on his Youtube channel), February 14, 2023, Pandemic unnecessary deaths, the data.

nature of the acute respiratory distress syndrome (ARDS) observed in COVID-19 patients.[165] Lung damage must be avoided, while giving the body time to fight the virus.

It is difficult to understand why health authorities continue to support intubation, despite evidence attesting to its negative impact on patient survival. Similarly, it is surprising that many doctors have persisted in this practice, even though some of their colleagues have observed its harmful effects.

Health authorities apply a biopolitical logic the point of which is to make an impact on people's minds. The high mortality rate in intensive care, partly due to this practice, helped to reinforce the discourse on the dangerous nature of the disease, fueling public fear. As for doctors, many are conformists, preferring official guidelines to clinical observation.

Unnecessary confinement
From a scientific point of view, quarantine and confinement measures appear to be the most disconcerting of all health decisions. The only way to understand confinement on a global scale is to see it as a global biopolitical strategy. The point of it being to create an international stupor so as to facilitate the adoption of measures already envisaged in the fictitious scenarios of pandemic simulations.

In fact, confinement used as a measure for the purpose of managing epidemics has long been abandoned. Experience shows that it is totally useless, even counter-productive, as it mixes healthy people with those potentially infected.[166] In any case, no scientific research justifies the reintroduction of the containment strategy as implemented during a health crisis, especially where potential treatments exist.

---

165. *COVID-19 Does Not Lead to a "Typical" Acute Respiratory Distress Syndrome*, Gattinoni et al., *American Journal of Respiratory and Critical Care Medicine*, 2020.
166. CSI, April 29, 2021, with Jean-Dominique Michel. Read also : *Depuis 600 ans, « la quarantaine n'est absolument pas une solution »*, France Culture, Pierre Ropert, March 4, 2020.

International studies,[167] particularly those carried out by the most renowned epidemiologists (before the pandemic at least, for they have since been denigrated and marginalized...), confirm the futility of confinement and closure of businesses and administrations. Among the most important is the meta-analysis,[168] carried out under the aegis of the Johns Hopkins Institute in 2022.

The mask masquerade

The narrative around masks during this health crisis is a textbook illustration of the contradictory and questionable recommendations to which we were exposed. At the start of the crisis, the French authorities rightly assured us that masks were unnecessary for the general public. A few weeks later, masks suddenly became indispensable. This about-turn contributed to generating a certain distrust of the government, at least among the most critically minded. Among others, the contradictory messages created confusion and obstructed rational thinking.

French surgeon Dr. Eric Loridan was one of the first to question the efficacy of face masks for the general public. According to his review of the literature, wearing a polypropylene face mask offered no protection against the transmission of viruses, and could possibly even pose a threat to the safety of those wearing it. The only reason behind the obligation to wear a mask was to remind everyone that an epidemic was persisting. His assertions got him into a lot of trouble.[169]

A US CDC study on influenza published in May 2020 concluded that the use of surgical masks did not prove significantly effective, nor did

167. *Assessing mandatory stay-at-home and business closure effects on the spread of Covid19*, E. Bendavid, C. Oh, J. Bhattacharya, J.P. A. Ioannidis, Eur J Clin Invest., 2021, PMID 33400268.
SARS-CoV-2 suppression and early closure of bars and restaurants: a longitudinal natural experiment, R. Takaku, I. Yokoyama, T. Tabuchi, et al., *Sci Rep,* 2022.
168. *A Literature Review and Meta-Analysis of the Effects of Lockdowns on COVID-19 Mortality,* J. Herby, L. Jonung, and S. H. Hanke (2021), *Studies in Applied Economics,* January 2022, Johns Hopkins Institute for Applied Economics, Global Health, and the Study of Business Enterprise.
169. *L'Ordre des médecins va juger le Docteur Loridan parce qu'il a entièrement raison sur les masques*, Aimsib.org, November 27, 2022.

it reduce transmission. The study also pointed out that the mode of transmission of respiratory viruses remained poorly understood.[170]

The WHO focused on "non-pharmaceutical measures" to control influenza epidemics. Such measures generally refer to hand hygiene, surface cleaning, ventilation, contact tracing, isolation of the sick, travel reduction and border closures... This comprehensive 120-page report,[171] was all the more interesting since it dated from 2019. What did the WHO conclude about masks? That they were relatively limited in terms of preventing influenza transmission. In fact, their use outside of healthcare institutions had not shown any significant efficacy. The WHO also noted that wearing masks can give a false sense of security and lead to neglect of other essential preventive measures, such as hand hygiene and social distancing. What's more, inappropriate use of masks could potentially increase the risk of infection!

It has to be said that the WHO recommendations for COVID-19 have evolved considerably, since it now recommends the use of masks to help prevent the spread of the COVID-19 virus, although the scientific literature has not really provided any new information in the meantime...

Tom Jefferson and international experts from the Cochrane collaborative network produced a meta-analysis,[172] confirming the futility of wearing of masks for the purpose of interrupting or reducing the spread of respiratory viruses. The analysis compiles 78 randomized trials conducted with healthcare workers and the general public. In neither group was there any significant reduction in influenza cases or similar diseases. What's more, no difference was found between the wearing of surgical masks and more elaborate protection, such as N95 masks, designed to filter out at least 95% of airborne particles.

---

170. *Nonpharmaceutical Measures for Pandemic Influenza in Nonhealthcare Settings-Personal Protective and Environmental Measures*, J. Xiao et al., *Emerging Infectious Diseases*, 2020.
171. *Non-pharmaceutical public health measures for mitigating the risk and impact of epidemic and pandemic influenza*, World Health Organization, 2019.
172. *Physical interventions to interrupt or reduce the spread of respiratory viruses*, T. Jefferson, et al., *Cochrane Database of Systematic Reviews*, Sept. 2023.

To conclude

It is important to refer to the scenarios of the pandemic simulations that preceded COVID-19. It was necessary to make the disease appear more severe than it really was by allowing the numbers of sick and dead to rise. It was also necessary to terrorize the population to maintain a maximum level of anxiety until the vaccines were available, deemed from the outset to be the sole and ultimate solution.

In the spring of 2021, the authorities assured us that the health pass would be highly respectful of individual liberties.[173] Nonetheless, the French government ultimately chose to pressure its citizens to vaccinate by making vaccination *de facto* mandatory in many sectors of society. In December 2021, France's Minister of Health came clean at last: "It's simple, crystal clear, and we admit it: we want the French to get vaccinated."

"Hot and cold" messaging is also part of the strategy, used to destabilize people's thinking. It serves to expedite acceptance of measures that are decided not on the basis of sound scientific evidence, but rather to willfully exercise control over the population and to stir up a particular measure of fear.

We must remain vigilant and continue to question the decisions taken by the authorities. The management of this crisis is having devastating and costly consequences on everyone's health. As we have seen, many treatments proved effective relatively quickly. At lower cost, they could have helped boost the population's immune health, making citizens less vulnerable not only to COVID-19, but also to other respiratory infections. Unfortunately, preventive measures capable of simultaneously combating multiple pathogens are not the preferred methods of the health authorities, and of pharmaceutical companies still less. The latter prefer to promote virus-specific remedies, to multiply their sources of revenue. Among these, vaccination is a remedy of choice.

---

173. *Passeport sanitaire : le " oui, mais " du CCNE, La Croix,* March 29, 2021.

PART III

VACCINES AT THE SERVICE OF BIOPOWER

Vaccines are widely recognized as essential public health instruments. Their importance is such that many vaccines are mandatory for children, whereas others are the subject of recurrent campaigns aiming to improve vaccination coverage for various viral diseases. This is particularly true of the flu vaccine, which is recommended every year for people over age 65 in France. In 2023, France launched a major HPV vaccination-awareness campaign for schoolchildren.

During the COVID-19 crisis, we witnessed and played a part, sometimes unwillingly, in the largest global immunization campaign ever undertaken. The inducement to get vaccinated, accompanied by pressure and blackmail with the vaccine pass, fueled intense debate, even among fervent defenders of vaccination. One key point of the controversy concerns use of the term "vaccine" for what instead appears to be experimental gene therapy. This semantic play makes it possible to circumvent constraints regulating the safety and efficacy of these new drugs before they can be marketed.

It ought to be known that traditional vaccines already benefit from a number of facilities designed to not obstruct their development and enable their rapid production. In her book *Le dernier langage de la médecine: histoire de l'immunologie, de Pasteur au Sida*,[174] Anne-Marie Moulin, director of research emeritus at the CNRS, reminds us of the lack of scientific grounds for vaccination: "The theories of immunity were at first a simple commentary on vaccination techniques" and "The rest of the history of vaccination after 1885 is not that of a victorious empiricism, but of an often clueless empiricism." She also points out that vaccinations have always been an instrument of power.[175]

---

174. 1991, PUF, with a preface by Niels K Jerne, Nobel Prize winner in physiology and medicine.
175. *La médecine plébiscitée ? Vaccins et démocratie*, Médecine/sciences 2016.

Similarly, Dr. Michel de Lorgeril's collection *Vaccins et Société* argues that vaccine science lacks rigor and does not follow the principles of evidence-based medicine. There are virtually no double-blind clinical trials demonstrating the efficacy and safety of conventional vaccines.

Since the H1N1 flu crisis, the first global "pandemic" for which a vaccine was developed as a matter of urgency, the main challenge has been to improve the speed of production. Another objective is to produce flu vaccines that are better adapted to emerging variants.

The production method of egg-based flu vaccines has been around for decades. It takes around six months, however, to produce enough vaccine for one flu season. The dominant influenza strains have to be predicted several months in advance, which can result in potential mismatches between the vaccine and the viral strain actually circulating. On the other hand, this process requires a large number of specially prepared hen eggs, which can be problematic in the event of egg shortages or avian disease. The mRNA platform is, a priori, less complicated from a technical standpoint and has the advantage, according to the experts, of being able to adapt rapidly to new variants.

At the Milken Institute Future of Health Summit in Washington in October 2019, during a debate on a "universal flu vaccine," prominent figures including Anthony Fauci and Margaret Hamburg, former commissioner of the US Food and Drug Administration, suggested, in a thinly veiled manner, bypassing clinical trials of mRNA vaccines. According to them, a major health crisis could avert a decade of testing. The COVID-19 crisis struck less than two months later: it appears plausible that these health officials were already aware of the emergence of SARS-CoV-2, and perhaps intended to make the most of it to meet their objectives. The coronavirus crisis presented an ideal opportunity to advance these therapies, which until that point had come up against major ethical and scientific hurdles.

This third and largest part of my book concerns the new vaccine methods introduced during the crisis, and which raised a number of problems. We will examine the repercussions of the COVID-19 vaccination policy on health, a textbook case of mismanagement. Far from producing the results expected, widespread vaccination has had considerable adverse effects on public health, the mechanisms and scale of which we are only beginning to understand.

In Part II, we discussed how traditional vaccines can facilitate certain infections; we will see that the efficacy of the anti-COVID-19 mRNA "vaccine" has been impacted by a similar phenomenon. It is now clear that this technology is not a miracle solution, nor does it eliminate all the problems associated with traditional vaccines. It does, however, offer the prospect of much higher profits, thanks to lower manufacturing costs.

Key points

Most research into post-vaccination immunity focuses on so-called "neutralizing" antibodies measured in vitro. However, these antibody levels may not reflect real protection. Indeed, although antibody levels are often higher after vaccination than after infection, cases of reinfection are far more common in vaccinated individuals than in those who have recovered from the disease.

Natural immunity to COVID-19, acquired after infection with the virus, is stronger and disappears more slowly. It is likely that the real protection against COVID-19 relies more on immune memory. This memory, provided by T and B cells that persist long after infection, seems to offer a better quality of defense than that provided by vaccines.

It is also important to note that vaccinating people who have already been infected could present risks. Indeed, systemic adverse reactions seem to be more frequent in these individuals than in those who have never been infected, especially after the first dose of vaccine.

Moreover, vaccination could have unintended consequences, including reducing the body's ability to cope with future variants. It could also reshape the innate immune response, reducing the body's ability to fight other viruses or cancers, and influence the evolution of inflammatory and autoimmune diseases.

3.1 Natural immunity versus vaccine immunity

In 2021, with the COVID-19 vaccination campaign already well underway, vaccine immunity was intensely promoted to the detriment of natural immunity. In addition, it was recommended that people who had already been infected with the COVID-19 virus should be vaccinated, even though this could present a real danger, according to existing studies.

Once again, I took to my pen for the AIMSIB website, to compare vaccine immunity with natural immunity. For the record, (the duration of) natural immunity was administratively reduced to six months in the context of the health pass. Was this motivated by scientific reality or was it political manipulation to prevent natural immunity from seeming more effective than vaccine immunity? This was clearly a political move, since we know that natural immunity lasts longer than six months (up to 18 years for SARS-CoV in 2003).

WHO wipes out natural immunity
I am intrigued by the WHO position and its recent about-turn: until June 2020, natural immunity was recognized by the WHO as a key component of herd (or population) immunity against new pathogens. But since November 13, 2020, the WHO has held that herd immunity can be attained only through vaccination and not through natural infection... This was reaffirmed on December 31, 2020, for COVID-19, while acknowledging that we do not actually know the vaccine coverage threshold required to achieve "herd immunity," a notion that remains somewhat nebulous to bona fide scientists.[176] On what basis did the WHO decide to depreciate natural immune functions in favor of artificial immunization, if not for the political priority of implementing global vaccination? Since the presence of life on Earth, natural immunity has developed continuously and adapted in all living beings in response to microbes, and all that time without vaccines.

---

176. See Vincent Pavan's work in CSI n°32, November 18, 2021. Denouncing false epidemiological science …
(*Dénoncer la fausse science épidémiologique* … (available in French only))
https://amu.hal.science/hal-02568133v3

Even the US CDC, known for strongly favoring vaccine immunity, which it considers to be superior to natural immunity, explained in 2021 that: "Data are currently insufficient to determine an antibody threshold that indicates when an individual is protected against infection. At this time, there is no FDA-cleared or approved test that providers or the public can use to reliably determine whether a person is protected from infection." In official language, this is tantamount to confirming that, as just indicated, we do not know the "correlate of protection" with regard to the protection conferred by infection. The question is: on what scientific basis have health authorities assessed, independently of manufacturers' claims, the vaccine efficacy of the products they have bought for billions of euros or dollars?

Vaccine antibodies: unreliable controls
As we saw in the previous section, antibodies are not necessarily the right marker for assessing immunity to a pathogen. Clinical studies by pharmaceutical companies rely solely on antibody levels to "demonstrate" that their vaccines are effective, but these levels represent, at best, only the quantity of so-called "neutralizing" antibodies, i.e. the quantity of antibodies capable of neutralizing the virus *in vitro* (in the laboratory). Sometimes, it is sufficient for the manufacturer to exhibit a high rate of virus-binding antibodies *in vitro* (without even "neutralizing" the virus) to have the vaccine approved. And the trend is to move towards approvals that are based solely on this efficacy criterion. Clinical studies do not measure the capacity of the cellular response, and even less do they measure the innate immune response, which is far more complex to assess.

Vaccination of convalescent subjects could present risks: more systemic adverse events are observed in convalescent subjects than in naive subjects (in the sense of "never having been infected") after the first dose of vaccine.[177]

In the case of Pfizer's COVID-19 vaccine, a 2022 study even showed that high antibody levels could be associated with more severe side effects. The antibody results nevertheless served as scientific validation for the generalized recommendation of a third Pfizer dose by the

---

177. 175 PMID 33691060, PMID 33803014, PMID 34062184, PMID 34400714, PMID 33930320.

European Medicines Agency. Regardless of whether this third dose increases the risk of adverse effects, the antibodies have spoken!

In February 2022, the French National Authority for Health (HAS) marked a high point in terms of issuing incoherent guidelines: in a special notice, it reduced the validity of the recovery certificate from six to four months in France, while emphasizing that this validity remained at six months internationally.[178] With no scientific ground to stand on, it validated the "rule of three" imposed by the Minister of Health, stipulating that one infection is equivalent to one injection, and that the primo-vaccination regimen must always include at least one injection. This logic is intrinsically contradictory: if one infection is indeed equivalent to one injection, then three infections should logically be equivalent to three injections.

The terminology used by the HAS was also confusing: it used the expression "primo-vaccination regimen" rather than referring to the acquisition of protection against COVID-19 infection. Clearly, the focus of concern was no longer protection or immunity, but injection. What's more, the HAS, still in contradiction mode, reminded us that a second dose was not recommended for a person who had already been infected. How then can we justify this "rule of three" for people who had been infected and then received a dose? Logically, they should not have received a third injection.

Hyper-targeted immunity
One of the main weaknesses of vaccination is that it does not provide broad-spectrum immunity, as does natural immunization. Natural infection stimulates mucosal immunity, unlike intramuscular vaccination. Vaccination only induces antibodies against a single protein, the Spike, whereas the virus possesses others. Subsequently developed inactivated whole-virus vaccines were able to induce antibodies against other viral proteins, but this did not make them any more effective.[179]

Immunity conferred by infection can protect against future variants, as it also affects non-variable parts of the virus; in contrast, vaccine antibodies are directed against the Spike, which mutates extensively

---

178. HAS, Avis n°2022.0012/SESPEV, February 14, 2022.
179. *Vaccins à virus inactivé anti-COVID-19 (Valneva et autres) : décevants !* Hélène Banoun, ResearchGate, January 2022.

in successive variants. We shall also see that vaccination can induce antibodies that facilitate infection.

What is more, vaccination appears to weaken the immune response to future infection. Even more importantly, it modifies the immune response of convalescents, and not necessarily in a good way: it could reduce convalescents' subsequent ability to react to future variants.

Immune restraint

In the course of my investigations, I came across several studies documenting this other worrying fact: immune response weakens following vaccination. This is related to the phenomenon of immune imprinting (or OAS), that was discussed in relation to influenza. I compiled my conclusions into an article on *COVID-19: Natural immunity versus vaccine immunity*, October 2021, and, since then, numerous articles have confirmed the OAS induced by repeat injections. It appears that the consequences are more severe for individuals who contracted the SARS-CoV-2 virus naturally before being vaccinated.

Vaccination does indeed increase the level of antibodies targeting the Spike protein, but these antibodies remain specific to the first "imprint," that is, to the Spike protein of the original Wuhan strain.

Vaccination narrows the spectrum of the immune system by preventing it from reacting to the Spike of new variants and also to other (non-Spike) antigens of viruses encountered. For example, the concentration of antibodies targeting the N protein is lower in vaccinated individuals compared with those who have recovered from COVID-19. However, the N protein mutates less frequently than the Spike, making anti-N antibodies particularly effective against successive variants. This phenomenon of immune imprinting is more developed in the elderly, who have fewer naive lymphocytes, as we have seen. This is a pity, because it is the elderly who need protection against COVID-19, not the young.

It is impossible to reference all the articles on this subject, but it is worth pointing out that articles that do allude to it often try to attribute the vaccine damage to a previous infection. Such is the case of a paper in *Science*,[180] which looks only at triple vaccinees and claims that OAS is due to previous infections and not to the vaccine.

---

180. *Immune boosting* by B.1.1.529 (Omicron) depends on previous SARS-CoV-2 exposure, C.J. Reynolds, et al., Science, 2022. PMID 35699621.

Does the vaccine protect against severe forms of COVID-19?
For a rigorous assessment of the immunity conferred by a vaccine, it is essential to measure protection against severe forms of the disease, for example on the basis of hospitalization or mortality rates. Clinical trials of vaccines, however, have failed to demonstrate this, owing to a lack of significant statistics. Granted, it is difficult to observe severe forms of the disease in trial participants selected for their good health. The claim that the vaccine protects against severe forms of the disease is a persistent one that, to date, has not been proven. Despite this, the notion is widely disseminated as an undisputed truth by media which are allied with the interests of biopower. For further details on this positioning, we refer to the research of biostatistician Christine Cotton, author of *Tous vaccinés, tous protégés*.

According to a retrospective cohort study,[181] involving 700,000 Israelis, vaccinees have a higher risk of COVID-19-related hospitalizations than the naturally infected (6.7 times higher). People who have already been infected with SARS-CoV-2 are 27 times less likely to develop a symptomatic infection a second time than are those who have been vaccinated.

Further reading
– *COVID-19: Natural immunity versus vaccine immunity*, October 2021, https://www.qeios.com/read/DP264J
– Banoun H. *Why are children and many adults not affected by COVID-19?* Role of the host immune response Infect Dis Res. 2022; 3(3):18. doi:10.53388/IDR20220825018
https://web.archive.org/web/20220820133628/https://www.tmrjournals.com/public/articlePDF/20220819/a4
– *Assessing natural anti-COVID-19 immunity: serology, cellular immunity*
https://www.qeios.com/read/STSOHC
– *Une troisième dose pour que ça marche enfin ?* Aimsib.org, November 26, 2021.

---

181. *Comparing SARS-CoV-2 natural immunity to vaccine-induced immunity: reinfections versus breakthrough infections*, Sivan Gazit et al., medRxiv, August 25, 2021.

3.2 When COVID-19 vaccines enable instead of prevent infection

We have already mentioned two immune mechanisms that facilitate infection: facilitating antibodies (ADE) and antigenic imprinting (OAS). Regardless of the technological differences between RNA and conventional vaccines, these two mechanisms are nonetheless also observed with COVID-19 vaccines. I alerted to the risks of OAS in two articles published in 2020,[182] even before the vaccines were released, based on earlier observations in 2003 SARS-CoV vaccine trials. Unfortunately, the hypotheses proved correct. Cases of post-vaccination COVID-19 were reported from the very start of the vaccination campaign.

Warnings ignored

At the start of 2020, all the coronavirus experts were concerned about the emergence of this fearsome deleterious phenomenon, well known since the animal trials for SARS-CoV-1 vaccines in 2003.[183] It is well known that ADE is caused by antibodies targeting the virus' famous Spike protein. This effect is even considered to be inevitable.[184]

The question then arises: why have all the vaccine manufacturers chosen the Spike protein as their particular antigen? It is present in large quantities on the virus membrane, and vaccine science focuses primarily on the production of antibodies, considered to be beneficial players in our immune system. So, it was logical to choose this protein as a target, for it could induce an abundance of neutralizing antibodies capable of binding to the viral membrane and preventing it from penetrating our cells.

---

182. *Covid-19 graves, admettre l'existence des anticorps facilitateurs et Vaccin anti-Covid-19 et immunité de groupe, c'est non... et encore non*, Aimsib.org.
183. *Antibody-Dependent Enhancement of Viral Infections, In: Dynamics of Immune Activation in Viral Diseases*, R. Kulkarni et al., Springer, Singapore, 2020. *Antibody-dependent SARS corona-virus infection is mediated by antibodies against Spike proteins*, S.F. Wang et al., Biochem Biophys Res Commun, August 2014. PMID 25073113.
184. *Antibody dependent enhancement: Unavoidable problems in vaccine development*, L. Xu et al., Adv Immunol, 2021.

Nonetheless, this approach is limited and reductive, since it "overlooks" the possibility of ADE. This occurrence, whereby some of the antibodies could actually facilitate infection rather than fight it, should have been taken into greater account in the vaccine design. The Risk Management Plan for the Pfizer vaccine clinical trial reports does state that ADE is a risk to be monitored, but no further details are given (this risk has since been removed without comment).[185]

Infections occurring immediately after vaccination in clinical trials

Peter Doshi, a professor at the University of Baltimore specializing in drug safety and editor of the BMJ, explains that such assessment has unfortunately not been carried out comprehensively.[186] Incidents of COVID-19 occurring immediately after injection of vaccine doses were not registered in clinical trial reports, and it can even be said that every effort has been made to eliminate them from both efficacy and toxicity outcomes. It is not possible to differentiate between a manifestation of ADE and a viral infection without ADE. Thus, when cases of disease or death occur shortly after vaccination, the vaccine cannot be ruled out as a likely cause. Accurate assessment of ADE requires careful monitoring of cases of COVID-19 occurring in the days following vaccination. And yet, in all published clinical trials, these periods are discreetly excluded. Vaccine manufacturers exclude post-injection surveillance of infection for seven to 15 days, on the pretext that patients were not yet protected during that time. While this may be a legitimate argument, it does not preclude analysis of the number of infections in the days following injection.

Clearly, vaccine efficacy is distorted by a major bias: only cases of COVID-19 occurring more than 14 days after each injection are considered. Having analyzed some of these clinical trials in several articles for the AIMSIB website, I see the same peculiarity visible in the figures for the fortnight after the injection.

In short, it is crucial to recognize that ADE is a worrisome phenomenon in the context of COVID-19 vaccination. Accurate monitoring

185. EMA_EPAR-Pfizer June 2023, RMP Version number: 10.0, https://www.ema.europa.eu/en/documents/rmp-summary/comirnaty-epar-riskmanagement-plan_en.pdf.
186. *Pfizer and Moderna's 95% effective vaccines? Let's be cautious and first see the full data*, November 26, 2020, on the BMJ blog.

and analysis of post-vaccination COVID-19 cases would have been essential.

ADE, observed in all COVID-19 vaccine trials, including the "classics"

The presence of ADE in mRNA vaccines shows that these new methods are not spared this phenomenon, which has already been observed in the past with all types of vaccine targeting the coronavirus Spike protein. In the case of SARS-CoV-2, conventional vaccines are unable to overcome the ADE barrier.

Regarding the Chinese inactivated-virus vaccine CoronaVac, from the Sinovac laboratory, it was noted that people who had received a single dose had a much higher risk of contracting COVID-19 than those who had not been vaccinated.[187]

The "classic" Novavax vaccine (based on Spike recombinant protein), developed by an American firm and intended for those "hesitant" about mRNA vaccination, gives the same type of result. On closer analysis,[188] it is not so classic, since the Spike protein is modified just as it is for the other vaccines and produced on insect cells. The point of this is about injecting the complete Spike protein, despite its toxicity. Furthermore, this Spike has been modified to boost its stability… The final preparation is adjuvanted with Matrix-M®, a new adjuvant tested in clinical trials for flu vaccines. Like all adjuvants, it increases inflammatory reactions and enables higher antibody production than a non-adjuvanted vaccine.

In the Novavax trial, to measure vaccine efficacy, only COVID-19 presenting more than 14 days after the second dose is recorded. Moreover, signs of COVID-19 within seven days of the first dose are not confirmed by PCR, which prevents their recognition as COVID-19-confirmed! In this study, as in others, data manipulation can produce inconsistent results which are evident under scrutiny, but very few people took a close look at the results when they were first published. I was strongly criticized in the summer of 2021 when I undertook such thorough analysis.

---

187. *Effectiveness of an Inactivated SARS-CoV-2 Vaccine in Chile*, PMID: 34233097

188. *Novavax : Bientôt un vaccin classique contre la COVID-19 ?*, H. Banoun, July 11, 2021.

To minimize the excess number of post-vaccination COVID-19 cases in the days following injection, manufacturers artificially inflate COVID-19 rates in subjects receiving placebo during the same period. This is likely achieved by testing participants in this group more intensively than those vaccinated (we know how easy it is to obtain a positive PCR result by increasing the number of amplification cycles). Subsequently, after this initial critical period, post-vaccination cases of COVID-19 decline, so there is no need to artificially increase the rate in placebo subjects. As a result, lower COVID-19 rates were observed in placebo subjects more than seven days after the second dose of saline, as if the latter offered protection against COVID-19!

I observed this same manipulation in the Pfizer trial with adolescents and also adults.[189] Comparing the incidence rate of the disease in the general population with that among clinical trial participants (particularly those in the placebo group) reveals the manipulation. For example, while the incidence of COVID-19 was 0.61% in the general population in the USA during the period corresponding to the Pfizer clinical trial, it was 3.1% in the placebo group. Data manipulation makes the placebo saline solution appear protective against COVID-19 once the period between the first dose and 15 days after the second dose has elapsed. The same problem (albeit less pronounced) was encountered in the Moderna trial, but it is important to note that a large number of vaccinated participants were excluded from the trial without explanation between the two doses.

I presented all this information at several CSI programs in July and August 2021. The results of the trials, however, were published as early as the end of 2020: apart from a few discerning scientists, who took interest in these results? Of the millions of biological researchers in the world, has no one else read them before me in the summer of 2021?

If I waited a few months before examining them, it was because I thought this had probably already been done by experts from the official agencies (EMA and FDA in particular), but also by researchers from other institutions. However, we later learned that, at the time, FDA experts had resigned, and that EMA experts were pressured to approve the vaccines despite these obvious flaws in the reporting.[190]

189. https://www.qeios.com/read/KP77NW, *Clinical trials of Covid vaccines in adolescents: do the EMA and FDA have access to the same data?* August 23, 2021.

190. *Biden's top-down booster plan sparks anger at FDA*, Adam Cancryn, Sarah

Did researchers at French state entities such as the CNRS and Inserm censor themselves, or were they subject to pressure? This question emerges clearly from Juliette Rouchier's interview with Toby Green, Professor of History at King's College.[191]

How long can the academic world avoid self-examination of its behavior during the COVID-19 pandemic?

In all the clinical trials, the rarity of severe cases of COVID-19 confirms that the pandemic may not have been as dangerous as announced. Most of the trial participants were young and healthy, individuals who generally had no fear of the virus. So why vaccinate them? For example, in the Novavax trial, the risk of contracting COVID-19 was around 1% during the trial period. We heard a lot about the protection offered by a supposedly "altruistic" vaccine, only to learn, once a large part of the world's population had been vaccinated, that it did not prevent transmission. There was, therefore, no justification for vaccinating healthy young people.

In 2023, these manipulations came as less of a surprise, as we now know that Pfizer delivered fraudulent clinical trials. A whistle-blower, Brook Jackson, revealed that the legal procedures of the clinical trial had not been respected. In particular, the trial staff knew who had been vaccinated and who was in the placebo group. It was therefore easy to manipulate the PCR test results for the latter group and overlook the COVID-19 symptoms of the vaccinated group.[192] Brook Jackson was fired immediately after her statements, and her complaint (before the law) was rejected. Nonetheless, examination of the records published following a FOIA request showed numerous irregularities.[193]

We also note that the toxicity of the vaccines was visible as soon as the trials were published at the end of 2020, but everyone turned a blind eye to this reality.

Owermohle, Politico, August 31, 2021. *Children's Health Defense Team, Government Officials Pressured EU Regulators to Rush Authorization of Pfizer Vaccine, Leaked Documents Reveal, Children's Health Defense*, July 11, 2023.

191. *Réflexions sur la soumission du monde académique durant la crise du COVID-19*, interview with Toby Green, June 23, 2023.

192. *COVID-19: Researcher blows the whistle on data integrity issues in Pfizer's vaccine trial*, P. D. Thacker, BMJ, 2021.

193. Pfizer/BioNTech C4591001 Trial, OpenVAET, April 2022.

Post-vaccination COVID-19 observation

Since the initial vaccination campaigns, many people have reported catching COVID-19 very soon after the injection. The observation of post-vaccination COVID-19 is confirmed by official figures, although the authorities have done their utmost to conceal this by invariably asserting the contrary. The websites ourworldindata.org,[194] and data from Johns Hopkins,[195] show large increases in COVID-19 cases with vaccination campaigns in countries where it had previously been unknown (e.g. Cambodia, Cuba, Mongolia, New Caledonia, Viet Nam) or was little known (Hungary, India, Palestine, Philippines).

The authorities had difficulty in recognizing this ADE effect, explaining that it was due to a change in the behavior of freshly vaccinated individuals who, as soon as they had been injected, refrained from practicing all barrier gestures. Outbreaks of COVID-19 in homes for the elderly in the UK as of December 2020 cannot be attributed to a behavioral change.[196]

When statistics show ADE

There are a staggering number of publications striving to demonstrate the efficacy of the vaccines, but as British mathematician and statistician Prof. Norman Fenton has pointed out, the same bias was already at work in clinical trials: deaths of people who had been vaccinated less than a week before (or a fortnight, depending on the publication) were classified among the deaths of non-vaccinated people. Correcting this error alone reveals the COVID-19 excess mortality immediately after vaccination. Of course, this only applies to the older age groups likely to die of COVID-19.[197]

In "real-life" efficacy studies, the same bias is sufficient to mask the ADE and artificially increase vaccine efficacy.

194. https://ourworldindata.org/COVID-19-vaccinations.
195. 193 https://corona-virus.jhu.edu/map.html.
196. *Rapid Response to: "Thinking beyond behavioural change as an explanation for increased COVID-19 post vaccination"*, Clare Craig, BMJ, March 2021.
197. Latest statistics on England mortality data suggest systematic miscategorisation of vaccine status and uncertain effectiveness of COVID-19 vaccination, Martin Neil et al., ResearchGate, 2021.

All this is confirmed by a fine Indian study,[198] which shows, based on a survey of healthcare workers, the total ineffectiveness of two doses of vaccine when a new wave of the virus arrives in India, as well as the facilitation that occurs just after the injection of the first or second dose of vaccine.

When clinical cases confirm ADE

There are reports of severe COVID-19 just after vaccination: Sridhar et al.[199] reported the case of a woman recently vaccinated (seven days) with Pfizer's mRNA vaccine, who died of acute respiratory distress syndrome. No evidence of COVID-19 infection was found, but anti-Spike antibodies were indeed detected 13 days after injection!

In Japan, Bando et al.[200] describe two patients with acute COVID-19 who were vaccinated with Pfizer's product. Both presented with acute respiratory syndrome not attributable to SARS-CoV-2. Imaging showed interstitial lung disease. The authors suggest that the immune response to COVID-19 was reactivated by vaccination, but they make no allusion to probable ADE or VAERD (Vaccine-associated enhanced respiratory disease).

Hirschbühl et al.[201] conducted autopsies on 170 people who had died of COVID-19 (or were carriers of the virus at the time of death). They found that fully vaccinated patients had much higher pulmonary viral loads than non-vaccinated patients. This finding was even more pronounced in partially vaccinated women. The authors do not rule out the role of ADE in this occurrence.

---

198. *Persistent Health Issues, Adverse Events, and Effectiveness of Vaccines during the Second Wave of COVID-19: A Cohort Study from a Tertiary Hospital in North India*, U. Kaur et al., *Vaccines* (Basel), 2022, PMID 35891317.
199. *Vaccine-Induced Antibody Dependent Enhancement in COVID-19*, P. Sridhar et al., Chest, 2022.
200. *Two cases of acute respiratory failure following SARS-CoV-2 vaccination in post-COVID-19 pneumonia*, T. Bando et al., *Respirology Case Reports*, 2022.
201. *High viral loads: what drives fatal cases of COVID-19 in vaccinees? an autopsy study*, K. Hirschbühl et al., *Modern Pathology*, 2022.

Biological elucidation of post-vaccinal ADE

Remember that ADE occurs when antibodies are produced in low quantities and with reduced affinity following injection, creating conditions similar to those seen in dengue-associated ADE.

Several 2021 and 2022 studies detail the biological mechanism of COVID-19 post-vaccine ADE. Its main features are as follows:

An American study shows that the ratio of binding to neutralizing antibodies after vaccination is higher than after natural infection. The majority of antibodies inducted by the vaccine have no neutralizing activity.[202]

A Japanese team has shown that antibodies in the serum of people vaccinated with anti-COVID-19 mRNA facilitate virus entry *in vitro*. There is indeed an imbalance between the concentration of neutralizing (beneficial) and facilitating (deleterious) antibodies, similar to that observed after measles vaccination.[203] Other research suggests that the imbalance may vary between Moderna and Pfizer vaccines.[204]

Prof. Jacques Fantini's team also showed that, for certain variants, neutralizing antibodies have a lower affinity for the Spike protein, while facilitating antibodies show a strikingly higher affinity.[205]

Facilitation takes place at the level of "epitopes," also known as "antigenic sites," which are the specific parts of an antigen to which antibodies can bind. An epitope is, in a way, the "target" recognized by the immune system. With the evolution of the virus and the successive emergence of SARS-CoV-2 variants, facilitating epitopes are conserved and neutralizing epitopes mutate, allowing the variants to escape neutralizing antibodies, thereby reinforcing the possibility of ADE after infection or vaccination against the original strain.[206]

---

202. *The plasmablast response to SARS-CoV-2 mRNA vaccination is dominated by non-neutralizing antibodies that target both the NTD and the RBD,* F. Amanat et al., medRxiv, 2021.
203. *Reevaluation of antibody-dependent enhancement of infection in anti-SARS-CoV-2 therapeutic antibodies and mRNA-vaccine antisera using FcRand ACE2-positive cells,* J. Shimizu et al., Scientific Reports, 2022.
204. *Subtle immunological differences in mRNA-1273 and BNT162b2 COVID-19 vaccine induced Fc-functional profiles,* P. Kaplonek et al., *bioRxiv,* 2021; Update in: *Sci Transl Med,* 2022.
205. *Infection-enhancing anti-SARS-CoV-2 antibodies recognize both the original Wuhan/D614G strain and Delta variants. A potential risk for mass vaccination,* N. Yahi, H. Chahinian, J. Fantini, J Infect, Dis. 2021.
206. *Structural Dynamics of the SARS-CoV-2 Spike Protein: A 2-Year Retro-*

Antibodies facilitating viral entry into cells can have a beneficial effect by enabling Natural Killers (NKs) to identify infected cells. The antibodies then help the NKs to phagocytize these cells, but it has been shown that these protective antibodies are less effective when induced by vaccination rather than by infection.[207]

In the complex landscape of biological processes, other phenomena contribute to the deleterious effect of antibodies induced by vaccination. One of the most remarkable effects, observed in mRNA vaccine trials, is the transient drop in blood lymphocytes immediately after injection. This effect, far from negligible, favors infections in general, and post-vaccination COVID-19 in particular. The discovery of this post-vaccinal lymphopenia in the week following injection is documented in a Pfizer trial in China,[208] and in the Pfizer Phase I/II trial.[209]

Further reading

– *Vaccination anti-Covid-19, état des lieux*, with Vincent Reliquet, Aimsib.org, February 7, 2021. See paragraphs 3 and 4, 6-3.

– *Comment expliquer biologiquement l'excès de Covid-19 post-vaccinaux*, Aimsib.org, July 30, 2021.

– *Covid graves, admettre l'existence des anticorps facilitateurs*, Aimsib.org, August 23, 2020.

– *Vaccin anti-Covid-19 et immunité de groupe, c'est non... et encore non*, Aimsib.org, May 3, 2020.

– *Les vaccins à virus inactivés, une solution ?*, Aimsib.org, August 1, 2021.

– *Novavax : Bientôt un vaccin classique contre la COVID-19 ?*, Aimsib. org, July 11, 2021.

spective Analysis of SARS-CoV-2 Variants (from Alpha to Omicron) Reveals an Early Divergence between Conserved and Variable Epitopes, P. Guérin, N. Yahi, F. Azzaz, H. Chahinian, J. M. Sabatier, J. Fantini, *Molecules*, 2022.

207. *Natural Killer Cell-Mediated Antibody-Dependent Cellular Cytotoxicity Against SARS-CoV-2 After Natural Infection Is More Potent Than After Vaccination*, G. J. Rieke et al., J. Infect. Dis., 2022.

208. PMID: 33888900.

209. *Phase I/II study of COVID-19 RNA vaccine BNT162b1 in adults*, M.J. Mulligan et al., *Nature*, 2020; *Safety and Immunogenicity of Two RNA-Based COVID-19 Vaccine Candidates*, E.E. Walsh et al., New England J Med, 2020.

3.3 Clinical trials: predictable failure with all types of vaccine?

Even before the vaccination campaign launched in December 2020, vaccine manufacturers and health authorities were well aware of the uncertainties surrounding the efficacy and safety of COVID-19 vaccines. Proof of this is provided by a US CDC document dated October 2020, signed by Tom Shimabukuro, on behalf of the vaccine safety group. This document details the follow-up that was slated to be put in place once the vaccines had been approved.[210]

The CDC had planned to closely monitor a whole range of potentially adverse effects, including death, neurological effects, infarction, anaphylactic shock, thrombosis and myocarditis. These very same adverse effects were monitored following vaccine approval.

The document also mentions the need to monitor women who declare pregnancy after vaccination. At the time, vaccination of this population segment was not yet recommended, no pregnant women had been included in clinical trials, and women of childbearing age were expected to take contraception. Men were also concerned: they were advised to abstain from sexual intercourse and sperm donation in the month following the vaccine injections. The question arises as to whether studies of the presence of mRNA in semen have been conducted, and how the authorities determined that this risk faded after one month.

With regard to efficacy, the document points out that the US CDC noted the absence of data on certain populations, such as the elderly, pregnant women, the immunocompromised, the chronically ill and children. The duration of protection offered by vaccines and their effectiveness against variants of the virus were also questioned at the time. All these concerns and monitoring points were justified when I examined the clinical trials.

In reality, as illustrated by the full-scale trial of Pfizer's vaccine in Israel, the risks quickly outweigh the benefits: a rise in deaths is reported within a month after the start of the vaccination campaign.

---

210. *CDC post-authorization/post-licensure safety monitoring of COVID-19 vaccines*, T. Shimabukuro, CDC, October 30, 2020.

Contrary to a study published in *The New England Journal of Medicine* (*NEJM*) on the efficacy of Pfizer's vaccine in Israel, there were more instances of COVID-19, sometimes severe, following injections.

Five biases that disqualify the "good results" of Pfizer's vaccine in Israel

The New England Journal of Medicine study claims to assess the vaccine's efficacy in the Israeli population after two doses received. The *NEJM* publication was scrutinized by two researchers, and I translated their work, later made available to AIMSIB readers.

Haim Yativ, an Israeli engineer, and Dr. Hervé Seligmann were quick to identify common biases when it came to reversing a reality that biopower considered disturbing.[1] These major biases were almost continuously present in studies brandished by the authorities for the purpose of legitimizing policies that do not correspond to effective health management based on sound scientific argument.

Lack of independence: the authors of the original study received funding from several pharmaceutical companies, including Pfizer.

Lack of randomization: the study did not use a random draw to select participants, which could possibly introduce selection bias.

Exclusion of certain populations: large segments of the population were excluded from the study, notably healthcare workers, retirement home residents, people confined at home, and those who had had contact with a healthcare worker within three days prior to vaccination. This limits the scope of the study outcomes applicable to the overall population.

Short surveillance period: patients were monitored for an average of 15 days (after injection), which is of course far too inadequate to assess the long-term efficacy of the vaccine and any potential adverse effects it may cause.

Lack of transparency: the study's raw data are no longer available, which curtails any possibility of verification or replication of study results.

---

1. https://www.aimsib.org/2021/03/05/critique-de-lessai-grandeur-nature-du-vaccin-pfizer-en-israel/

Adenovirus vaccines from Janssen and AstraZeneca

As for the adenovirus vaccines that have been withdrawn from the market, a review of the clinical trials suggests that they should never have been made available in the first place.[211] One has only to look at the dossier for the conditional authorization of AstraZeneca's Vaxzevria vaccine to understand that the EMA acted in a sea of unknowns:

– efficacy had not been demonstrated in people over age 55;

– efficacy against severe forms of COVID-19 and hospitalization had not been demonstrated;

– the duration of protection was not known;

– efficacy against asymptomatic infections and in HIV-positive subjects had not been demonstrated;

– Phase III clinical data, with trials still in progress at the time of writing, did not allow us to draw any conclusions regarding protection in patients with comorbidities or autoimmune diseases;

– lastly, efficacy on circulating and future variants remained absolutely unknown.

In fact, the AstraZeneca vaccine proved so toxic during the trial that the manufacturers replaced the saline placebo (during the course of the study!) with a highly reactogenic vaccine, MenACWY, an anti-meningococcal... This ironed out the differences between the two groups in terms of adverse effects.

With regard to Janssen's adenovirus vaccine, the FDA made no secret of the increased risk of embolisms and thromboses, even though its conditional marketing authorization in Europe had just been granted. It called for monitoring of seizures (and other neurological diseases), inner ear disorders and pericarditis.

A number of major anomalies in the analysis of the Johnson & Johnson (Janssen) dossier unveiled by the FDA suggest that the random selection of vaccine/placebo groups may have been biased: there are more exclusions for cause of death in the placebo group than in the vaccine group. In the placebo group, 11 participants died (from causes other than COVID-19), compared with one in the vaccine

---

211. RéinfoCOVID-19/Aimsib (10/04/2021), *Note de synthèse sur les vaccins Vaxzevria (AstraZeneca)TM et COVID-19 Janssen (Johnson&Johnson) TM.*

group, i.e. 11 times as many. If these deaths were independent of COVID-19, there should have been the same number in each group. This disparity raises the question: were more frail or older individuals intentionally selected for the placebo group, in order to bias the benefit/risk ratio in favor of the vaccine?

The European Medicines Agency also suspended the AstraZeneca,[212] vaccine for a few days, following reports of serious cases of thrombosis throughout Europe. This suspension was eventually transformed into a restriction of recommendation, for the over-55s only. The vaccine was still authorized in a large number of countries in 2023,[213] but was ultimately withdrawn from sale in May 2024 on the pretext of a drop in demand.

Are clinical trials of conventional vaccines conclusive?

As part of my research, I also examined the clinical trials of so-called "classic" vaccines, i.e. protein and inactivated virus vaccines. Novavax, a modified Spike protein vaccine, is adjuvanted with a new molecule that has already demonstrated high toxicity in a malaria vaccine trial. As with other vaccines, ADE cannot be ruled out when looking at animal trials. What's more, here again, cases of COVID-19 occurring in the days following vaccination are not considered or excluded, giving the impression that the placebo is almost as protective as the vaccine... Adverse effects are numerous and some serious, including deaths, severe cases of COVID-19, myocarditis and neurological disease.

As regards the inactivated virus vaccines such as Sinovac, Sinopharm, Coronavac and Valneva, clinical trial results are no more reassuring. These vaccines contain an aluminic adjuvant which is used only in the "placebo" group, which means that the trials do not contain a true placebo group. The clinical trial shows facilitation of infection in the 14 days following injection, which is confirmed very early on in a post-marketing observational study. The clinical trial gave no indication of protection against symptomatic forms of COVID-19, nor

212. *European Medicines Agency. COVID-19 Vaccine AstraZeneca: benefits still outweigh the risks despite possible link to rare blood clots with low platelets,* Eur Med Agency, 2021.
213. Particularly in Europe: https://www.ema.europa.eu/en/medicines/ human/EPAR/vaxzevria

against severe forms, nor against death. Serious adverse events were also reported, including allergic reactions, neurological disorders and local tumors at the injection site.

Further reading

– https://www.researchgate.net/publication/366605160_What_do_the_Moderna_and_Pfizer_preclinical_studies_recently_unveiled_by_FOIA_reveal

What do the Moderna and Pfizer preclinical studies recently unveiled by FOIA reveal?

– *Review of: Neutralization of SARS-CoV-2 Spike 69/70 deletion, E484K, and N501Y variants by BNT162b2 vaccine-elicited sera (review of an in vitro efficacy essay), Qeios*, April 19, 2021. https://doi.org/10.32388/HGI4LE

– *Les vaccins à virus inactivé, une solution ?* Aimsib.org, August 1, 2021.

– *Vaccins à virus inactivé anti-Covid-19 (Valneva et autres) : décevants !*, Aimsib.org, January 16, 2022.

– *Novavax, bientôt un vaccin « classique » contre la COVID-19 ?*, Aimsib.org, July 11, 2021.

– https://www.qeios.com/read/KP77NW: *Clinical trials of COVID vaccines in adolescents: do the EMA and FDA have access to the same data?*, August 23, 2021.

– *Critique de l'essai grandeur nature du vaccin Pfizer en Israel*, Aimsib.org, March 5, 2021.

– *Vaccination anti-Covid-19, état des lieux*, Aimsib.org, February 7, 2021.

– *Note de synthèse sur les vaccins Vaxzevria (Astrazeneca)TM et Covid-19 Janssen (Johnson&Johnson)TM*, co-edited by Aimsib/ReinfoCovid, April 10, 2021.

The different types of vaccines

Like the Pfizer-BioNTech product, mRNA vaccines apply a radically new approach to protecting against viral infections. They do not contain the virus that causes COVID-19. Instead, they carry the genetic code (messenger RNA or mRNA) needed to produce the modified Spike protein of the SARS-CoV-2 virus. Once injected, our body uses this code to produce Spike. This protein triggers an immune response, producing antibodies and activating T cells to fight the virus in case of exposure.

Adenoviral vector vaccines, like AstraZeneca's, use a weaker version of a different virus (in this case, an adenovirus that causes the common cold in chimpanzees) to deliver the genetic material of the SARS-CoV-2 virus into human cells. This genetic material is used by our cells to produce the virus Spike, triggering an immune response. Unlike mRNA vaccines, adenoviral vector vaccines do not require ultra-low temperature storage, making them easy to distribute.

Protein vaccines, like Novavax, are based on the use of proteins or protein fragments from the virus to stimulate an immune response. In the case of Novavax's COVID-19 vaccine, the modified SARS-CoV-2 Spike protein is used. This protein is produced in the laboratory (from insect virus grown on insect cells) and encapsulated in nanoparticles. The vaccine is also adjuvanted, which means that it contains a substance that boosts the immune response to the vaccine; this particular adjuvant has never been marketed before.

Inactivated virus vaccines use an inactivated or "killed" version of the whole virus to stimulate an immune response. These have been used for many years to prevent diseases such as influenza. The SARS-CoV-2 virus is grown in the laboratory and then inactivated, so that it cannot cause disease. When injected, the immune system recognizes the virus as a threat and produces an immune response.

3.4 High-risk vaccination policies

Vaccination against COVID-19 has been the subject of worldwide debate, particularly with respect to vulnerable groups: infants, children, adolescents and pregnant women. On what scientific basis did health authorities give the go-ahead to administer vaccines to these populations? We are going to discover that the data available at the time offered no guarantee of efficacy and already then pointed to major risks for these groups, notably that of endangering the lives of thousands of babies in the womb.

3.4.1 Should infants, young people and pregnant women be vaccinated?

Vaccinating the very young: scientific heresy

It is particularly disturbing that the authorities approved the use of COVID-19 mRNA vaccines for infants as young as six months of age. It is obvious, as we have repeatedly emphasized, that children are generally not seriously affected by COVID-19. Of course, this does not mean that they cannot be carriers of the virus. Most experience only minor symptoms, similar to a mild cold. It is essential to remember, however, that only children with severe chronic illnesses may be susceptible to developing a severe form of the disease.

Like many others, I am shocked by the authorization granted to administer anti-COVID-19 mRNA vaccines to infants, which is why I undertook to investigate the reasons behind this authorization for several media. (Aimsib, CSI, *InfoDuJour*).

On June 15, 2022, the FDA approved the Pfizer and Moderna vaccines for infants and children up to five years of age. A close look at the FDA report reveals that the efficacy of these vaccines is based primarily on the rate of antibodies produced. Even by this measure, which is far from the most rigorous, efficacy barely reaches 50%, or even less, depending on the method of calculation.

It is important to recall that 50% is normally the minimum efficacy threshold for vaccine approval. The FDA admits to departing from this rule. But this is not the only departure from good scientific practice: in assessing the degree of protection afforded by the vaccine against infection, so many participants were excluded from assessment that the results became virtually unfeasible. And despite even these exclusions, the efficacy of the vaccine remains questionable for some groups, presenting a greater risk of infection between the first and second doses. Even more disturbing, severe cases of COVID-19 have been reported in vaccinated children, whereas this is not the case in non-vaccinated children. The FDA even identified 12 cases of vaccinated children showing repeated occurrence of COVID-19 disease during the trial.

Not a single child who had already acquired natural immunity following a previous infection was reinfected. This highlights the strength of natural immunity to disease.

The series of serious adverse reactions suffered by vaccinated children is alarmingly similar to that observed in other, older groups. These include convulsions, high fevers, anaphylactic shock, appendicitis, epilepsy, hypersensitivity reactions, and Kawasaki disease (systemic multi-inflammation), to name but a few. Add to this respiratory infections, chest pain, allergic rashes, viral infections, diabetes, severe urticaria and liver damage, all observed within two months of follow-up. And for those who escape these serious effects, their future antiviral immunity may be compromised by the immune imprinting phenomenon described earlier.

In view of all this, it is shocking that FDA, recognizing the inefficacy and potential dangers of mRNA vaccines for infants, approves them, nonetheless. Robert F. Kennedy Jr. sheds light on this decision, which some consider outright criminal: "Vaccine manufacturers are not liable for injury or death associated with urgently licensed vaccines but may be held liable once the vaccine is fully licensed – unless the vaccine is added to the CDC's childhood immunization schedule."[214]

This authorization, lacking any scientific basis whatsoever, is a typical biopolitical rule. Trials on infants should never have even started! Why initiate trials on infants when we know that children are generally spared from the disease, and that vaccines do not prevent transmission?

---

214. *H.R.5546 National Childhood Vaccine Injury Act of 1986.*

Vaccination of adolescents: between data manipulation and risks ignored

In spring 2021, mRNA vaccines were authorized for adolescents, notably the Pfizer product on May 10, 2021. Clinical trial results clearly indicate, however, that this authorization was a mistake.

In the EMA report published on May 28, 2021, evaluating the Pfizer vaccine, many passages concerning adverse events in adolescents were redacted. The link to this report now displays a version modified in July 2021: certain previously redacted passages have been restored, clearly declaring adverse events in adolescents but other passages concerning these same adverse events have disappeared. It is common that modifications to official EMA documents are not signaled in successive versions posted on the same web link. Nevertheless, the report shows that a large number of adolescents avoided follow-up visits, with no explanation given for this fact. Serious adverse events forced the withdrawal of two adolescents from the trial.

In the case of the Moderna vaccine, the FDA refused to authorize it for adolescents, whereas the EMA gave its unconditional approval on July 23, 2021. A review of the clinical trial outcomes for this population segment reveals flagrant manipulation of the figures used to calculate efficacy, and the EMA report itself cited above highlights the risks of myocarditis and pericarditis, particularly in young men and after the second dose. On reading what is published about this trial, it is clear that safety is not guaranteed.

Lymphadenopathies, headaches, myalgias and arthralgias, high fevers, nausea and vomiting are very frequent occurrences after vaccination; anaphylaxis and hypersensitivity are noted at an "unknown" frequency! Facial paralysis and severe swelling of the face have also been reported; all this for less than 3,000 vaccinated subjects, which suggests that there will be many serious adverse effects in adolescents from the marketing phase onwards.

Benefits for pregnant women: where is the evidence?

It is crucial to recall that no pregnant women were included in the COVID-19 vaccine trials. Indeed, it is standard practice to exclude pregnant women from all vaccine trials! What's more, contraception is strictly required for young women participating in these trials, and men are asked to abstain from sexual intercourse and sperm donation for the duration of the study. These precautions are understandable, given that mRNAs are in fact gene therapies.

In the spring of 2021, following the HAS recommendation to vaccinate pregnant women, whom it considered to be at risk, I started a new article to explore the grounds for this highly puzzling directive. During my professional training, we were taught that it was inadvisable to vaccinate pregnant women. How, then, is it possible to justify authorizing a vaccine for pregnant women without any prior testing?

The official Ministry of Health guidance appeared to be applicable to all pregnant women, without distinction. I proved, and other studies subsequently confirmed, that pregnancy in itself does not constitute a risk factor for severe forms of COVID-19. Women with risk factors prior to pregnancy, such as obesity, diabetes or hypertension, naturally retained those risk factors during pregnancy.

Despite strict contraception recommendations during clinical trials, some trial participants do nonetheless become pregnant. Surprisingly, neither the vaccine manufacturers nor the health authorities see fit to monitor them in particular. That is a problem in itself.

In addition, a study under the auspices of the V-Safe active pharmacovigilance program was published, but only 15% of the women concerned responded, rendering the study not significantly representative. Moreover, the results for vaccine-related risk of spontaneous abortion were clearly manipulated. To estimate the percentage of miscarriages among women vaccinated during the first 20 weeks of pregnancy, the study set women vaccinated before 20 weeks as the numerator and the total number of women in the study (including those vaccinated after 20 weeks) as the denominator. This is incorrect, because it dilutes the risk. The correct way of calculating the risk would have been to divide the number of miscarriages among women vaccinated before 20 weeks by the total number of women vaccinated before 20 weeks. This would have given an accurate estimate of the risk for women vaccinated during this specific period. A miscarriage is defined as a spontaneous abortion before 20 weeks of gestation. By using the wrong denominator, the study potentially underestimates the risk of miscarriage associated with the vaccine for women vaccinated during the first 20 weeks of pregnancy.

The authors, in charge of vaccino-vigilance at the CDC, seem to have been so baffled by their own maneuvering that they finally admitted their study's incoherence. They even pointed out that during the 2009 influenza A (H1N1) pandemic, after the introduction of the inactivated H1N1 2009 vaccine, miscarriage was the most frequently reported side effect among the pregnant women who received it. Is this their way of expressing remorse for publishing such a misleading study? It is regrettable that science should be tainted by the moral dilemmas of scientists under pressure.

In August 2022, a new, equally dubious study was conducted by the Canadian National Vaccine Safety Network on 200,000 women (no less!) and published in *The Lancet*. It asserts that "the data constitute evidence that messenger RNA vaccines are safe during pregnancy." This assertion is in total contradiction to their own results. Yet it is easy to identify the many scientific biases and communicate them to the public. The study in fact lists a multitude of adverse effects, and monitors pregnancy for only a ridiculously short period of seven days after injection![215] Despite its demonstration that the risk of adverse effects is due to vaccination, false information about the safety of this vaccine in pregnant women is repeated over and over again in all the conventional media to uphold public confidence in the official recommendations.

Even more surprisingly, declassified documents reveal that the FDA was aware as early as February 2021 that the mRNA vaccine could cross into the placenta, end up in breast milk and result in adverse effects in breast-fed infants.[216] This fact was already known and foreseeable. We will come back to this later.

"Unexpected" disturbances to the menstrual cycle
Signs of menstrual cycle disturbances emerge from the very first days of vaccination, with many women soon reporting various "disturbances." In view of these reports, from April 2021 onwards, researchers called for clinical trials to monitor monthly changes in vaccinated women.[217]

215. *Est-ce que l'étude du Lancet permet d'affirmer que la vaccination est sans danger pour les femmes enceintes ?*, CSI, April 2023.
216. https://www.researchgate.net/publication/370107164_FDA_knew_as_ of_February_2021_that_the_mRNA_vaccine_crosses_the_pl acenta_passes_into_milk_and_causes_adverse_events_in_breastfed_infants
217. *Can the COVID-19 vaccine affect women's menstrual cycles?*", ABC7 News, April 23, 2021.

The "Clancy Investigation" is further evidence of the unexpected emergence of these cycle disorders. "Unexpected" in the sense that these adverse effects were "not anticipated" and therefore not originally listed in the product notice. Kate Clancy, a researcher at the University of Illinois, shared her own experience on Twitter, asking her followers to notify possible post-vaccination menstrual changes.[218] Confronted with a multitude of responses, with the help of a colleague at Washington University in St. Louis, she set out to produce a structured survey (University of Illinois, *Survey on post-vaccination menstrual changes*).

According to data presented in the Clancy study,[219] 42.1% of women surveyed reported an increase in menstrual flow following vaccination against COVID-19. For some, this change occurred within the first seven days after vaccination, but for the majority, it occurred between eight and 14 days. Surprisingly, unexpected bleeding was reported not only by menstruating women, but also by two-thirds of those in the menopause. This type of side effect was not anticipated and has not been specifically investigated in vaccine clinical trials.

It should be noted that, according to the study, this heavier bleeding seems to affect more people already suffering from reproductive problems, such as endometriosis,[220] fibroids, PCOS (polycystic ovary syndrome) ...

Other studies highlight various disruptions to the fertility cycle in women. Among them, the Rodríguez Quejada et al. study examines menstrual cycle disturbances after COVID-19 vaccination. Similarly, another study (Al-Mehaisen et al.) investigates the short-term effect of the COVID-19 vaccine on menstrual cycles.[221]

---

218. Kate Clancy on Twitter, tweet from February 24, 2021.
219. *Investigating trends in those who experience menstrual bleeding changes after SARS-CoV-2 vaccination*, K. M. N. Lee, E. J. Junkins, C. Luo, U. A. Fatima, M. L. Cox, K. B. H. Clancy, *Sci Adv.* 2022, PMID 35857495.
220. *The effect of SARS-CoV-2 BNT162b2 vaccine on the symptoms of women with endometriosis*, A. Gilan et al., *Archives of Gynecology and Obstetrics*, 2023.
221. *Menstrual cycle disturbances after Covid19 vaccination,* L. Rodríguez Quejada et al., *Womens' Health*, 2022.
Short Term Effect of Corona Virus Diseases Vaccine on the Menstrual Cycles, M. M. Al-Mehaisen L. et al., Int *J Women's Health*, 2022.

After the usual rebuttals by official bodies and aligned researchers, the impact of mRNAs on menstruation was at last admitted as a common side-effect. This effect could even be linked to the lower birth rate observed in countries that have massively vaccinated their populations.

As could be expected, a study,[222] whose methodology is largely questionable, has sought to prove the contrary, with a major bias consisting of excluding a large majority of subjects during the course of the study. Here is how: the study focused on women who consulted in hospital for menstrual problems, rather than on a larger sample of women who reported changes in their cycle after vaccination. In addition, it did not consider cycle changes occurring within the first seven days after vaccination, considering this period to be a negative control. A "negative control" means that the researchers do not expect any menstrual cycle changes during this period and use it as a reference for comparing effects observed later. Only the period from eight to 90 days after vaccination is considered, and the diagnosis must have been made during this timeframe. Women with a history of cycle problems are also excluded, even though they are potentially at greater risk of adverse vaccine reactions. Ultimately, nearly half the participants were excluded from the study.

In March 2023, the pharmacovigilance service of the French National Agency for Medicines and Health Products Safety finally recognized menstrual cycle disturbances due to COVID-19 vaccines.[223] Unfortunately, French pharmacovigilance experts still seem to confuse passive pharmacovigilance (based on spontaneous case reports from victims, their relatives or healthcare professionals) with active pharmacovigilance (based on systematic surveillance through questioning of a group of vaccinated individuals).

The major problem with this type of spontaneous pharmacovigilance is under-reporting. All figures would probably have to be multiplied by 10 or even 100, since international studies estimate that only 1 to 10% of adverse reactions are reported.[224]

---

222. *Association between SARS-CoV-2 vaccination and healthcare contacts for menstrual disturbance and bleeding in women before and after menopause: nationwide, register based cohort study*, R. Ljung et al., BMJ, 2023, PMID 37137493.

223. M. B. Valnet-Rabier et al., *Pharmacovigilance signals from active surveillance of mRNA platform vaccines* (tozinameran and elasomeran), *Therapie*, 2023, PMID 37012149.

224. See my summary of studies on this well-known phenomenon: *Sous-noti-*

A historic drop in birth rate

Another concern is emerging: since the end of 2021, a drop in the birth rate has been observed throughout Europe. Prof. Konstantin Beck, a statistics expert and former adviser to the Swiss government, has shown the causal link between COVID-19 vaccines and the sharp drop in the birth rate in Switzerland, down to figures comparable to those during mobilization in 1914. Based on publicly available Swiss and German data from scientific publications, health insurance companies and the Swiss Federal Statistical Office (FSO), Beck eliminates all other explanations put forward: behavioral change due to the pandemic, reduced fertility, with the cause of the drop in birth rate attributed to a rise in miscarriages and stillbirths. He also signals the excess mortality in young adults and of pulmonary embolism, cardiac arrest and stroke in 0–14-year-olds following COVID-19 vaccinations.[225]

Further reading

– *Vacciner les femmes enceintes contre la COVID-19 ?* Aimsib.org, May 9, 2021.

– *Is The CDC Safety Study Following Covid-19 Vaccines Hiding Risks Of Miscarriages?* (France) on May 3, 2021, by Emma Kahn, https://childrenshealthdefense.eu/eu-issues/is-the-cdc-safety-study-following-covid-19-vaccines-hiding-a-high-number-of-miscarriages-from-france/

– *FDA approves COVID-19 vaccine for babies (6 months and older) : non-existent "scientific bases »* https://www.researchgate.net/publication/366440489_FDA_approves_COVID-19_vaccine_for_babies_6_months_and_older_non-existent_scientific_bases

---

fication des effets indésirables des vaccins: quelques références utiles, Aimsib. org, August 22, 2022.

225. *Increase in Miscarriages, Stillbirths Directly Linked to COVID-19 Shots, Data ShowHealth Officials 'Should Have Known'*, childrenshealthdefense.org, July 28, 2023.

See also the video on Rumble.com: *Women and children first! Baby gap and young people's excess mortality in Switzerland*, June 22, 2023, presentation for Doctors for COVID-19 Ethics, Zurich.

3.4.2 Scientific fact "adjusted" by the authorities

As early as July 2020, the French Scientific Advisory Board formulated a lengthy, fairly honest and well-documented opinion on future anti-COVID-19 vaccines. In November of that year, the French National Authority for Health (HAS) launched a process to ensure the transparency of the vaccination campaign scheduled for December 2020.

It seems that official French experts had their doubts about these future vaccines. And yet, as early as November 2020, the European Commission had already concluded secret agreements providing for six vaccine doses for every European citizen, all age groups combined. It should also be remembered that vaccination began before the clinical trials were completed, with phase III initially running until 2024.

The Scientific Advisory Board noted that clinical trials did not allow it to be determined whether the vaccines could effectively reduce virus transmission. In November 2020, manufacturers were communicating mainly through press releases aimed at investors, overlooking the fact that the few clinical trials published at that time were already revealing disquieting adverse effects.

The Scientific Advisory Board also addressed several issues raised by skeptical scientists: potential cross-immunity with coronaviruses causing common colds, which would render a vaccine specific to SARS-CoV-2 useless; the risks associated with ADE; the duration of protection offered by vaccines; and potential mutations in the virus that could compromise this protection.

From its earliest deliberations, the Scientific Advisory Board anticipated a potential influx of vaccine-related adverse events and called for reinforced vaccino-vigilance, which the ANSM was apparently doing.[226] This concern over possible adverse effects was shared beyond France's borders. In fact, an official UK Department of Health document, published in the Official Journal of the European Community, disclosed a similar concern. Anticipating a high volume of adverse events, the UK issued a call for tenders, acknowledging that it did not have technology needed to deal with the situation.[227] Later, in 2023,

226. See *Un dispositif de surveillance renforcée*, ansm.sante.fr.
227. *United Kingdom-London: Software package and information systems,* ted.europa.eu., October 23, 2020.

many experts claimed to have been taken by surprise and misled by vaccine manufacturers. However, cumulated evidence shows that they were well aware of the potential risks.

A document issued in April 2021 by the French Council of State (Conseil d'État) clearly shows that France's highest government authorities were aware of the potential ineffectiveness and risks associated with the vaccine. For example, in response to a request from a vacationing citizen for an exemption from barrier and containment measures on account of protection acquired through vaccination, the Ministry of Health stated that vaccination does not guarantee total immunity against infection, nor against transmission of the virus. Moreover, it points out that "vaccinated persons are also those most at risk of severe forms of the disease and death in the event of initial vaccine inefficacy or reinfection after vaccination."[228]

In passing, it should be noted that neither the Ministry of Health nor the Council of State had understood the ADE occurrence, and perhaps had never even heard of it!

If further examples are needed of the authorities' disregard for expert opinion, the introduction in late 2021 of the third vaccine dose (or booster, administered only with an mRNA vaccine) speaks for itself. Neither the HAS nor the French Academy of Medicine approved this decision. The HAS emphasized the value of natural immunity acquired post infection, challenging thereby the need to revaccinate those who had already contracted COVID-19. For its part, the French Academy of Medicine recommended in October 2021 that the validity of the health pass not be linked to booster inoculation.

Abroad, the Israeli Ministry of Health had acknowledged the "fantastic" protection conferred by a previous infection.[229] And an Israeli study,[230] concluded that a third dose was ineffective.

For its part, the FDA was already giving the green light for a third dose in November 2021. Jacqueline A. O'Shaughnessy, Chief Scientist, stated that, based on available scientific data, it was "reasonable

---

228. *Conseil d'État, juge des référés, 01/04/2021, 450956, Inédit au recueil Lebon*, April 1, 2021.
229. *Israeli study: Recovered COVID-19 patients with one vaccine protected like three doses*, Israeli Ministry of Health, Haaretz.com.
230. *Green Pass and COVID-19 Vaccine Booster Shots in Israel – A More 'Realistic' Empirical Assessment Analyzing the National Airport Data*, O. Koren, R. Levi, S. Altuvia, SSRN, November 7, 2021.

to believe" that the Pfizer-BioNTech COVID-19 vaccine could be effective. Since when are terms like "reasonable" and "believe" scientific criteria? The FDA relied on small studies of individuals who had received the third dose. The efficacy of this dose was assessed exclusively by means of immuno-bridging, i.e. on the basis of induced antibody levels, and only against the original 2019 strain of Wuhan, which was no longer in circulation!

We have often been told that mRNA technology is highly adaptable. However, the third dose was still based on the genetic code of the 2019 Spike protein, with no adaptation to the variants in circulation at that time. It was already known that adaptation to the delta variant would be dangerous, and even that infection or vaccination could promote the production of facilitating antibodies active above all on the new variants in circulation. The balance between neutralizing and facilitating antibodies seems to have tipped more towards facilitation for the variants, and neutralization of the original Wuhan strain.[231]

As always, scientific observation perceived the consequences of the vaccination strategy adopted by governments. All warnings were nonetheless systematically dismissed in favor of rigid biopolitical measures, heading straight for disaster.

Rebuttal of the reasons cited in favor of the vaccine pass
In January 2022, France adopted the vaccination pass, replacing the health pass. From then on, access to certain areas required proof of vaccination instead of a negative virological test. And yet, there was no justification for this quasi-obligation to vaccinate in order to lead a normal life. In fact, from the beginning of 2022, the Omicron variant had become the predominant variant, supplanting the others, while resisting the antibodies generated by vaccines. Numerous studies had already shown that those vaccinated were more likely to carry the Omicron variant than the non-vaccinated. Furthermore, Omicron does not cause an increase in case of pneumonia or death.

In mid-2022, both the FDA and the EMA announced that mRNA vaccines would be adapted to the new variants by autumn. The MHRA, the UK regulator of the medical device market, followed suit in August.

To avoid scrapping vaccines originally designed for the Wuhan strain, the FDA asserted, despite the evidence, that the vaccine "prototype"

---

231. PMID 35744971 and PMID 34580004.

was effective against Omicron. It did, however, acknowledge the decline in efficacy against severe forms. The contorted efforts of the experts to align their narrative with the manufacturers' guidelines were remarkable.

If the FDA implicitly recognized that the vaccines being marketed did not prevent severe forms of COVID-19,[232] it was also because the decision to change the target strain could only be taken if the vaccine's efficacy against severe forms was in doubt. These observations were corroborated by an Israeli study, which showed that in previously uninfected over-60s, the risk of developing a severe form of COVID-19 was much higher after the third vaccine dose than in those protected by natural infection.[233] Once again, the continuous evolution of the virus was overlooked. The virus will always be one step ahead of adapted vaccines. Surprisingly, the first vaccine adaptation still included the mRNA encoding the 2019 Spike protein. The expectation of diminished efficacy, due to immune imprinting (or "original antigenic sin"), reinforced by revaccination with the same 2019 antigen, remained ignored. However, tests carried out by Moderna in 2021 showed that the immune response was clearly biased in favor of the original strain, and the more this strain was vaccinated with, the stronger this immune imprint became.[234]

That same error was repeated in 2023, as the "adapted" autumn vaccines targeted the previous spring vaccines.

It is essential to emphasize the challenges and failures encountered each year in adapting influenza vaccines to seasonal variants. The CDC admits a 0% efficacy against the A H3N3 clade during a university epidemic in 2021. In addition, an overall efficacy of 8% has been observed for individuals over 6 months of age, and 14% against A/H3N2 after adjustment.[235]

FDA experts and manufacturers alike were aware that adapting COVID-19 vaccines would not work. Yet it was authorized, as were

232. *Vaccines and Related Biological Products Advisory Committee Meeting Report*, April 2022, Safety Platforms for Emergency Vaccines (SPEAC), Brighton Collaboration.

233. *Protection and Waning of Natural and Hybrid Immunity to SARS-CoV-2*, Y. Goldberg, M. Mandel, Y. M. Bar-On, et al., New England J Med, 2022, PMID 35613036.

234. *Immune imprinting and SARSCoV-2 vaccine design*, A. K. Wheatley, A. Fox, H. X. Tan, et al., Trends Immunol, 2021

235. *Efficacy of flu vaccines*, FDA report, 2021.

vaccines for infants and young children aged 6 months to 5 years. Authorized despite no safety data being presented, which is a cause for concern, especially in light of information indicating facilitation and aggravation of infection by the original vaccine versus current variants.

One study revealed that among Omicron-infected subjects, those who had received the booster vaccination were contagious for a longer period of time than non-vaccinated subjects who had already contracted the disease.[236]

A CDC document,[237] from September 2022, shows the total failure of adapted vaccines on mice having undergone the different vaccine regimens and re-infected with the Omicron BA.5 sub-variant to estimate the protection conferred by the different boosters (Wuhan strain or bivalent vaccine): all vaccinated and boosted mice caught COVID-19!

We note that the authorities were quickly made aware of the risks and limited efficacy of this vaccination, whether through the recommendations of expert groups or the analyses carried out by various scientific academies. How, then, are we to understand this discrepancy between the internal discourse of those in power and that destined for the public?

Politicians and official experts are swept along by the tide of biosecurity policy, caught up in a headlong rush of inconsistencies and untruths. It is not always a matter of direct corruption. Politicians risk their careers, and those who rise to power the quickest are the ones who best defend the biosecurity discourse.

Some scientists receive "gifts" directly from industry, or through the funding of their laboratories or hospitals: for the most part, they repeat the rhetoric of consultancy companies and industry without seeking to learn more. Others are well aware that the official discourse is at odds with what they know, but they are victims of the "doublethink" described by George Orwell in his novel 1984: they know, but at the same time they forget what they know so as not to jeopardize their careers or funding of the lab to which they have devoted most of their lives.

---

236. *Duration of Shedding of Culturable Virus in SARS-CoV-2 Omicron (BA.1)*, NEJM, 2022.
237. *Booster Doses of Moderna COVID-19 Vaccines in Adults, Adolescents & Children*, September 1, 2022, ACIP meeting COVID-19 Vaccines.

Further reading

– *Vaccins anti-COVID-19, surs et efficaces ? Avis du Conseil Scientifique, de la HAS, ce qu'en a fait la Commission Européenne*, Aimsib. org, November 29, 2021.

– *Une troisième dose pour que ça marche enfin ?*, Aimsib.org, November 26, 2021.

– *Réfutation des arguments « scientifiques » justifiant le passe vaccinal*, ReinfoCovid, January 5, 2022.

– *Adaptation of COVID-19 vaccines for fall 2022*, https://www.researchgate.net/publication/362355889_Adaptation_ of_COVID-19_vaccines_for_fall_2022

3.5 Biopolitics seriously harms health

According to analyses by independent researchers, the strategy of mass vaccination against COVID-19 was a dismal failure. The explosion in the number of cases of adverse drug reactions recorded in pharmacovigilance registers cannot but jump out at observers accustomed to such data. Everyone knows that this is just the tip of the iceberg, but the authorities persist in denial, surfing on "passive" pharmacovigilance to conceal the harmful consequences of biopolitics.

3.5.1 Predictable side effects ignored

It is alarming to see that health authorities continued to promote anti-COVID-19 vaccination despite the overwhelming evidence. In a collaborative article published in July 2023, other independent researchers and I highlighted the alarming number of post-vaccination adverse events.[238] Although the data evolved rapidly, it was clear that by the end of the first half of 2022, the authorities had all the information they needed to halt the vaccination campaign. Yet they persisted in this course in autumn 2023, which was inexcusable from a scientific standpoint.

Pfizer's pharmacovigilance documents, requested by the European Medicines Agency and made public, are particularly revealing.[239] They show 508,351 reports of individual adverse reaction, containing 1,597,673 events, one-third of which are classified as serious. These figures cover the first quarter of 2022. Since the start of vaccination, Pfizer had accumulated 1.5 million individual reports and almost 5 million adverse events. Clearly, Pfizer was quickly aware that almost every organ was affected, with vascular, nerve, eye, hearing, respiratory, reproductive and psychiatric disorders, among others.

Why wasn't this information shared with the general public? To what extent were certain politicians aware of the situation? Investigations will be necessary to provide the answers.

---

238. *Chères élites, prenez soin de nous*, Aimsib.org, July 16, 2023.
239. *Confidential Pfizer Document Shows the Company Observed 1.6 Million Adverse Events Covering Nearly Every Organ System*, Global Research, June 21, 2023, see details of adverse events in Appendix 2.2: http://tiny.cc/El-Pfizer.

Furthermore, our collaborative article also pointed to the unexplained excess mortality in several countries, particularly among young people. In France, according to provisional Insee figures, excess mortality in 2022 was 9.8% compared with 2019, i.e. an increase of 60,181 deaths,[240] including young people who did not die from COVID-19.[241] This deliberate ignorance of the facts causes concern and raises questions about the motivations behind these decisions.

From the start of the vaccination campaign in December 2020, health authorities were aware of the potential adverse effects of vaccines (see box below), not least because these adverse effects had already been announced in clinical trials, as we saw in section 3.3 on *Clinical trials: predictable failure with all types of vaccine?*

Not surprisingly, many side effects were reported by subjects as soon as vaccinations were launched. These reports, whether from the victims themselves, their families or their doctors, were recorded in various databases of pharmacovigilance systems such as the American VAERS, EudraVigilance in Europe, the French ANSM, the British MHRA, and others.

Media silence

Clearly, we have seen a time of unprecedented censorship in media coverage of the health crisis, particularly in the treatment of adverse events. Whereas traditional media adopted a common editorial line, several alternative platforms came under accrued scrutiny. This led to targeted attempts to silence dissident voices, particularly those of independent researchers.

One emblematic case is that of Laurent Mucchielli, French sociologist and director of research at the CNRS. He was removed from *Mediapart* after questioning the failure on the part of pharmacovigilance. The newspaper *France Soir* decided to republish his work, which contributed to reopening the debate on a crucial issue. Mucchielli did not remain speechless for long, however. He coordinated a collective publication, *The COVID Doxa*, comprising a collection of his writings previously available on *Mediapart*, and integrating contributions from other authors, including myself.

---

240. According to France's national statistics institute, https://www.insee.fr/fr/statistiques/6206305?sommaire=4487854
241. *Insee Première*, no. 1951, June 2023, https://www.insee.fr/fr/statistiques/7628176.

Suffice to look at the list of adverse effects published in May 2023 by the ANSM to understand that the French regulatory authority was two years behind the information reported by Laurent Mucchielli... Without listing the undesirable effects published in case reports or international meta-analyses, the list includes all the pathologies announced by the FDA in October 2020.

Adverse effects known to the FDA as of October 2020

Adverse effects had been anticipated by the authorities: as early as October 2020, with the Food and Drug Administration calling for special monitoring in case of the following issues:

– COVID-19 disease [Author's note: the FDA thus implicitly recognized the ADE effect, facilitation of infection by the vaccine].
– death
– optic neuritis
– encephalitis
– myelitis
– ataxia
– vaccination during pregnancy and adverse effects on pregnancy
– Guillain-Barré syndrome
– acute disseminated encephalomyelitis
– chronic inflammatory demyelinating polyneuropathy
– transverse myelitis
– multiple sclerosis
– meningoencephalitis
– epileptic seizures / convulsions
– narcolepsy / cataplexy
– stroke
– autoimmune disease
– non-anaphylactic allergic reactions
– anaphylaxis
– acute myocardial infarction
– myocarditis / pericarditis
– disseminated intravascular coagulation (dic)
– venous thromboembolism
– arthritis and arthralgia
– multisystemic inflammatory syndrome (mis-c, mis-a), Kawasaki disease
– immune thrombocytopenia (itp).

Source: *CDC post-authorization/post-licensure safety monitoring of COVID-19 vaccines*, Tom Shimabukuro. MD, MPH, MBA CDC COVID-19 Vaccine Task Force Vaccine Safety Team, October 22, 2020.

ANSM update in May 2023: adverse reactions to COVID-19 vaccines

The French National Agency for the Safety of Medicines (ANSM) published an update on adverse reactions associated with COVID-19 vaccines. Dated May 11, 2023, the update classifies reactions in three categories: confirmed, potential under surveillance, and already under surveillance.

Confirmed signals
– hypertension
– myo/pericarditis
– heavy menstrual bleeding
– delayed injection-site reaction (painful, erythematous, pruritic)
– erythema multiforme

Potential signals under surveillance
– shingles and viral reactivation
– heart rhythm disorders
– glomerular nephropathy
– pancreatitis
– rheumatoid arthritis
– acquired hemophilia
– Parsonage-Turner syndrome
– menstrual disorders (excluding heavy menstrual bleeding)
– rhizomelic pseudo-polyarthritis
– autoimmune hepatitis
– deafness
– loss of consciousness (whether or not associated with falls)
– autoimmune hemolytic anemia

Signals already under surveillance
– cerebral venous thrombosis
– thrombocytopenia and variants
– diabetic imbalance due to reactogenicity
– vaccine failure
– macrophagic activation syndrome
– zoster meningoencephalitis
– medullar aplasia
– Guillain-Barré syndrome

- corneal graft rejection
- imbalance/recurrence of chronic pathology
- amnesic ictus
- tinnitus
- ANCA systemic vasculitis
- musculoskeletal disorders
- thyroiditis
- uveitis

The Spike protein and its role in SARS-CoV-2 pathogenicity
All current COVID-19 vaccines target the SARS-CoV-2 Spike protein. This protein is now widely recognized as one of the causes, if not the main cause, of the virus' pathogenicity. As early as spring 2020, Jean-Marc Sabatier explained the potentially harmful effects of SARS-CoV-2 infection through the interaction of the Spike protein with the human cellular receptor ACE2. This receptor plays a crucial role in the renin-angiotensin system, which not only regulates blood pressure and water balance, but is also involved in inflammatory and coagulation processes.

Thus, the toxicity associated with the vaccine Spike protein could lead to complications similar to those observed in COVID-19 patients, notably by affecting endothelial cells, which are abundant in ACE2 receptors and line the inside of our blood vessels. The quantities of Spike circulating in vaccinated individuals may be equivalent to, or much greater than, those produced during severe COVID-19 infection.[242]

Persistence of Spike protein and viral RNA in long Covid
It should be noted that Spike protein and virus RNA can persist for a prolonged period in individuals suffering from what is known as *long Covid*. However, these elements are generally not detected in people who have been infected but do not show prolonged COVID-19 symptoms. A single study shows the opposite.[243] Another investiga-

242. H. Banoun, *mRNA: Vaccine or Gene Therapy? The Safety Regulatory Issues*, Int. J. Mol. Sci. 2023, https://www.mdpi.com/1422-0067/24/13/10514.
243. *Liquid biomarkers of macrophage dysregulation and circulating Spike protein illustrate the biological heterogeneity in patients with post-acute sequelae of COVID-19*, C. Schultheiß, E. Willscher, L. Paschold, et al., *J Med Virol*, 2022.

tion finds no persistent trace of Spike protein in individuals without prolonged symptoms.[244] In addition, a separate study examines the presence of viral antigens in the gut and finds that only patients with long COVID have persistent viral antigens in this region, although no cultivable virus was detected.[245] This evidence confirms the role of Spike toxicity in the pathogenic effect of the SARS-CoV-2 virus. It is possible that genetic predispositions may influence the way in which individuals react to the Spike protein.

Vaccine Spike toxicity

In 2021, I translated and supplemented an article by Stephanie Seneff and Greg Nigh listing and explaining the adverse reactions observed as of May 2021 following vaccines based on Spike modified from the toxic Spike of SARS-CoV-2. My report includes details of the mechanism described by Jean-Marc Sabatier. In October 2021, Prof. Jean-Paul Bourdineaud and Dr. Jean-François Lesgards published an article in France Soir reminding us that the problem with these vaccines is that the protein they produce is as toxic as the virus' Spike protein.[246]

It is now known that the Spike protein can cross the blood-brain barrier and is neurotoxic. It has also been discovered that Spike causes agglutination of blood cells,[247] and it can, along with its viral mRNA, enter cell nuclei.[248]

Another potential toxicity, and not the least significant, is that many of the vaccinated person's cell types will integrate the mRNA and produce Spike. This protein, once on the surface of these cells, will be identified as foreign by the immune system, which could then eliminate them. This action could cause necrosis in essential organs. It

244. *Persistent Circulating Severe Acute Respiratory Syndrome Coronavirus 2 Spike Is Associated With Post-acute Coronavirus Disease 2019 Sequelae*, Zoe Swank et al., *Clinical Infectious Diseases*, 2023.
245. *Postacute COVID-19 is Characterized by Gut Viral Antigen Persistence in Inflammatory Bowel Diseases*, A. Zollner, R. Koch, A. Jukic, et al., *Gastroenterology*, 2022.
246. *Nous ne sommes pas « anti-vax », nous sommes « anti-spike » !* October 13, 2021.
247. *SARS-CoV-2 Spike Protein Induces Hemagglutination: Implications for COVID-19 Morbidities and Therapeutics and for Vaccine Adverse Effects*, C. Boschi et al., *bioRxiv*, 2022.
248. S. Sattar et al., *bioRxiv*, 2022.

should also be noted that Spike has similarities with human proteins, which could lead to autoimmune diseases following immunization against it.

It is important to remember that asymptomatic people, when infected with the virus, resist the disease thanks to their innate immune system. A robust mucosal barrier, including macrophages and neutrophils, eliminates the virus before it can spread throughout the body. The majority of people exposed to the virus will not develop systemic infection and will be protected from the harmful effects of Spike. Conversely, after vaccination, mRNA and Spike spread throughout the body and remain there. More importantly, the more stable vaccine Spike could be expected to be more toxic than the viral Spike.

Indeed, it is notable that the mRNA used in COVID-19 vaccines has been modified to make it more stable, i.e. less biodegradable. It is therefore not a "natural" mRNA. To achieve this, all natural uridine molecules have been replaced by N1-methyl-pseudouridine. In addition, the mRNA sequence was adjusted (by codon optimization) to enhance Spike protein production (to produce more antibodies) and increase its similarity to human RNAs. This similarity is intended to prevent the mRNA from being rapidly identified and destroyed as an intruder.

These modifications are not without risk, however. The enhanced stability of the Spike protein produced on the basis of this mRNA could make it more toxic than its original version. This is a mutated Spike protein. Produced from the vaccine, it is deliberately different from the viral Spike. What's more, the mRNA modification could lead to copy errors and incorrect folding of the Spike protein. In some cases, this could lead to the protein acting as a prion, causing degenerative diseases similar to Creutzfeldt-Jakob disease.

In addition, mRNA is encapsulated in lipid nanoparticles to protect it and facilitate its mobility. These particles also act as adjuvants, the exact effects of which remain poorly understood. Among the components of these nanoparticles is PEG (polyethylene glycol), a substance that has been associated with anaphylactic reactions.

Higher risk of cancer

Since the beginning of 2023, doctors have been signaling the emergence of turbo-cancers (de novo cancers or reactivation of cancers in remission that flare up and resist treatment). These serious adverse effects will be discussed in the section on gene therapy products (GTP). Cancers are indeed among the risks associated with this class of drugs, but this risk has been underestimated for mRNA vaccines due to their categorization as vaccines. This illogical classification has prevented pharmacovigilance from carrying out the particularly close monitoring needed of cancers.

Risk of myocarditis: vaccines more dangerous than the infection

Every time a vaccinated young athlete dies, the media insist that COVID-19 infection causes more myocarditis than the vaccine. Nevertheless, all serious studies confirm the data published by the CDC's vaccino-vigilance team, a source that can hardly be considered conspiratorial. In the case of COVID-19 infection, the CDC tells us that young people aged 16 to 39 are 7.5 times more likely to develop myocarditis after catching COVID-19 than would be expected without infection.[249] The CDC also publishes that boys and young men aged 12 to 24 have a 100-fold greater risk of myocarditis within 21 days of the second dose of mRNA than would be expected.[250] So there would be a 7.5 times greater risk of myocarditis after catching COVID-19, but 100 times more after two doses of mRNA vaccines. This should have been enough to withdraw these products from the market.

One of the most convincing publications is a Swiss prospective study,[251] which monitored participants over a given period to observe the effects of a treatment. Nearly 3% of those vaccinated showed signs of myocarditis. The study, which focused on young, healthy healthcare workers, also showed that women were more likely to be affected. In Thailand, another study of 300 teenagers aged 13 to 18

249. *Association Between COVID-19 and Myocarditis Using Hospital-Based Administrative Data – United States, March 2020-January 2021*, T. K. Boehmer et al., *Morb Mortal Wkly Rep*, 2021, PMID 34473684.
250. *COVID-19 Vaccine safety updates Advisory Committee on Immunization Practices (ACIP)* June 23, 2021, Tom Shimabukuro, page 27.
251. *Sex-specific differences in myocardial injury incidence after COVID-19 mRNA-1273 Booster Vaccination*, N. Buergin et al., Eur J Heart Fail. July 20, 2023. PMID 37470105.

after their second dose of the Pfizer vaccine found that almost one-third of vaccinated teenagers showed cardiac symptoms.

> **Further reading**: In an article co-authored with Patrick Provost, we provided references to studies showing a higher incidence of myo/pericarditis post vaccination compared with the rate of incidence before infection. I supplemented these references in August 2023 in an article available on my ResearchGate page: What are the real risks of myocarditis after Covid infection and after Covid vaccine?

Probable mechanisms of thrombosis and myocarditis

The Spike protein, whether from the virus or the vaccine, can trigger several mechanisms that increase the risk of thrombosis. Here is a summary of these pathophysiological disturbances:

– disruption of the renin-angiotensin system (RAS), as per the work of Jean-Marc Sabatier. A study confirms the mechanism linked to RAS deregulation.[252] This mechanism is associated with thrombosis;

– anti-FP4 antibodies: following injection of the vaccine, a high level of anti-FP4 (anti-platelet factor 4) antibodies is observed. These antibodies could cause blood clots in unusual places. This is an autoimmune mechanism;

– Spike protein and vascular permeability: the Spike protein can increase (through binding to ACE2) vascular permeability and the amount of prothrombotic von Willebrand factor. It can also bind to another endothelial cell receptor involved in permeability, and even generate autoantibodies against it;

– molecular mimicry of Spike: this protein can mimic other proteins involved in coagulation. This can lead to an autoimmune mechanism whereby the body produces antibodies against Spike, which can also react with these coagulation proteins;

– anti-idiotype antibodies: secondary antibodies, called "anti-idiotypes," may share certain biological properties of Spike. Let's try to understand this via an image: imagine an impression of your teeth made at the dentist's; it's like a first antibody (Ab1), which recognizes

---

252. *COVID-19 Vaccine-Related Thrombosis: A Systematic Review and Exploratory Analysis*, C. Bilotta et al., Front Immunol, 2021, PMID 34912330.

a virus; then, the dentist uses this impression to make a mold of your teeth; this mold is like a second antibody (Ab2 or anti-idiotype), which recognizes and adapts to the first impression: the mold reproduces the structure of the Spike. These anti-idiotype antibodies can bind to ACE2, just as the Spike protein would. This could explain why certain effects persist even after the Spike protein has disappeared. They are due to anti-idiotypic antibodies, which can sometimes mimic the original antigen (in this case, the Spike protein) and interact with the same targets as the antigen;[253]

– in the case of myocarditis, several mechanisms are currently being investigated, ranging from the presence of impurities in the vaccine to specific and non-specific immune reactions;

– impurities in mRNA vaccines: impurities in mRNA vaccines (mentioned by manufacturers Pfizer and Moderna themselves) could be the cause of cases of myocarditis;[254]

– production of Spike protein by cardiac cells: cardiac cells producing Spike protein after vaccination can be attacked by the immune system, causing myocarditis;[255]

– non-specific reaction to systemic inflammation: myocarditis could result from systemic inflammation caused by the vaccine, independently of the production of anti-Spike antibodies;[256]

– a study on mice shows that intramuscular and intravenous injection of anti-COVID-19 mRNA leads to cardiac necrosis in all animals after the second dose;

253. *Immune Response and Molecular Mechanisms of Cardiovascular Adverse Effects of Spike Proteins from SARS-CoV-2 and mRNA Vaccines*, P. Bellavite, A. Ferraresi, C. Isidoro, Biomedicines 2023, https://doi. org/10.3390/biomedicines11020451.
254. *The Novel Platform of mRNA COVID-19 Vaccines and Myocarditis: Clues into the Potential Underlying Mechanism*, G. Lazaros et al., Vaccine, 2021, PMID 34312010.
Innate immune mechanisms of mRNA vaccines, R. Verbeke, M. J. Hogan, K. Loré, N. Pardi, Immunity, 2022, PMID 36351374
255. *Case report: SARS-CoV-2 specific T-cells are associated with myocarditis after COVID-19 vaccination with mRNA-1273*, U. Stervbo et al., Front. Med. 2023.
256. *Cytokinopathy with aberrant cytotoxic lymphocytes and profibrotic myeloid response in SARS-CoV-2 mRNA vaccine-associated myocarditis*, A. Barmada et al., Sci Immunol, 2023.

– mRNA toxicity: mRNA vaccines could have an inflammatory effect, particularly on the heart, when they reach this vital organ. I discuss this in an article on ResearchGate.[257] LNPs (lipid nanoparticles) re-circulate in a re-petalled manner in the heart, and the contaminants present in the final product could be largely responsible for this inflammation, according to the manufacturers themselves.

Further reading

– *Pire que la maladie, les conséquences involontaires des injections anti-COVID-19*, Aimsib.org, June 27, 2021.

– *Explications biologiques du mécanisme des effets indésirables des vaccins anti-COVID-19*, Aimsib.org, October 2, 2022.

– *A 6-Week Time Period May Not Be Sufficient to Identify Potential Adverse Events Following COVID-19 Vaccination*, H. Banoun and P. Provost, *International Journal of Vaccine Theory, Practice and Research*, 2023. https://ijvtpr.com/index.php/IJVTPR/article/view/67

– *What are the real risks of myocarditis after COVID infection and after COVID vaccine?*

https://www.researchgate.net/publication/373236772_What_are_the_real_risks_of_myocarditis_after_Covid_infection_and_after_Covid_vaccine?

– *mRNA: Vaccine or Gene Therapy? The Safety Regulatory Issues*, H. Banoun, *Int. J. Mol. Sci.* 2023.

---

257. *About the mechanisms and long-term follow-up of post-COVID mRNA injection myocarditis*
https://www.researchgate.net/publication/373302824_About_the_mechanisms_and_long-term_follow-up_of_post-COVID_mRNA_injection_myocarditis

3.5.2 Underestimating the risk of genome modification

In an article published in March 2022 : *Rétrotranscription et intégration dans le génome de l'ARN viral et/ou vaccinal : que sait-on ?* (*Retrotranscription and integration of viral and/or vaccine RNA into the genome: what do we know?*), I analyzed the probability of vaccine mRNA integrating into the genome of vaccinees. Here, I would like to take this opportunity to thank Alexandra Henrion-Caude, PhD. in genetics and a specialist in RNA, for carefully reviewing and critiquing my article.

At the time, two studies were causing a stir, for they suggested that there could be a possible risk of viral or vaccine RNA transforming into DNA, and subsequently integrating into our genome. This is a crucial issue, because if this were to happen, it would mean that mRNA would be permanently inserted into our DNA, which forms the genome of our cells. Note that the SARS-CoV-2 virus is an RNA virus that multiplies without needing to enter the cell nucleus. The virus genome is therefore not expected to integrate into our genome.

In simple terms, this is how protein production works in our bodies: our DNA, located in the cell nucleus, contains the information. This is copied (transcribed) into messenger RNA, which then travels out of the cell nucleus. There, it is "read" and transformed (translated) into proteins.

If the RNA from the virus or vaccine manages to integrate with our DNA, it could have unexpected and potentially dangerous consequences. For example, our body could continuously produce an undesirable protein. What's more, this modification could be passed on to our children via our reproductive cells. And even if no protein is produced, the addition of a foreign sequence to our DNA could disrupt the normal functioning of our cells, leading to various diseases and even cancers. For RNA to integrate with DNA, it must first be transformed (retrotranscribed) into DNA and enter the cell nucleus. It is easy to see why the media react so strongly to any hint of the possibility of viral or vaccine RNA integrating into DNA.

A study published in 2021 in the renowned journal PNAS,[258] (acronym

---

258. *Reverse-transcribed SARSCoV-2 RNA can integrate into the genome of cultured human cells and can be expressed in patient- derived tissues*, L. Zhang, A. Richards, M. I. Barrasa, et al., Proc Natl Acad Sci USA, 2021.

of the *Proceedings of the US National Academy of Sciences*) was conducted by recognized experts in their field. The study reveals that parts of the genetic code of the SARS-CoV-2 virus can be copied and integrated as DNA into the genetic code of human cells grown in the laboratory. Furthermore, the researchers found evidence of this integration in cells taken from deceased COVID-19 patients, which came from organs such as the lungs, heart, brain and stomach.

For this transformation and integration to occur, a special enzyme called "reverse transcriptase" is required. It is naturally present in certain cell types, notably cancer cells and embryonic cells. The study shows that one of these enzymes, called LINE-1 reverse transcriptase, can transform the RNA of the SARS-CoV-2 virus and convert it into the genetic code of the infected cell. This very enzyme is activated during viral infection or vaccination.

Another study,[259] reveals that vaccine mRNA (which contains the instructions to produce the virus' Spike protein) can be converted into DNA six hours after cells have been exposed to the vaccine. This transformation is observed in laboratory-grown cells derived from liver cancer. However, some critics point out that it is difficult to generalize these results to all cells in the human body, since the cells used in this study are cancer cells and therefore have particular characteristics, including high production of the LINE-1 enzyme. This is a legitimate criticism, but there are healthy cells in our bodies that multiply rapidly, such as those in bone marrow, the intestine, the skin, the respiratory tract and the embryo. The LINE-1 enzyme is also present in non-dividing cells, such as muscle cells and neurons. In addition, viral infection can increase the enzyme's activity. So, getting vaccinated during or after an infection could theoretically increase the risk of vaccine mRNA integrating into our DNA, if such integration were confirmed.

In conclusion, although it has not been clearly demonstrated that the vaccine's mRNA can integrate into the genome of a vaccinated person, this remains biologically plausible. This risk should therefore have been seriously studied BEFORE administering a product still in the experimental phase to billions of people.

---

259. *Intracellular Reverse Transcription of Pfizer BioNTech COVID-19 mRNA Vaccine BNT162b2 In Vitro in Human Liver Cell Line*, M. Aldén et al., Curr. Issues *Mol. Biol.* 2022.

However, as a ReinfoCovid[260] article on the same subject points out, it would be useful to check whether DNA is already present in the vaccine before administration. This would allow us to determine whether the DNA detected in human cells after vaccination comes from the vaccine itself, or is the result of mRNA conversion into DNA by the cells. If DNA is already present in the vaccine, this would mean that mRNA conversion into DNA in the human body is not necessary to explain the presence of this DNA in our cells. This would call into question the hypothesis of *in vitro* reverse transcription by human cells in the Aldén study.

The possibility that the DNA detected in mRNA vaccines may in fact be a residual "impurity" from the manufacturing process, rather than the result of mRNA conversion into DNA by human cells, is not incongruous. As we shall see,[261] Pfizer and Moderna vaccine vials contain significant quantities of contaminating DNA.

That said, since my 2022 synthesis, new information has emerged, reinforcing initial concerns and providing further disturbing details about the possibility of DNA integration.

After infection with the virus, some people who have had COVID-19 show persistent traces of the Spike protein for up to a year after infection. This persistence could be due to the integration of the mRNA virus into the human genome. This hypothesis is suggested by a study that observed both vaccinated and non-vaccinated patients.[262]

Further research examines the continued presence of viral antigens in the gut. Only people with prolonged COVID-19 sequelae show these antigens and viral RNA, although no viable virus is detected.[263]

---

260. *Retro-transcription de l'ARNm du vaccin Pfizer/BioNtech : un début de preuve in vitro*, Reinfocovid.fr, March 8, 2022.
261. Speicher et al., *Quantification of residual plasmid DNA and SV40 promoter-enhancer sequences in Pfizer/BioNTech and Moderna modRNA COVID-19 vaccines from Ontario, Canada. Autoimmunity*. 2025 Dec;58(1):2551517 PMID: 40913499. https://pubmed.ncbi.nlm.nih.gov/40913499/
262. *Persistent circulating SARS-CoV-2 Spike is associated with post-acute COVID-19 sequelae*, Z. Swank et al., *Clin Infect Dis*, 2022.
263. *Postacute COVID-19 is Characterized by Gut Viral Antigen Persistence in Inflammatory Bowel Diseases*, A. Zollner et al., Gastroenterology, 2022.

It is also possible that the SARS-CoV-2 virus can activate endogenous retroviruses, called HERVs. These viruses, which lie dormant in our bodies, possess the enzyme reverse transcription.[264]

In 2022, we also learned that the SARS-CoV-2 Spike protein can penetrate the nucleus of cells and introduce the mRNA of this protein. It is possible that the Spike protein produced by the vaccine will act in the same way with the vaccine mRNA.[265]

With regard to adenovirus-based vaccines, such as those from Astra-Zeneca and Janssen, an expert in the integration of foreign DNA into human cells points out that the DNA of an adenovirus, similar to that of the COVID-19 vaccines, can integrate into the genome of mice.[266] Did the DNA corresponding to the RNA of the vaccine's Spike protein integrate into the genome of people vaccinated with Astra-Zeneca or Janssen products? It would be surprising if researchers did not address this question someday.

What to retain about mRNA reverse transcription (virus and Pfizer vaccine)[267]

In vitro reverse transcription: Pfizer-BioNTech vaccine mRNA can be converted to DNA when studied in the laboratory (*in vitro*).

– Virus RNA integration: RNA from the SARS-CoV-2 virus, responsible for COVID-19, can integrate into the genome of human cells grown in the laboratory, and has been found in various organs of patients who have died of severe COVID-19.

– mRNA and retro-transcription: mRNAs, whether natural, foreign or even artificial, can be converted to DNA in human cells, even in the absence of viruses. Molecular biology "dogma" is often more complex than biology students may retain: DNA is transcribed into RNA,

264. *SARS-CoV-2 awakens ancient retroviral genes and the expression of pro-inflammatory HERV-W envelope protein in COVID-19 patients*, B. Charvet et al., ISCIENCE, 2023.
265. *Nuclear translocation of Spike mRNA and protein is a novel feature of SARS-CoV-2*, S. Sattar et al., Front. Microbiol, 2023.
266. *Adenoviral Vector DNAand SARS-CoV-2 mRNA-Based COVID-19 Vaccines: Possible Integration into the Human Genome*, W. Doerfler, Virus Res., 2021, PMID 34087261.
267. *Retro-transcription de l'ARNm du vaccin Pfizer/BioNtech : un début de preuve in vitro*, Reinfocovid.fr, March 8, 2022.

but the reverse is also possible, and this was suggested by Francis Crick as early as 1956.

– DNA contaminating mRNA vaccines is more likely to become integrated into the genome.

Further reading
– *Rétrotranscription et intégration dans le génome de l'ARN viral et/ou vaccinal : que sait-on ?*, Aimsib.org, March 20, 2022.

3.5.3 Vaccino-vigilance: institutional blindness

Surveillance of adverse drug and vaccine reactions is crucial to patient protection. It is nonetheless far from infallible. The under-notification of adverse reactions in databases for this purpose has long been acknowledged.

In the context of COVID-19, the shortcomings of vaccino-vigilance have become particularly glaring. Yet, even before the vaccination campaign began in December 2020, the authorities were warned of the nature and extent of potential adverse effects. This information was nevertheless neglected. Why this omission, and how have the experts managed to conceal the adverse effects?

It is worth remembering that the COVID-19 crisis presented a unique opportunity to showcase mRNA vaccines. These vaccines were eagerly awaited by vaccination promoters as a solution to the recurring inefficacy of flu vaccines. This perspective was even underscored at the Milken conference in October 2019, where experts discussed the promising future of mRNA vaccines.[268]

In a note published in August 2022 on the AIMSIB blog, I shared a list of publications highlighting a major problem: the under-reporting of adverse vaccine reactions. To give you an idea, in 1998, Spanish experts estimated that only one adverse reaction in 1,000 was actually reported. More recently, this estimate suggests that only between 1 and 10 adverse reactions out of 100 are actually reported.

---

268. *Universal Flu Vaccine, Milken Institute Future of Health Summit, Washington*, October 28-30, 2019.

Take, for example, an Italian study on the measles-mumps-rubella-varicella (MMRV) vaccine. It revealed that non-serious side-effects were reported 1,529 times more frequently, and serious side-effects 339 times more frequently, when "active surveillance" was implemented. This type of surveillance involves close monitoring of each vaccinated person using a detailed questionnaire to identify any changes in their state of health.

In current practice, "passive monitoring" is the most widespread: patients or their doctors are expected to report any adverse effects spontaneously. This type of monitoring can greatly underestimate the frequency and severity of undesirable effects.

There seems, however, to be some confusion among some experts as to what active pharmacovigilance is in fact. For example, the French ANSM published an article in March 2023,[269] the very title of which refers to "active surveillance," when it is clearly just a matter of spontaneous reports. Is this a deliberate error or a misunderstanding? This conjures notions of George Orwell's doublethink. In any case, such confusion casts doubt on the rigor of the study and the relevance of its conclusions.

Most international experts agree that only 1% (or even less) of adverse reactions are in fact reported. According to Dr. Phillip Altman, an Australian pharmacovigilance specialist, the under-reporting rate of AEs following anti-COVID-19 vaccination is close to 100% on account of the pressure exerted on doctors. One Australian expert even estimates that the rate could be as low as 0% for adverse reactions to COVID-19 vaccines in Australia, due to the pressure exerted on doctors.

Insufficient follow-up
Another reason why the adverse effects of vaccines are underestimated is that the observation period after vaccination is too short. I address this subject in an article co-authored with Prof. Patrick Provost of Montreal's Laval University (see box at the end of the chapter), who invited me to co-author it. Although other researchers also contributed, they did not sign the article for fear of reprisals, Patrick Provost having been sanctioned by Laval University.

---

269. *Pharmacovigilance signals from active surveillance of mRNA platform vaccines (tozinameran and elasomeran)*, M. B. Valnet- Rabier et al., *Therapies*, 2023.

Our publication appeared in the *International Journal of Vaccine Theory, Practice, and Research*. This journal is not listed in PubMed owing to its critical nature, but it is nevertheless a peer-reviewed journal. The publisher, aware that it would be censored anyway, did not wish to even attempt indexation on the international PubMed database.

RNA specialist Patrick Provost trusted his colleagues and received an mRNA vaccine. Unfortunately, he experienced a number of undesirable side effects. When he tried to report them, he realized that many of them would not be considered since they had occurred more than six weeks after vaccination. In partnership with a Quebec pharmacy closely monitoring changes in the health status of its post-vaccination patients, we observed that many people report adverse effects well beyond the six-week mark.

The recommended period for monitoring vaccine side effects is unclear and often contradictory. Brighton Collaboration,[270] an organization that monitors vaccine safety, generally recommends a follow-up period of 42 days, or six weeks. An FDA study on COVID-19 vaccines also indicates a follow- up period of 42 days. This recommendation seems to be based on doctors' opinions rather than on scientific evidence. This is circular reasoning: since doctors generally only report adverse events (AEs) occurring within six weeks of an injection, the FDA is content with this timeframe. Obviously, doctors are not likely to be interested in AEs that occur beyond this timeframe. For mRNA vaccines, which are similar to gene therapies, this observation period should be much longer.

Children who contract COVID-19 are monitored for 120 days, to assess the risk of post-infectious cardiac complications. This prolonged follow-up is used to compare this risk with that associated with vaccination. The question then arises: why is post-vaccination follow-up shorter than post-infection follow-up?[271]

---

270. https://brightoncollaboration.us.
271. *BNT162b2 Vaccine-Associated Myo/Pericarditis in Adolescents: A Stratified Risk-Benefit Analysis*, A. Krug, J. Stevenson, T.B. Høeg, *European Journal of Clinical Investigation*, 2022.

Vaccine risks vs. COVID-19: the verdict of an Indian study

I wish to highlight a significant study,[272] from India, which seems to have escaped the attention of the authorities. I have already referred to this study in the chapter on ADE.

Its strength lies in its simple yet effective methodology. To eliminate the biases commonly observed in case control studies (where the same individuals change status as soon as they are vaccinated), the researchers directly compared vaccinated healthcare professionals with their unvaccinated counterparts. Strangely, this direct method is rarely adopted, particularly by those who might be reluctant to highlight the adverse effects or inefficacy of vaccines.

The study focuses on persistent health problems, adverse events and vaccine efficacy during the second wave of COVID-19. It offers a comparative assessment with pathologies associated with COVID-19 infection. The observations are clear: pathologies associated with COVID-19 infection in young, healthy individuals are far less frequent and diversified than vaccine-related adverse events. What's more, the risk is accentuated in people who have already contracted the virus prior to vaccination. The study confirms what has already been observed many times: vaccinating a person who has already had COVID-19 exposes them to an increased risk of adverse effects. In fact, before COVID-19, which has virtually succeeded in making doctors and scientists forget what they already knew, people who had been infected naturally were never vaccinated subsequently.

Clearly, more rigorous methods could be employed to identify adverse effects associated with COVID-19 vaccines. Unfortunately, health authorities are often content to produce confusing, even deliberately biased studies, and refuse to share the raw data with independent scientists.

---

272. *Persistent Health Issues, Adverse Events, and Effectiveness of Vaccines during the Second Wave of COVID-19: A Cohort Study from a Tertiary Hospital in North India*, U. Kaur et al., *Vaccines*, 20

The main flaws in vaccino-vigilance

Under-reporting of adverse events
It is well known that many adverse reactions are never reported. This may be for a number of reasons, including pressure on healthcare professionals, lack of awareness, or the belief that only a serious effect is worth reporting.

Limited monitoring time
The period during which adverse reactions are monitored after vaccination is often very short, typically six weeks. This is not sufficient to detect long-term or rare effects. Additionally, this period seems to be determined arbitrarily, with no clear scientific justification.

Monitoring methodology
There are two main surveillance methods: active and passive. Active surveillance involves proactive monitoring of individuals after vaccination, while passive surveillance relies on spontaneous reports of adverse events. Unfortunately, passive surveillance is the most commonly used method, which minimizes the estimation of adverse events.

Lack of clarity and transparency
Regulators and vaccine manufacturers are not transparent when it comes to their analytical methods. They do not provide full data. Specialists have also identified gaps or errors in data registries. There is no way of verifying the information provided in official reports.

The enigma of vaccine batch variability
As soon as the first vaccine-related adverse events appeared, certain batch series were identified as being responsible for the majority of serious incidents. This observation is based on data from the VAERS (Vaccine Adverse Effect Reporting System) managed by the CDC in the US. The ANSM in France does not provide access to the batch numbers responsible for adverse events, so verification is impossible.

The subject came to the attention of the general public in 2022, when a website, howbad.info, was set up to check the adverse events associated with each batch: it revealed a great deal of heterogeneity, with some batches appearing significantly more toxic in terms of the number of reports to pharmacovigilance.

In 2023, a study,[273] confirmed the heterogeneity of toxic effects associated with different vaccine batches. The researchers accessed batch numbers linked to adverse reaction reports in Denmark. Where vaccines are produced according to good practice standards, each batch is homogeneous and therefore is expected to appear proportionally in adverse event reports. However, this study reveals that batches fall into three distinct categories according to their frequency of appearance in these notifications.

Batches with the highest number of doses distributed are associated with fewer adverse reactions than smaller batches. It should be pointed out that batches are not distributed uniformly in a single region. On the contrary, doses from each batch are dispersed across different countries or regions. This method of distribution is a strategy long adopted by vaccine manufacturers to minimize the detection of potential adverse events in a specific geographical area, such as a small town that would only receive doses from a particular batch.

According to several sources, the health authorities seem to have been informed of this heterogeneity. In any case, it is undoubtedly known to manufacturers, since in Australia Pfizer vaccinates its employees with a batch specifically designated for them, which the regulatory authority does not consider worth testing. This information is documented in the list of batches tested, available on the Australian Therapeutic Products Regulatory Agency website.[274]

In the United States, access to batch expiry dates is controlled for "security reasons" on the CDC website and issued in dribs and drabs.[275] People who have benefited from this system claim that non-toxic batches have no expiration date, unlike batches that have caused numerous adverse events, as if the CDC knew the numbers of inactive batches that do not require an expiration date.[276]

---

273. *Batch-dependent safety of the BNT162b2 mRNA COVID-19 vaccine*, M. Schmeling, V. Manniche, P. R. Hansen, *Eur J Clin Invest*, 2023.
274. https://www.tga.gov.au/batch-release-assessment-COVID-19-vaccines
275. https://vaccinecodeset.cdc.gov/LotNumber/
276. *CDC's Expiry List and Biologically Active Lots*, Craig Paardekooper, https://howbad.info/cdcexpiry3.pdf

And finally, German chemistry professors have access to batch release data from the Paul Ehrlich Institute (PEI), responsible for testing Pfizer batches in Europe. They published several articles in the *Berliner Zeitung*,[277] to explain that the batches found to be of low toxicity in Denmark were hardly ever tested by the PEI, whereas the toxic batches were all tested. In an interview published in June 2023, they also reported that some batches have a strange color. They asked BioNTech for explanations, but the lab provided only grotesque answers.[278]

The German chemists make an important point: it is normal for the vaccine suspension to appear colored in low-angled light, precisely because of the small size of the lipid nanoparticles (LNPs, which envelop the vaccinal mRNA). If they agglomerate, the coloration disappears. Strangely enough, the manufacturer advises discarding the vial if it is colored. However, according to these chemists, this is the opposite of what should be done.

A random manufacturing process

This is a very confusing story. Here's how I understand it. First, it is important to clarify that the term "placebo" is specific to clinical trials, where it usually refers to a neutral, transparent-looking saline solution. Such a placebo is therefore visually different from COVID-19 vaccines, which contain suspensions of nanoparticles containing mRNA. Why would the manufacturers have marketed batches that were deliberately inactive and easy to spot? In my opinion, the idea of a global clinical trial mixing placebos and active batches seems unlikely, especially when you consider the inability of laboratories to carry out official clinical trials on only 40,000 participants...

On the other hand, it is plausible that the heterogeneity observed in vaccine batches is due to insufficient control of the manufacturing process. The European Medicines Agency (EMA) has highlighted this variability in its reports on vaccine quality. The amount of intact mRNA varies considerably from batch to batch. The LNPs enveloping the mRNA in vaccines are highly variable in size. The size of these LNPs is essential to the vaccine's efficacy. LNPs are fragile. As of 2021, it is

---

277. *Chemiker an BioNTech: "Diese Antwort finden wir etwas irritierend"*, February 1, 2022.
278. Interview from June 2023 on punkt-preradovic.com, *Lots de vaccination: Une étude prouve l'effrayant – with Prof Dr. Gerald Dyker and Prof Dr. Jorg Matysik.*

recommended not to shake the vials nor transport them in motor vehicles (sic!). If the LNPs break up, releasing the mRNA, the latter could be destroyed or fail to reach target. What's more, if the LNPs clump together, they could become inactive.[279]

Given the delicate nature of LNPs, it is crucial to strike a balance between effective homogenization and preservation of particle integrity. When handling tanks of several hundred liters, mixing may be poorly achieved, with variations in LNP concentration between the top and bottom of the tank. In addition, the size of the LNPs could also vary according to their position in the tank. These variations could have implications for the quality and efficacy of the final product. It is also surprising that the optimal storage temperature remains a moot point, as recommendations have varied continuously since 2021[280]: from -80°C to 8°C, depending on the state of dilution and the shelf life...

Who is in charge of product quality control, and what type of controls are carried out? I have asked the ANSM and the EMA about this and have received no reply.

The analysis of batch heterogeneity is, however, a matter of concern. Academic researcher Hervé Seligmann studies the VAERS reports and has identified a potential link with the delay in publication of pharmacovigilance reports.[281] These delays could introduce a bias, giving the illusion that certain batches of vaccines are less toxic than others. As a result, reports of serious adverse reactions in children and women of childbearing age appear to be published later, some as much as two years later.

The question arises: is there a deliberate attempt to conceal these cases, or is it simply because these incidents are examined at greater length by pharmacovigilance experts? In addition, Seligmann identifies numerous errors in the batch numbers mentioned in the notifications. His conclusion is that the differences between batches are not qualitative, but rather gradual. In other words, they are more

---

279. *Stability testing of the PfizerBioNTech BNT162b2 COVID-19 vaccine: a translational study in UK vaccination centers*, L. Kudsiova, A. Lansley, G. Scutt, et al., *BMJ Open Science*, 2021.

280. *Addressing the Cold Reality of mRNA Vaccine Stability*, Crommelin et al., *J Pharm Sci*, 2021.

281. *COVID-19 vaccine batches with apparent low toxicity are not placebos, but have delayed publication of adverse reports in VAERS*, H. Seligmann, ResearchGate, July 2023.

subtle variations between batches, manifesting in terms of degree or intensity rather than nature or type.

To conclude, in my opinion, there are no "intentional" placebos in the mRNA vaccines injected into the world's population, merely the desire to sell at any price, regardless of product quality. This is confirmed by Pfizer itself, which explains certain undesirable effects such as myocarditis by the manufacturing problems mentioned above.[282]

Further information
– A 6-Week Time Period May Not Be Sufficient To Identify Potential Adverse Events Following COVID-19 Vaccination, H. Banoun, P. Provost, *International Journal of Vaccine Theory, Practice and Research*, 2023.

3.5.4 Can vaccinated individuals disseminate vaccine mRNA?

I would like to share with you here the contents of an article I am publishing in a peer-reviewed journal which, though little-known, sheds light on vaccine shedding, a sensitive subject, to say the least

I thought long and hard before deciding to look into this matter, reluctant as I was to explore the possibility of vaccine transmission from the vaccinated to the non-vaccinated. If this phenomenon were proven, it could accentuate division within the population. Let's not forget that in 2021, the authorities treated the unvaccinated as second-class citizens. The notion of vaccine transmission could generate even more animosity, but this time against the vaccinated.

In view of the many misinterpretations circulating on both sides of the matter, I decided to get to work and try to clarify the situation. On the one hand, the authorities maintain that shedding is impossible with anti-COVID-19 vaccines. For them, this notion refers only to the transmission of a live vaccine virus by a recently vaccinated person and applies only in the case of live attenuated virus vaccines (such as MMR—measles-mumps-rubeola). The authorities are thus

282. *The Novel Platform of mRNA COVID-19 Vaccines and Myocarditis: Clues into the Potential Underlying Mechanism*, G. Lazaros et al., *Vaccine*, 2021.

taking a back seat, since the dissemination of mRNA or Spike does not fall within this framework. On the other hand, some critics confuse transmission of the vaccine component (mRNA or Spike protein) with transmission of the virus itself by a vaccinated but unprotected person. However, a vaccinated but infected person can, of course, transmit the virus, since the vaccine does not prevent transmission, as we have already mentioned.

Initial feedback from the field

For the record, the COVID-19 vaccination campaign was launched in December 2020. The first account I read of shedding dates back to the summer of 2021 and originates with a doctor.[283] He mentioned strange cases among medical and scientific colleagues, who experienced symptoms similar to vaccine side effects after contact with recently vaccinated people. He suggested that vaccine components could be transmitted through the skin or breath and called for further studies on the subject.

At first, I found such testimonials unconvincing. Over time, however, their number increased. In October 2021, I was informed of a particularly alarming case: a group of healthcare professionals in France reported a stroke in a 7-year-old child with no previous medical history, whose parents had just been vaccinated.

There were also discussion groups collecting similar testimonials on the Telegram messaging app, from both patients and doctors. These testimonials described symptoms identical to those experienced by vaccine recipients. What's more, some official Pfizer documents relating to clinical trials (phase I/II/III trial protocols) made vague mention of the possibility of vaccine transmission, whether through mishandling or even intimate contact with a vaccinated person.

---

283. *Covid Vaccine Side Effects*, raysahelian.com, accessed June 2021, updated December 2021.

Where do the vaccine's mRNA and the Spike protein it produces go?

Before answering this question, I tried to understand how the vaccine mRNA and the Spike protein that our cells then produce spread through our bodies. We have been assured that mRNA remains only in the muscle where the vaccine was injected and is eliminated within 48 hours. Similarly, the Spike protein is supposed to be produced only during this period, and exclusively by the cells of the muscle concerned. Those who make such claims, however, are either misinformed or dishonest, or perhaps both. Indeed, many scientific studies and preliminary animal tests of COVID-19 vaccines already demonstrate the contrary.

The public should also be aware that, compared with the amount of viral mRNA circulating during a natural infection, the mRNA doses injected are massive: up to 107 times more, as Prof. Jean-Michel Claverie emphasizes.

Before delving into the details, first a brief overview of the trajectory of vaccine components in the body: after injection, the vaccine mRNA, encapsulated in lipid nanoparticles, circulates in the lymph and bloodstream, entering the cells where the Spike protein is then produced. The undegraded mRNA and Spike protein circulate back into the body via "natural exosomes." These exosomes form after the lipid nanoparticles have diffused throughout the body, releasing the mRNA and producing the Spike protein.

LNPs: nanometric transporters

To understand the vaccine's biodistribution within the body, we need to look at the structure of its active ingredient. The vaccine's mRNA is protected and transported by lipid nanoparticles (LNPs), artificial vesicles formed from an assembly of natural and artificial lipids.

The LNPs contained in vaccines have the same structure as the natural exosomes or extra-cellular vesicles (EVs) they seek to mimic. First, we'll look at how LNPs travel through the body after injection. Then we will look at how EVs are ultimately involved in the biodistribution of vaccine components.

> **Lipid nanoparticles (LNPs)**: nanometric lipid structures, often used in mRNA vaccines to protect and transport mRNA inside cells. In the context of COVID-19 vaccines, they have a specific size of between 60 and 100 nm.
>
> **Extracellular vesicles (EVs)**: spherical, bilayer proteolipid structures generated naturally by most living cells, serving to transport various molecules, including lipids, proteins and nucleic acids, between cells. EVs can vary considerably in size (from 20 to 4,000 nm).

1/ Biodistribution of mRNA transported by LNPs

Before the arrival of COVID-19 vaccines, we already knew that LNPs could be administered by a variety of routes: intramuscular, subcutaneous, intra-dermal, intra-tracheal, oral, ophthalmic and even topical. The mRNA inside these LNPs, whatever the route of administration, can be converted to protein over several days. Preclinical animal studies have shown that some LNP constituents are eliminated in the urine and feces.

Studies (pre-2020) in mice show that mRNA-containing LNPs, when injected intramuscularly, migrate from the injection site to the lymph nodes and then into the systemic circulation, concentrating mainly in the liver and spleen. This is confirmed by preclinical trials of COVID-19 mRNA vaccines.

These results are reported in EMA (European Medicines Agency) documents: the RNA encapsulated in LNPs can be distributed to many organs, such as the spleen, heart, kidneys, lungs and brain. Animal studies reveal a concentration of LNPs in specific organs such as the adrenal glands, bone marrow, eyes, intestine, liver, lymph nodes, ovaries, spleen and testes.

Vaccine mRNA is detectable in humans from day one and remains in the blood for at least two weeks after injection. This mRNA can be converted into Spike protein in affected cells and tissues. It was found in axillary lymph nodes 60 days after injection, and one month later in the deltoid muscle at the injection site.

Vaccine mRNA is encapsulated in LNPs but released inside cells. As we will see later, the cells that absorb the vaccine mRNA can in turn encapsulate it in another transporter, the natural "exosomes." These extracellular vesicles (EVs) will then distribute it to other cells. In fact, EVs are produced after endocytosis (cellular uptake) of mRNA-containing LNPs. This mRNA, re-encapsulated in EVs, remains functional and can be converted into Spike protein.

2/ Production of Spike protein and generalized diffusion
When vaccine mRNA enters a cell, it is transformed into Spike protein by the cellular machinery. This protein does not remain confined within the cell. In theory, the vaccine is designed to expose this protein to the cell surface, enabling the immune system to recognize it and trigger an immune response. But the cells don't obey the vaccinologists' wishes, and the Spike protein escapes.

In the blood...
The Spike protein produced by the vaccine can be found in the bloodstream, at levels similar to those observed in patients with severe forms of COVID-19. Its concentration may even exceed that observed in these patients. Free Spike persists for several days in the bloodstream and has been detected within three weeks of injection in boys suffering from post-vaccinal myocarditis, and months after injection in circulating monocytes (white blood cells).

In the organs...
Spike protein is also found in specific areas of lymph nodes for at least 60 days after the second vaccine dose. It is also detected in the heart of patients with myocarditis, from the first day after vaccination and up to three weeks later.

Autopsies reveal the presence of this protein in various organs, such as the heart, brain, muscles and even in certain areas of the lymph nodes, three weeks after vaccination.

3/ Circulation of Spike and mRNA via natural exosomes
Before we look at how our body handles the circulation of Spike protein and residual mRNA, let's recall the essential role of the extracellular vesicles (EVs) produced by our body.

Before COVID-19 vaccines, much was already known about these natural vesicles, also known as exosomes. The presence of EVs in all biofluids is well documented. Exosomes play an essential role in the transport of mRNAs, other types of RNA and proteins. For example, our sweat contains vesicles that carry small fragments of mRNA from our cells (20 to 200 bp,[284] much smaller than vaccine mRNA). These mRNA fragments are still functional, i.e. they can be translated into proteins. What's more, they are protected from the enzymes that normally break down RNA thanks to their packaging in these vesicles.

Certain types of RNA, called microRNA, are more concentrated in sweat than in blood. These microRNAs do not end up in our sweat by chance: they are actively carried there. Similarly, our skin cells can release vesicles carrying microRNAs. These vesicles are also present in saliva and have been identified in the sputum of mild asthma sufferers.

Another fascinating aspect of these natural vesicles is their bidirectional nature during pregnancy. They can travel between mother and fetus, crossing the barrier that separates them in either direction. In fact, they can even be used to deliver drugs to the fetus during pregnancy, demonstrating their potential for healthcare.

Returning to our subject, the main revelation brought by independent research is that exosomes can also transport vaccine mRNA, and the Spike protein once produced in the vaccine recipient's body. Exosomes are therefore also involved in the bio-distribution of vaccine components, which do not necessarily remain confined to the injection site.

Spike wrapped in EVs
It has now been established that the virus' Spike protein circulates in the form of exosomes: the SARS-CoV-2 Spike protein and its fragments have been identified in the extracellular vesicles of COVID-19 patients.

Similarly, after mRNA-based vaccination, once the vaccine's lipid nanoparticles are internalized and the mRNA is translated into Spike protein, cells can encapsulate this vaccine Spike in exosomes, just as they would for viral Spike, and release it into the bloodstream.

Traces of this vaccine Spike were detected in keratinocyte vesicles (skin cells) in a patient with skin lesions three months after receiving

---

284. In molecular biology, the number of "base pairs" (bp) is often used to measure the size of a nucleic acid (DNA or RNA).

the Pfizer-BioNTech vaccine, and also in a persistent rash 100 days after vaccination.

This confirms that the vaccine mRNA and Spike protein circulate and remain throughout the body for an extended period. The natural exosomes that carry them can pass into various body fluids, such as milk, sweat or sputum.

Can mRNA or Spike from the vaccine infect another person?

First of all, it should be remembered that artificial lipid nanoparticles (LNPs) and natural lipid nanoparticles (exosomes) are already used therapeutically via inhalation, transdermal, *in utero* and conjunctival vectors.

Lipid nanoparticles

LNPs are remarkable structures capable of crossing the skin barrier to transport genetic material. Thanks to their composition, similar to that of cell membranes, they can infiltrate the skin, either through hair follicles or by penetrating keratinocytes directly. Their capacity doesn't stop there: they can also carry molecules into the eye, more specifically into its posterior chamber, when administered conjunctivally.

LNPs are now being actively tested in clinical trials for gene therapy and vaccination. For example, when nebulized, these particles can transport nucleic acids directly into the lungs, where the mRNA they contain is efficiently translated. Clinical trials of inhaled anti-graft vaccines based on mRNA-containing LNPs demonstrate that this mRNA can be converted into protein in the body, inducing antibody production. The intranasal route is also explored for administering treatments via LNPs.

Finally, transcutaneous vaccination with LNP is currently under study. These particles are able to penetrate the skin through the hair follicles and accumulate in the sebaceous glands. Initial results show that their efficacy is similar to that of intramuscular injections when the particles are of the same size as those used in COVID-19 vaccines.

Extracellular vesicles

Extracellular vesicles (EVs or natural exosomes) are not new to the medical field. They are already used to deliver a variety of treatments, notably locally to treat conditions such as periodontitis, ulcers or epidermolysis bullosa. They are also successfully used for inhalation, intranasal, oral, intra-ocular and subconjunctival administration, transporting drugs to the desired location. When ingested, cow's milk EVs are resistant to gastric juices, as demonstrated by studies on mice.

These nanovesicles are also showing their potential in oncology. They can be used to deliver RNA directly into a brain tumor via intranasal introduction.

In the context of the COVID-19 pandemic, EVs are also being studied as a therapeutic option. Currently, some 60 clinical trials are underway, using exosomes loaded with mesenchymal stem cells. These stem cells have the potential to repair lung cells damaged by the SARS-CoV-2 virus.

The exosomes, which carry a specific part of the Spike protein (the receptor-binding domain), proved their ability to introduce this antigen into the lung cells of mice by inhalation, triggering an immune response. Similarly, inhalation of exosomes containing mRNA or Spike protein has shown the ability to immunize mice and monkeys against SARS-CoV-2.

Interestingly, these natural EVs appear to be more efficient than LNPs, their synthetic counterparts.

Naked RNA?

Naked mRNA (not encapsulated in LNPs or EVs) may also be able to penetrate the skin and be inhaled: the feasibility of inhaled RNA for passive transfection has been demonstrated in a number of studies. Inhaled RNA can lead to Spike synthesis, resulting in immunization of the individual, i.e. antibody production.

My conclusion

It is clear that natural extracellular vesicles (EVs) carrying mRNA and Spike protein could be excreted via various body fluids. These EVs could then be absorbed by unvaccinated individuals, whether through skin contact, inhalation, breast-feeding or even transplacental transmission in fetuses. Nor can it be ruled out that semen could be a transport vector. Naked mRNA can also be excreted and absorbed. It is therefore biologically plausible that vaccinated individuals could transmit mRNA or Spike protein to non-vaccinated individuals by proximity.

It is unfortunate that in-depth studies were not carried out before marketing and clinical trials. If bio-distribution in animals was widely known, other aspects, such as transmission via breast milk, should have been examined. At least five independent studies show the presence of exosomes carrying vaccine mRNA in breast milk within 48 hours of injection.[285]

As for transmission via sperm, no one has mentioned this, even though this should be studied for any gene therapy product. We shall see that mRNAs are objectively GTPs, gene therapy products.

My work was published in November 2022 in a modest scientific journal, but it quickly attracted attention because it addressed a widely debated, and above all highly sensitive, issue. It was even attacked by AFP Canada in a dispatch entitled *COVID-19 vaccinated do not 'shed' mRNA to unvaccinated*, published on December 14, 2022.[286]

A few days after publication, the publisher sent me an e-mail announcing, without any further explanation, that he had received a request for additional proofreading, three reviewers having been called in to help. I am still waiting for the result of this review. He added the words *"Being questioned"* in red just before the title of my article on his website. Today, it is labeled as an *Editorial expression of concern*. And still no response from the editor.

I contacted all the experts who had read my work on ResearchGate, a platform for exchange between researchers, to ask for their criticism. Since its publication, I have received more and more testimonials and questions. It is embarrassing at times: how do you answer someone who is worried about being intimate with their partner? My reluctance to work on this subject was well-founded.

---

285. See *Biodistribution of mRNA COVID-19 vaccines in human breast milk*, Hanna et al., *eBioMedicine*, October 2023.
286. Accessible via the following link: https://factcheck.afp.com/doc.afp.com.33398EC.

Further reading

Current state of knowledge on the excretion of mRNA and Spike produced by anti-COVID-19 mRNA vaccines; possibility of contamination of the entourage of those vaccinated by these products, H. Banoun, *Infect Dis Res*, 2022.

https://web.archive.org/web/20221115065725 / https://www.tmrjournals.com/public/articlePDF/20221114/48 3e983160eb24f1ef94bdd666603ac9.pdf

---

The FDA aware as early as February 2021 that vaccine mRNA passes into placenta and breast milk

The FDA has decided not to release its files on COVID-19 vaccines for 75 years, on the pretext that these documents are extremely voluminous, and officials must reread them before publishing. Reread, or censor them? This discounts the perseverance of citizens who succeed in obtaining certain files through FOIA requests (Freedom of Information Act, which authorizes anyone to request the disclosure of a document from a US federal agency).

For example, a declassified document tells us a great deal about the adverse effects of Pfizer's BNT162b2 vaccine, based on spontaneous declarations collected between December 11, 2020, and February 28, 2021. It is still necessary for many independent citizens to examine hundreds of thousands of pages to extract the key information.

The majority of those who received the vaccine before it was authorized for pregnant women were caregivers. Inevitably, some became pregnant and then breastfed. Others were vaccinated while breast-feeding, which should never have been the case, given the total absence of clinical data and official re-recommendations for the general public at the time.

It should be remembered that no pregnant women, let alone nursing mothers, were included in the clinical trials. Administering the vaccine to this population was tantamount to conducting a savage clinical trial, all the more so since the first victims were virtually forced to oblige: young women working in the healthcare or a related sector, and who were often vaccinated under duress, to keep their jobs.

.../...

There exists a double standard when it comes to vaccines: how can we explain the relentless attacks on the medical professors at the Marseille IHU, who treated patients and were bashed for conducting an uncontrolled clinical trial with a drug that has been in use for 70 years?

Consequences for breast-fed infants
Adverse reactions observed in some infants are compatible with the passage of vaccine mRNA into breast milk during the week following vaccine administration: these symptoms appear within seven days post-vaccination. In infants, these symptoms include scaling. of the skin, increased irritability, rashes and urticaria, angioedema, undefined illnesses (sometimes leading to hospitalization), lethargy, diarrhea, fever... Cases of cessation of lactation and change in milk color have also been reported.

It wasn't until the vaccine was marketed and administered to breast-feeding mothers that researchers independent of the manufacturers began studying breast milk. Five studies confirm the passage of vaccine mRNA into breast milk during the first week after injection.

Pregnancy and post-vaccination complications
As for pregnant women, a large number of miscarriages (spontaneous termination before 20 weeks' gestation) were reported within three weeks of vaccination. Some miscarriages occurring later may not have been reported.

Premature births have also been reported, accompanied by newborn complications similar to the adverse effects of the vaccine, such as tachycardia, respiratory distress and thrombosis. The FDA has clearly stated that these infants were exposed to the vaccine via the placenta but does not comment further on this. The disorders observed in these premature infants could result from the toxicity of the Spike protein, which could have been transmitted from the mother's body to the fetus, or even produced directly by the fetus following translation by its cells of the vaccine's mRNA.

.../...

Sources

– FDA knew as of February 2021 that the mRNA vaccine crosses the placenta, passes into milk, and causes adverse events in breastfed infants, H. Banoun, ResearchGate, April 2023.

https://www.researchgate.net/publication/370107164_FDA_knew_as_of_February_2021_that_the_mRNA_vaccine_crosses_the_placenta_passes_into_milk_and_causes_adverse_events_in_breastfed_infants

3.5.5 What tests should be required in the event of death following a COVID-19 vaccine?

From the beginning of 2023, judges presiding over complaints from the families of victims of the effects of anti-COVID-19 vaccines have been seeking to know how and in what cases to order an autopsy of the deceased after vaccine injection. Scientists, doctors, jurists and lawyers are working together to answer these questions.

This guide was originally intended for judges, but it is addressed to the general public as we are striving to facilitate understanding outside specialist circles of how COVID-19 mRNA vaccines work, and why they are dangerous to a degree that could potentially cause death.

Initially, I proposed to translate a document written by German forensic pathologist Prof. Arne Burkhardt, who laid out the methods he uses for this type of inquiry. With other collaborators, we then thought it would be useful to add a lengthy introduction, to broaden understanding of the dangers of mRNA vaccines and their specific mode of action. Indeed, this new technology and the targeted antigen (the Spike protein) can potentially bring about multiple pathologies with immeasurable (or indefinite) onset times, until the duration of Spike expression can be ascertained.

The scientific literature has presented a considerable number of autopsy reports. When a team of independent researchers attempted to publish an analysis of these, it was immediately censored by the preprint server on which the analysis was posted. It became impossible to download the full text, later available on another platform.[287] The study[288] shows that the main vulnerabilities to death following COVID-19 vaccination involve the cardiovascular, hematological and respiratory systems, and multisystemic damage. The average time to death was 14 days after vaccination, and 74% of the deaths examined were attributed to the COVID-19 vaccine.

In our collaborative work, we look back at the artificial origin of the virus and the toxicity of the Spike protein responsible for the pathologies associated with infection by the SARS-CoV-2 virus and the adverse effects of the vaccine, which cause it to be produced in uncontrolled quantities over an unknown duration. Spike also disrupts the renin-angiotensin system. In addition to these pathologies, there are also diseases specifically caused by the synthetic modification of Spike (Creutzfeldt-Jakob prion diseases) and the gene therapy technology employed (see next chapter), such as cancers.

The carcinogenic effects of these vaccines may present with significant delay, up to as much as several years after injection, which explains why this type of risk is difficult to identify. The long development period of cancer and the relatively low incidence of individual cancers prevent traditional pharmacovigilance systems from identifying drug associations with cancer.

For all other drugs, the carcinogenic effect is closely monitored, and where doubt prevails, drugs are withdrawn from the market. For all drugs, that is, with the exception of anti-COVID-19 vaccines, pre- and post-marketing analyses attempt to identify the slightest carcinogenic effects of new products. To the contrary, in the case of anti-COVID-19 vaccines, the mainstream media try to censor or disqualify signs of increased cancer occurrence resulting from these vaccines.

RNAs play an important role in the regulation of gene expression and, as such, in cancer control. Moreover, for gene therapy products, of which mRNAs are an objective element, it is recommended to pay particular attention to the detection and monitoring of the carcinogenic effect.[289]

287. https://zenodo.org/record/8120771
288. *A Systematic Review of Autopsy Findings in Deaths after COVID-19 Vaccination*, N. Hulscher, P. McCullough, et al., *SSRN*, 2023.
289. *Negative Evidence: COVID-19 Vaccines and Cancer*, Jane M. Orient, M.D. Guest Editorial, *Journal of American Physicians and Surgeons*, 2023.

The mRNA technology is also likely to generate many autoimmune diseases, as Spike production by many cell types turns these cells into targets for the immune system.

Consequently, there is no reason to set a time limit for imputing a causal link between vaccine injection and an adverse event, or to limit the search for vaccine-induced pathologies to signals recognized by pharmacovigilance. This applies in particular to cancers: numerous testimonials from patients and healthcare professionals report atypical cancers and "turbo-cancers" (reactivation of stabilized cancers in remission, with a very rapid and often fatal course). It is deplorable that suspicious deaths occurring within seven days of vaccine injection are not systematically investigated.

A recent Japanese scientific publication covering 46 autopsies shows that most deaths were due to post-vaccination cardiac or thrombotic events. *A priori*, all post-vaccination deaths (even accidents and suicides) should be investigated for a potential causal relationship with the vaccine. Ultimately, fatal falls, with or without fractures, could also be linked to mRNA vaccines. Indeed, they can cause sudden necrosis of the shoulder joint, probably through hypercoagulability and thrombosis. It is not impossible that the vaccine could cause the same phenomenon in the femoral head.

The essential points of the proposed autopsy protocol include:

– search for thrombo-embolic events (both macroscopic and microscopic), vasculitis and myocarditis, particular inflammatory reactions, autoimmune reactions and foreign matter (lipids in nanolipid vaccine carrier particles, for example, or metallic or other impurities);

– search for Spike protein and mRNA in damaged organs. The search for the vaccine Spike protein in inflamed and necrotic tissues. This involves immunohistochemistry (using antibodies directed against the proteins to be tested), to detect Spike protein and Nucleocapsid protein (two proteins of the SARS-CoV-2 virus) in tissues. The abundant presence of Spike (present in the virus and produced after the vaccine) and the absence of Nucleocapsid protein (present only in the virus and not produced after the vaccine) indicates the responsibility of the vaccine and not of infection by the SARS-CoV-2 virus.

Vaccine mRNA can also be detected by PCR, but the problem with these assays is that they do not distinguish between vaccine mRNA and viral mRNA (the same applies to Spike). Vaccine manufacturers can therefore claim that this is a viral Spike produced continuously in a person previously infected with the virus. This is why we need to develop specific assay techniques that allow us to differentiate the two proteins: by mass spectrometry, for example.[290] For mRNA, a specific PCR of modified vaccine mRNA is required to differentiate it from viral mRNA.

Critical scientists still have their work cut out for them to perfect these techniques. To this end, we can't count on forensic scientists and molecular biologists who have remained within the doxa.

Why request an autopsy after the death of a person vaccinated with a messenger RNA "vaccine" against COVID-19?

https://www.researchgate.net/publication/372365662_Why_request_an_autopsy_after_the_death_of_a_person_vaccinated_with_a_messenger_RNA_vaccine_against_COVID-19

---

290. *Detection of recombinant Spike protein in the blood of individuals vaccinated against SARS-CoV-2: Possible molecular mechanisms*, Brogna et al., Proteomics Clin Appl, 2023, PMID 37650258.

PART IV

BIOPOLITICS OF THE FUTURE...
WHAT'S IN STORE FOR US?

As stated earlier, biopolitics is a concept developed by Michel Foucault in the late 1970s. The philosopher and chair of "History of Systems of Thought" at the Collège de France conceptualized biopolitics and biopower as elements of a broader strategy of power, which is exercised over the individual as a biological entity. This theoretical framework offers a valuable perspective for understanding the power dynamics surrounding such complex issues as vaccination and public health. Until the 18th century, states exercised their power over political subjects without taking their biological nature into account. For example, during epidemics, only policing measures were taken.

We have seen that the results of biopolitics are moving away from their intended goal, which is, among other things, to protect people's health, and notably through vaccination. We shall see how biopower is now trying to take advantage of the COVID-19 pandemic to advance on two fronts: research into the functional gains of viruses and acceleration of generalized vaccination. We will see that the biological normalization of human populations continues along with that of wild and domestic animal populations.

I have neither the expertise nor the space required to discuss other means of population control, such as, for example, digital identification,[291] even if it is linked to the widespread use of vaccination.

My main aim is to shed light on future vaccines and the tactics used to evade the fundamental principles of medicine. Ironically, these same principles are often put forth by biopower, which nevertheless never fails to violate them.

---

291. See CSI n°102, April 27, 2023: Fréderic Boutet – *Identité numérique* – with Emmanuelle Darles and Dr. Eric Ménat. See also World Economic Forum reports: *Advancing Digital Agency: The Power of Data Intermediaries*, Insight Report, February 2022, *Identity in a Digital World. A new chapter in the social contract*, Insight Report, September 2018.

4.1 mRNA: vaccines or gene therapy?

The regulatory challenge

The subject of drug regulation may seem tedious, but it is essential in view of biopolitics and its vaccine orientation. We will see how anti-COVID-19 mRNAs managed to escape gene therapy product (GTP) regulation to benefit from the far more relaxed vaccine regulations.

I discuss this subject in depth in one of my articles. After a rocky road, it was published in a PubMed-indexed peer-reviewed journal. Initially rejected by two different journals, the article was accepted by the *International Journal of Molecular Sciences* (publisher MDPI, a journal ranked by Google in eighth place out of the top 100 life science journals), but only after a complete rewrite. To meet publication standards, I had to tone down certain assertions. For example, it was impossible for me to express the wish that mRNAs be not better regulated but banned altogether from the context of vaccines.

As theoretically promising as mRNAs may be, they have been tested for years against genetic diseases and cancers, and the results have always shown their toxicity and inefficacy. At the very least, they could be used on a "compassionate" basis for patients who are terminally ill and for whom no other therapy is possible. In summary, this is what the article says:

The active substance in COVID-19 vaccines is a nucleic acid (mRNA) which introduces a genetic sequence that must be translated into a protein (Spike, in this case) to produce the desired prophylactic effect. In terms of their mode of action, these vaccines fittingly correspond to the notion of gene therapy product (GTP) as established by the EMA, the European Medicines Agency, and the American Society for Gene and Cell Therapy.[292] However, because they are used as vaccines against an infectious disease, mRNAs have been excluded from gene therapy product regulation in the United-States and the European Union. Consequently, the same formulation based on mRNA encapsulated in lipid nanoparticles (LNP) will be classified as a gene therapy product if it is intended to treat cancer or another disease but will be exempt from this classification if the use motivation is to prevent an infectious disease.

---

292. ASGCT: *Comirnaty Becomes First-Ever mRNA Vaccine to Receive FDA Approval*, August 27, 2021.

There is no clear scientific or ethical justification for this distinction. Why impose less rigorous controls on a product intended to be administered to a large part of the world's healthy population, compared with GTPs reserved for rare diseases or certain cancers?

As a result, some of the controls required for gene therapy products have not been applied to mRNA COVID-19 vaccines, raising obvious safety issues.

What's more, manufacturers are planning to replace traditional vaccines with mRNA vaccines, starting with influenza vaccines. These therapeutic products could, in a median solution, be considered "pro-drug" or "pro-vaccine" (see reference in "Further information"). Specific regulations would have to be drawn up for this type of product, insisting on control of potency, i.e. the quality, quantity, duration and sites of expression of the antigen of interest, as well as the toxicity of the antigen produced on mRNA instruction.

Semantic hijacking

Initially, gene therapy was mainly seen as a way of modifying or repairing a defective gene directly in the genome. This often involved working with DNA, the molecule that constitutes our genes. As science progressed, however, researchers have developed methods for introducing "added" nucleic acids into a patient's cells. These nucleic acids can be DNA or RNA. The term "added" means that these nucleic acids are introduced into the cells in a way that does not modify the individual's genome (the complete set of genes), but nevertheless allows them to influence cell function.

In the early 2000s, a narrow view of gene therapy still prevailed, prior to the use of plasmid DNA,[293] and, even more so, mRNAs. Since mRNAs are not intended to directly modify the genome, this may have served as a fallacious contention by those arguing that mRNAs should not be classified as gene therapy products (GTPs).

---

293. A plasmid DNA, or simply plasmid, is a small circular DNA molecule that is distinct from the main bacterial chromosome and capable of independent replication. Plasmids are commonly found in bacteria, but can also be found in some eukaryotes, notably yeast.

In an article published in 2019,[294] in one of the oldest scientific journals devoted to gene therapy, we are reminded that gene therapy today concerns any strategy that modifies gene expression or repairs an abnormal gene, and in particular includes the introduction of RNA into a patient's cells in order to make them produce a protein.

However, as I point out in my article, regulatory agencies have introduced an exceptional clause for GTPs designed to combat infectious diseases: they can be called "vaccines" for this purpose and thus, under mere semantic cover, escape the specific controls on GTPs.

It is noteworthy that Japan stands out in this respect: mRNA-based vaccines are subject to GTP regulation. Despite my few Japanese contacts, I have not yet been able to determine how the country's health authorities have approached and resolved this complex issue.

Clinical trials and gene therapy products: a series of failures
To understand the biopolitical significance of regulating these products, we need to step back a few years. It was the profit motive that led private companies to develop these products (biotech start-ups, a field in revolution). At first, the aim was to cure cancer. Then the biopolitical leaders joined forces with the private sector to push for the development of mRNA vaccines, particularly against influenza. The COVID-19 pandemic presented the perfect opportunity to move to the global commercial stage, brushing aside the "petty" problems of toxicity and inefficacy.

The first gene therapy for adenovirus-induced cancer was approved in China in 2003,[295] followed by authorizations in Europe and the United States, but the companies could not make these products profitable owing to the small number of target patients. High prices and doubts about efficacy and safety were obstacles to their cost reimbursement by health insurance systems.[296]

---

294. *The Landscape of Cellular and Gene Therapy Products: Authorization, Discontinuations, and Cost*, V. Shukla et al., *Hum Gene Ther Clin Dev*, 2019, PMID 30968714.
295. *An overview of development in gene therapeutics in China*, D. Wang, K. Wang, Y. Cai, *Gene Ther*, 2020.
296. *Comparison of Current Regulatory Status for Gene-Based Vaccines in the U.S., Europe and Japan*, Y. Nakayama, A. Aruga, *Vaccines*, 2015.

Definitions

Traditional vaccines. They use diminished or inactivated forms of the pathogen, or parts of it (such as proteins). Once administered, these elements trigger an immune response which, without causing disease, prepares the immune system to react quickly and effectively if the actual pathogen is encountered later.

Gene vaccines. According to European and French regulations, a vaccine must contain an antigen, which is not the case for mRNA vaccines. Instead of introducing a form of the pathogen (or part of it) into the body, these products use nucleic acids (such as mRNA) to instruct the patient's cells to produce part of the pathogen (usually a protein). This protein then triggers an immune response. These products are often called "vaccines" because they also aim to prevent disease by training the immune system, but their mechanism of action is closer to that of gene therapies, since they involve the introduction of genetic material into the patient's cells. We could call them pro-vaccines.

Moderna and Pfizer: a strategic shift towards mRNA vaccines

Founded in 2010, Moderna, whose name stands for *Modified RNA*, initially aimed to develop RNA-based drugs to combat cancers and genetic diseases. In 2011, Frenchman Stéphane Bancel became CEO. In 2014, Moderna opted for a major strategic shift: the lab turned to the development of mRNA vaccines, deemed more profitable than gene therapies. In 2013, the US Defense Advanced Research Projects Agency (DARPA) granted Moderna funding for research into these vaccines. The involvement of this US military agency is explained by the potential of mRNA vaccines to provide a rapid response in the event of a biological weapon attack.

In 2015, Moderna embarked on the development of an mRNA influenza vaccine and initiated a clinical trial in 2017. The results of this trial proved disappointing. Lack of efficacy, signs of toxicity, in a 2016 interview,[297] Bancel expressed his concerns about the potential health hazards of mRNAs. How can we explain the fact that a company with

---

297. *Ego, ambition, and turmoil: Inside one of biotech's most secretive start-ups, Stat*, September 13, 2016.

a record of failure and no sales has survived until its success with COVID-19?

BARDA (*Biomedical Advanced Research and Development Authority*) and CEPI (*Coalition for Epidemic Preparedness Innovations*) are among Moderna's active supporters in the development of these mRNA vaccines.[298]

In 2018, Moderna announced that it had found a solution to the problems of mRNA stability and distribution. It is based on two key elements: the use of efficient lipid nanoparticles, the famous LNPs serving as vectors, and the modification of uridines by pseudouridines. Pseudouridine is a molecule that resembles uridine, one of the four base components of RNA. In natural RNAs, pseudouridine sometimes replaces some uridines, but not all. An RNA composed exclusively of pseudouridines is not a natural phenomenon.[299]

In September 2019, Moderna announced the "promising" results of a clinical trial for an mRNA vaccine against the Chikungunya virus.[300] These results, however, showed a rapid drop in the level of antibodies produced and non-negligible adverse effects. The doses injected were considerable: from 0.1 to 0.6 mg/ kg, i.e. up to 42 mg for an individual. By comparison, the dose of mRNA in the Moderna COVID-19 vaccine is 100 micrograms/kg, or 400 times less. Only four years ago, dosage research was still in its infancy.

Another textbook case, this time on the European side, is a German biotech company that plays a key role in the development of mRNAs. Founded in 2008, BioNTech began its activities in 2012 by producing mRNA prototypes designed to fight cancer, like Moderna. In 2015, the company shifted its focus to the development of mRNA vaccines. By 2018, it was working alongside Pfizer to develop mRNA vaccines against influenza. In 2019, BioNTech attracted significant investment, notably from Sanofi and the Bill & Melinda Gates Foundation. In October of the same year, BioNTech was listed on Nasdaq.

---

298. *mRNA vaccines a new era in vaccinology*, N. Pardi, M. Hogan, F. Porter, et al., Nat Rev Drug Discov 2018.

299. *Regulation and Function of RNA Pseudouridylation in Human Cells*, E. K. Borchardt, N. M. Martinez, W. V. Gilbert, Annu Rev Genet, 2020.

300. *A Phase 1 Trial of Lipid-Encapsulated mRNA Encoding a Monoclonal Antibody with Neutralizing Activity Against Chikungunya Virus*, A. August et al., Nat Med, 2021. Erratum in Nat Med, May 2022, PMID 34887572.

It is important to recall some warnings from Ugur Sahin, the founder of BioNTech himself. In 2014, he expressed concerns about the use of codon optimization, which can affect mRNA translation speed and potentially lead to protein misfolding.[301] Sahin also drew attention to the potential toxicity of the unnatural nucleotides used in these mRNAs (pseudouridines). In addition, he pointed to the wide biodistribution of mRNA when injected intramuscularly, and also raised the risk that patients with autoimmune diseases may develop autoantibodies directed against mRNA.

Clearly, the heads of these major laboratories were the first to know about the potential risks of their products. Astonishingly, the public has never heard of these warnings, and their authors remained silent given the unprecedented financial prospects for COVID-19 mRNA vaccines.

When lobbies unravel regulations

As revealed in a European Medicines Agency document on the regulation of "advanced therapies,"[302] intense lobbying by industry was already tending in 2008 to exclude gene vaccines from the strict regulation of GTPs. In 2007 and 2008, the EMA classified nucleic acid vaccines as GTPs. The regulations changed in September 2009, just after the H1N1 influenza epidemic, when the EMA excluded mRNA vaccines from the GTP regulations.

In the United States, the FDA is responsible for issuing recommendations to drug manufacturers. Unlike the EMA, which requires

301. *mRNA-based therapeutics—developing a new class of drugs*, U. Sahin, K. Karikó, Ö. Türeci, Nat Rev Drug Discov., 2014, PMID 25233993.
302. This document summarizes stakeholder contributions to the EU Enterprise and Industry Directorate General's public consultation on proposals to amend Annex I of Directive 2001/83/EC on advanced therapy medicinal products. The consultation runs from April 8 to June 10, 2008. Patient organizations, universities and public organizations, industry, regulatory authorities, individuals and other stakeholders are invited to express their views. The long list of laboratories involved in the discussions shows that they had plenty to say. These include MedImmune, Merck Sharp & Dohme (Europe) Inc. and Pfizer, among others. *Implementation of the 'Advanced Therapies' Regulation Amendments to Annex I to Directive 2001/83/EC as Regards Advanced Therapy Medicinal Products*, European Commission, Directorate, https://health.ec.europa.eu/consultations/public-consultation-proposals-amend-annex-i-directive-200183ec-regards-advanced-therapy-medicinal_en

manufacturers to justify any failure to comply, FDA guidelines are non-binding. In 1998, it introduced special rules for nucleic acids used for prophylactic purposes, which are quite similar to those established for gene therapy products (GTP). In 2013, it took the explicit decision to exclude infectious disease vaccines from GTP regulation. This decision coincided with the start of DARPA's collaboration with Moderna. Although we are often reminded that correlation does not necessarily mean causation, these coincidences are nonetheless noteworthy.

Apparently more concerned about drug control, the EMA has surprisingly eased the constraints on product quality for mRNA vaccines. Indeed, in contrast to the 95% purity generally required for any drug designed for human use, the EMA accepts a much lower threshold: an integrity of only 50% of the expected mRNA in a vial is sufficient to approve a batch. What's more, it is not clear who carries out the tests independently of the manufacturers, or how they are carried out. The competent authorities, such as the ANSM (Agence nationale de sécurité du médicament) in France and the EMA itself, have not responded to my questions on this subject. What do these 50% authorized impurities represent? Is it degraded mRNA? Or is the quantity of active ingredient simply lower than indicated on the label? All still a mystery.

Impure products contaminated with DNA
The EMA had already reported the presence of residual DNA in Covid-19 vaccines, at widely varying levels. This observation has now been confirmed by independent researchers, including Kevin McKernan and his team: they have discovered contaminating DNA in the vaccines, a contamination which appears to originate in the mRNA manufacturing process. To produce this mRNA, a DNA plasmid is first synthesized by bacteria, then transcribed in vitro into RNA. Before encapsulating this mRNA in lipid nanoparticles (LNPs), it is essential to completely eliminate this DNA and bacterial toxins. The DNA contamination observed could therefore be the result of incomplete removal of these residues during the purification process.[303] We have already discussed this possible contamination in the chapter on *Genome modification, an underestimated risk* (Part III).

303. *Sequencing of Bivalent Moderna and Pfizer mRNA Vaccines Reveals Nanogram to Microgram Quantities of Expression Vector dsDNA per Dose*, K. McKernan et al., OSF Preprints, April 10, 2023.

Even more alarming, in the contaminating DNA present in the Pfizer vaccine, the researchers identified specific elements of the SV40 virus, known to be oncogenic, i.e. capable of causing the development of cancer in animals. It could also play a role in the development of malignant tumors in humans.

So, what is this genetic sequence doing in the DNA used to make a vaccine for humans?

SV40, or simian virus 40, was first discovered in monkeys. This polyomavirus has been widely studied for its ability to transform normal cells into cancerous ones in the laboratory. Historically, it came to prominence after being discovered in the 1960s in batches of polio vaccine grown on monkey kidney cells. This led to a growing awareness of the need for rigorous controls in the vaccine manufacturing process.

It turns out that the SV40 promoter, part of the virus' genetic sequence, is widely used in biotechnology. It enables the increase of RNA production from a plasmid (the small circular piece of DNA used in the laboratory). The use of this promoter is therefore a laboratory strategy to make the manufacturing process more efficient and profitable. Its presence is not necessarily attributable to malicious intent on the part of the manufacturer. The fact remains that SV40 should never have found its way, even partially, into a product intended for administration to the world's population. This raises serious questions about the purification and quality-control processes used to manufacture COVID-19 vaccines, which, as we know, were manufactured in a haste.

It should be noted that the high degree of impurities present is not a feature of mRNA vaccines alone: AstraZeneca and Janssen adenovirus vaccines also contain many proteins from manufacturing, which could be responsible for inflammation and autoimmune problems.[304]

Let's not forget the case of the Moderna batches in Japan, contaminated by metallic particles. The Spanish subcontractor Rovi claimed that these particles originated from a friction problem on the packaging line. Following two suspicious deaths, Japan withdrew 1.6 million doses in August 2021.[305]

304. *Process and product-related impurities in the ChAdOx1 nCov-19 vaccine*, L. Krutzke et al., eLife, 2022.
305. *Japan suspends 1.6M doses of Moderna shot after contamination reports* Aug 26, 2021, by Reuters https://www.nbcnews.com/news/world/japan-suspends-1-6m-doses-moderna-shot-after-contamination-reports-n1277669

No pharmacokinetic studies

I would like to point out in particular that the pharmacokinetic studies required for gene therapy products (GTP) were carried out in a highly cursory manner for mRNA vaccines. These studies, designed to investigate the fate of the vaccine's active substances within the body, should have highlighted the widespread and persistent distribution of mRNA and its product, the Spike protein, throughout the human body. They should also have examined its possible excretion, and even its probable transmission, as demonstrated in the case of breast milk. We touched on this in *Can vaccinated people disseminate vaccine mRNA?* (Section 3.5.4.).

Given this broad biodistribution, it would have been essential to study mRNA integration in the genome and in germ cells (ova and spermatozoa). In addition, potential toxicity to embryos should have been assessed. Limited studies on rats revealed skeletal malformations. Finally, genotoxicity and potential cancer risk would have had to be examined in depth. The results obtained from animal studies are, to date, ambiguous on this point, underscoring the need for further investigation.

No long-term monitoring!

Long-term safety monitoring of GTPs must extend over several years (30 years for the EMA), whereas for vaccines, it is generally only carried out over a few weeks. This should not be acceptable, given the persistence of the product being injected and the protein expressed. This follow-up is particularly fundamental for certain categories of pathology, which are also reported as adverse effects of COVID-19 mRNA vaccines: cancers, hematological and neurological disorders, rheumatic and autoimmune diseases, as well as infections. These diseases are listed in pharmacovigilance databases, including cancers for which no causal link has yet been officially recognized.

Outbreak of cancer and leprosy

As far as cancers are concerned, many independent interpretations of the official data show a rise in cancers after the COVID-19 vaccination campaign.[306] At the CSI program on June 15, 2023,[307] Viviane Cuendet presented the official Swiss figures, which show, among other pathologies, a rise in certain cancers from 2021 onwards, particularly in the 15-39 age group. She asked the Swiss health authorities whether they suspected a particular cause. The answer was negative, but the authorities did not deny the increases.

Could disruption of natural immunity be linked to the cancer recurrences that many doctors report following mRNA injections in their patients? At the International Covid Summit organized by Reinfo Liberté in Marseille in April 2022, American pathologist Dr. Ryan Cole presented the higher risk of cancer triggering or reactivation induced by the "modulation" of the immune response following mRNA vaccination. This was explained by an alteration in gene expression for a large number of immune cells, notably CD8 lymphocytes, which kill cancer cells. The disorganization of the innate immune system and its receptors also contributes to the activation of other viruses present in the body in a latent state (herpes, shingles, papillomavirus, respiratory syncytial virus). Without going into too much detail, let's not forget that in biology, a phenomenon can rarely be explained by a single mechanism: to explain this Spike-induced immunotolerance, the role of anti-Spike IgG4, which takes over from other IgG after repeated vaccinations, has also been suggested, as has the increased expression of the PD-L1 factor induced by vaccine Spike.

Leprosy or leprosy-type reactions are another example of an "unforeseen" pathology that could also be linked to immune system deregulation. Several publications document cases following mRNA anti-COVID-19 injections observed in various countries, including

306. *Negative Evidence: COVID-19 Vaccines and Cancer, Jane M. Orient, J of American Physicians and Surgeons*, Vol. 28, 2023, jpands.org/vol28no1/ orient.pdf.

307. N° 108, Conseil Scientifique Indépendant, https://www.conseil-scientifique-independant.org/csi-n-108-viviane-cuendet-15-06-23-plongee-dans-les-statistiques-covid-et-post-vaccinales-suisses-2/

the UK,[308] India,[309] Singapore,[310] Israel,[311] Indonesia,[312] and Brazil.[313] Despite the sophistication of mRNA vaccines, some side effects apparently re-emerge diseases thought to have been relegated to the past.

Deliberate omission?

In view of the issues that I have developed here, no mRNA should ever again be injected into a healthy person. Surprisingly, in the EMA document that sets out the framework for the clinical evaluation of new vaccines from 2023 onwards, no specific regulations are mentioned explicitly for mRNA vaccines. This document does apply to vaccines containing nucleic acids (without any further precision), so mRNAs are indeed concerned but not expressly named! Moreover, there are no mRNA specialists on vaccine expert committees.

Could this omission be interpreted as deliberate and planned? In autumn 2023, the EMA, like health agencies around the world, persisted in recommending anti-COVID-19 booster mRNA vaccination, adapted to the variants in circulation in spring 2023. Has this body learned nothing from its failures? This is no doubt more recklessness feigning as "action." Health authorities seem utterly incapable of acknowledging their errors.

In future, particular vigilance will also have to be paid to people suffering from genetic diseases or cancer. They are the ideal targets for mRNA treatment, which should never be called anti-cancer vaccines, since they are, in effect, gene therapies. This change in terminology is most likely intended to exempt such treatment from the rigorous

308. *COVID-19 Vaccination and Leprosy – A UK Hospital-Based Retrospective Cohort Study*, B. De Barros et al., *PLoS Negl Trop Dis*, 2023.
309. *A Spectrum of Leprosy Reactions Triggered by COVID-19 Vaccination: A Series of Four Cases*, N. Saraswat et al., *J Eur Acad Dermatol Venereol*, 2022.
310. *Multibacillary leprosy unmasked by COVID-19 vaccination*, S. Aponso et al., *JAAD Case Rep*, 2022 PMID 34841026.
311. *Erythema nodosum leprosum post-COVID-19 vaccination: endemic while pandemic*, T. Fachler et al., *J Eur Acad Dermatol Venereol*, 2022.
312. *Reversal Reaction in A Borderline Lepromatous Leprosy Patient after COVID-19 Vaccine: Prevention or Risks*, O. J. J. Fantoni, *J Pak Assoc Dermatol*, [internet] 2022.
313. *Erythema nodosum leprosum and active leprosy after ChAdOx1-S/nCoV-19 recombinant vaccine. A report of two cases*, Bessa Rebello Frassinetti et al., *Leprosy Review*, 2021.

controls imposed on GTPs. We now have good reason to suspect this is indeed so.

I hope that this book will contribute to raising awareness of the issues surrounding mRNA technologies. On a hopeful note, I see that the scientific article I published on this subject has been read and shared, albeit censored by the official media. Information must continue to circulate, as the EMA seems determined to promote mRNA therapies, inspired by the precedent of anti-COVID-19 vaccines. At least, this is what was suggested at an EMA meeting in February 2023,[314] where personalized therapeutic vaccines were discussed and industry sought to relax controls on gene therapies. Is the EMA planning to apply the same regulations initially designed for mRNA vaccines to all gene therapy products? Here again, vigilance is imperative.

Further reading
– *mRNA: Vaccine or Gene Therapy? The Safety Regulatory Issues*, H. Banoun, Int. J. Mol. Sci. 2023, 24, 10514, PMID 37445690.

314. *Report of the Regulatory and Scientific Virtual Conference on RNA-Based Medicines*, February 2, 2023, European Medicines Agency.

4.2 Gain of function after the emergence of SARS-CoV-2

It is now certain that the search for gain of function (GoF) in viruses is at the root of the COVID-19 pandemic. This is now accepted at the highest level in the US. Robert Kadlec, the US military officer in charge of bioterrorism response and pandemic preparedness, and also responsible for the creation of the COVID-19 vaccine development program Operation Warp Speed,[315] confirmed that the origin of the pandemic lies in vaccine research on emerging viruses. In July 2023,[316] in an article in the Australian press, he openly accused Anthony Fauci of being primarily responsible for the situation. In fact, Fauci had funded research on functional gains in China, through the National Institutes of Health (NIH) and the EcoHealth Alliance. Since February 2020, Fauci has been doing everything in his power to conceal this information.

However, Robert Kadlec completely disregards the role of Ralph Baric and the University of North Carolina (UNC) in this GoF research for the creation of vaccines against future viruses. This omission probably serves to conceal the potential American origin of the virus, whether at Fort Detrick or UNC, as we discussed in Part 1, *Origins of the Pandemic*.

It is worth pointing out here that the moratorium on GoF research introduced in 2014 included a major exception: it stated that research conducted for the purpose of protecting public health was exempt from the moratorium. EcoHealth Alliance's DEFUSE project, which combined GoF research with the development of vaccines against manipulated viruses, fell within the scope of this exception (see section 1.2, Origin of the COVID-19 virus: result of a laboratory leak?).

The designers of the EcoHealth Alliance project seemed so certain that they had modeled future pandemic viruses that they were planning to vaccinate bats against these as-yet-unseen viruses, using live

---

315. In early 2020, Operation Warp Speed, a public-private partnership initiated by the US government, sought to radically accelerate the development, manufacture and distribution of a vaccine against COVID-19.
316. *COVID-19 cover-up: Wuhan lab leak suspicions, Anthony Fauci and how the science was silenced*, Weekend Australian Magazine, July 28, 2023.

synthetic viruses. In their view, these viruses would emerge naturally in bats, so it was necessary to immunize these animals to prevent transmission to humans. As we have already pointed out, however, this approach was based on pure speculation.

Not a conspiracy, but a systemic convergence of interests
Despite the lessons that this pandemic could have brought, the outcome of the COVID-19 crisis management does not seem to be altering the trajectory of current and future biopolitics. For those holding the reins of biopower there is no question of curtailing gain-of-function research on viruses, nor of abandoning generalized vaccination as a priority response to all infectious diseases.

The kingpins at the heart of this biopower are the military-industrial-financial complex harboring the decision-makers in the USA, and the teams of researchers who make these functional gains to develop vaccines against future pandemics. On the one hand, there is a clear political will to maintain this direction; on the other, a kind of cecity on the part of the research teams, who don't seem to be fully aware of the implications of their work. Both elements are necessary to maintain the biopolitical orientation.

George Orwell describes this phenomenon of doublethink in his novel *1984: they know, but they forget that they know*. This ability to hold two contradictory beliefs simultaneously in people's minds seems to be one of the keys to success for those wielding biopower.

It is impossible to dissociate the search for gain of function from the quest for vaccines to protect populations against future emerging viruses. It would be wrong, however, to conclude that viruses are created in the laboratory with the deliberate aim of causing a pandemic and selling vaccines accordingly. What we observe is a systemic convergence of interests that has given rise to the COVID-19 crisis and its biopolitical management.

The colossal profits generated by pharmaceutical companies in this context hold sway. These financial rewards in turn reinforce the power of these industrialists, enabling them to exert considerable influence on the future trajectory of this biosecurity drift. The vaccine model, which favors vaccination as the main and often exclusive response to infectious threats, is thus becoming increasingly entrenched in public health strategy, fueled by a vicious circle in which power and profit reinforce each other.

A political-military-industrial complex

Why didn't the FDA, the US Food and Drug Administration, assess COVID-19 vaccines, unlike the EMA, the European Medicines Agency? Across the Atlantic, the COVID-19 health crisis was managed by the US military. This was so blatant that senior FDA officials were resigning in protest in 2021, feeling excluded from key decisions concerning COVID-19 vaccines.[317]

In fact, the various measures taken in response to the COVID-19 pandemic in the United States were considered as countermeasures to a potential biological weapon. This classification skirted the need for traditional clinical trials or rigorous proof of safety or efficacy.

Health crisis management influenced by the PREP Act

On February 4, 2020, a crucial milestone was reached in the United States in the management of the COVID-19 health crisis: the Department of Health and Human Services (HHS) declared total immunity for activities related to "countermeasures" against COVID-19, under the PREP Act (The Public Readiness and Emergency Preparedness Act).[318]

Originally conceived in 2005 and adapted in 2013 to respond to pandemics, the PREP Act is a legislative scheme that grants legal immunity to companies and individuals acting in response to a public health emergency by proposing countermeasures, via products for diagnosis, treatment, prevention and protection against COVID-19.

Under the PREP Act, the US Department of Defense (DoD) established contracts with industries around the world that could potentially be involved in the manufacture of countermeasures. Known as Other Transaction Agreements or OTAs,[319] these contracts bound the

317. *Biden's top-down booster plan sparks anger at FDA*, Politico, August 31, 2021.
318. *Department of Health and Human Services, Declaration Under the Public Readiness and Emergency Preparedness Act for Medical Countermeasures Against COVID-19-19*, March 10, 2020.
319. In the United States, Other Transaction Agreements (OTAs) were an essential tool in managing the health crisis, speeding up the development of vaccines and treatments. These contracts, authorized by a special entity under Congressional control (Other Transaction Authority), were used in particular by certain departments such as the Department of Defense (DoD) to respond to the pandemic.

signatories to the DoD and engaged them to produce equipment and medicines, including vaccines, to defined specifications. For example, in December 2020, the DoD awarded Sanofi $1.8 billion to produce an adult and pediatric vaccine according to FDA recommendations.[320] This immunity, while designed to spur speed and innovation in times of crisis, *de facto* placed the military at the heart of the health response.

Despite the declared end of the pandemic emergency by the United States on May 11, 2023, the Department of Health and Human Services decided to extend the PREP Act coverage of COVID-19 and influenza vaccines, as well as COVID-19 testing, until December 31, 2024.[321] This decision to protract legal immunity for the manufacturers of these medical products was made in a context in which the COVID-19 pandemic appeared to be under control in the country. Why maintain these exceptional measures at a time when the public health emergency had officially lifted? The immunity thus extended signaled that, despite the official end of the pandemic, US health authorities were preparing for possible new biological threats and still claiming to be managing them under military control.

We have seen the close ties between Moderna and the DoD, but Pfizer would not be outdone. In 2013, DARPA awarded the pharmaceutical giant a $7.7 million contract to work on a new immunization concept.[322] The aim was to investigate the possibility of directly inducing the production of protective antibodies against an emerging pathogen in an infected or exposed individual. This approach sought to bypass the usual method of vaccine creation, which involves *in vitro* steps. Instead, DARPA wanted Pfizer to explore an *in vivo* method, to accelerate the response time to a new disease. This is science fiction; it has no basis on any known hypothesis.

---

320. Department of Defense, Technical Direction Letter for Medical CRBN Defense Consortium (MCDC), Request for Prototype Proposals (RPP) 20-11, Objective PRE-20-11 for Definitized "Adjuvanted Recombinant COVID-19 Vaccine Development" Sanofi Pasteur, Inc. (Sanofi), December 2020, http://tiny.cc/sanofi-États-Unis.
321. *Eleventh Amendment to Declaration Under the Public Readiness and Emergency Preparedness Act for Medical Countermeasures Against Covid19, A Notice by the Health and Human Services Department*, May 12, 2023, federalegister.gov.
322. *DARPA Hires Pfizer to Perform Groundbreaking Vaccine Research*, Rich Smith, fool.com, December 5, 2013.

In any case, Pfizer was involved in the vaccine response to pandemics before 2020. As early as 2018, the laboratory collaborated with German biotech company BioNTech to develop anti-flu mRNA vaccines. Thanks to documents obtained through a FOIA (Freedom of Information Act) request, we know that BioNTech, Pfizer's future partner in 2020 for COVID-19 vaccines, was already working on LNPs (Lipid Nanoparticles) and mRNA purification,[323] in May 2019.

The work of critical scientists and politicians began at last to yield tangible results, timid though they were. In July 2023, pressured by revelations in the US about the virus possibly originating in connection with Sino-American collaboration, an amendment was passed in the House of Representatives to prohibit the US Department of Defense from continuing to fund EcoHealth Alliance and the Wuhan laboratory.[324]

French Health Defense Council

In France, health crisis management is marked by the pre-eminent role of the Health Defense Council. Comprising the President of the Republic, the Prime Minister, the Ministers of Health, Defense, the Interior, the Economy and Labor, this council is responsible for "taking crisis decisions in the field of health."

The existence of this state body is not defined in either the law or the Constitution. The Senate's Social Affairs Committee expressed its concern in its information report on the health pass (February 2022), underscoring the "substitution of the Defense Council for the Council of Ministers, and thus the removal of decision-making from the normal interplay of institutions."[325] This departure from the usual regulatory framework also caused a stir in the National Assembly. A bill[326] was

---

323. *Nonclinical Evaluation Report BNT162b2 [mRNA] COVID-19 vaccine,* Therapeutic Goods Administration, January 2021.
324. Rules Report, July 13, 2023, US House of Representatives, p. 46, no. 15. *An amendment to be offered by Representative McClain of Michigan or her designee, Defund Wuhan Institute of Virology and EcoHealth Alliance, Inc.*
325. *Rapport d'information fait au nom de la commission des affaires sociales sur l'adéquation de la passe vaccinal à l'évolution de l'épidémie de COVID-19,* No. 537, February 23, 2022.
326. *Proposition de Loi visant à lever le secret défense des délibérations du Conseil de défense sanitaire,* dated February 8, 2022, *French National Assembly.*

introduced to lift the confidential nature of Health Defense Council deliberations but was tabled without success.

Exceptional crisis management in Europe
In Europe, Regulation EU/2020/521 of April 14, 2020, effective retroactively from February 1, 2020, and applicable until January 31, 2022, released emergency aid under Council Regulation (EU) 2016/369.[327] Its purpose: to respond to a severe threat of disaster of natural or man-made origin. Eligible actions, or countermeasures, include the organization of ad hoc clinical trials of potential therapies or diagnostics according to testing standards agreed at European Union level, the list being non-exhaustive.

This regulation makes it possible to escape the usual standards of good manufacturing practice and clinical trials. It undoubtedly justifies and explains the exceptional way in which the European Medicines Agency (EMA) controlled anti-COVID-19 vaccine trials without applying all the controls required for gene therapy.

Towards loss of sovereignty?
The management of the health crisis also raises questions about the sovereignty of NATO member states. If the US Department of Defense declares a biological weapons threat, is the defense of NATO member states subordinate to Washington? Specialized lawyers could answer this question by referring to the EU Treaty (Title V on the Common Security Policy). This question is beyond my capabilities, but it deserves to be raised and examined.

While many would like to turn the page on COVID-19, it is crucial not to forget that sovereign states and supra-national bodies are busy militarizing preparedness for future pandemics. In the United States, a military officer, Colonel Paul Friedrichs, is in charge of this preparedness at the White House. The Council on Foreign Relations (CFR), a powerful think tank specializing in international politics, advises bypassing the World Health Organization (WHO) and placing the response to the next pandemic under the aegis of the UN Security Council. This approach would be coordinated with the G7 and G20,

---

327. *Regulation (EU) 2020/521* of the European Parliament and of the Council of April 14, 2020.

the International Monetary Fund (IMF), the World Bank and other international financial institutions.[328]

Ralph Baric, a living paradox

Ralph Baric of the University of North Carolina (UNC) and his team were singled out in early 2020 as potentially responsible for the creation of SARS-CoV-2, the virus responsible for the COVID-19 pandemic.[329] In response to these attacks, Baric literally took refuge in his laboratory, even sleeping there with his team to escape criticism.

He is the perfect embodiment of Orwell's doublethink. He claims that a deadly coronavirus epidemic was unheard of in 2003 (year of the emergence of SARS-CoV-1) and a second one a few years later even more so (MERS in 2012). He recalls that when he began studying coronaviruses in 1980, only those benign to humans were known. Today, we know of three capable of causing massive death. He acknowledges, therefore, that coronaviruses were not dangerous to humans until he himself began manipulating them. He cannot, however, conceive the possibility that he may have conferred this danger on them .....

Despite the controversy, Baric firmly denies his involvement in the origin of SARS-CoV-2 and continues frantically to build viruses with pandemic potential and search for vaccines. It was he who tested Moderna's anti-COVID-19 vaccine candidates on his humanized mice, which express the human ACE2 receptor, making these animals susceptible to infection by SARS-CoV-2.

Baric is thus a living paradox: a scientist specializing in pandemic prevention, but whose work on viral gain of function is considered by some to be a potential threat to global security. His situation illustrates the fundamental tension at the heart of gain of function research: the potential to both prevent and provoke health disasters.

In 2007, Ralph Baric recognized that it is difficult to distinguish between fundamental academic research and the development of biological weapons: to defend against this bioterrorism, researchers

---

328. *Pandemic Preparedness Lessons from COVID-19*, Council on Foreign Relations, Independent Task Force Report No. 78.

329. *The US Scientist At the Heart of COVID-19 Lab Leak Conspiracies Is Still Trying to Save the World From the Next Pandemic, Time Magazine*, July 11, 2023.

need to understand the mechanisms that make viruses more pathogenic, in order to develop possible countermeasures.[330]

In 2014, in the midst of an international debate on the risks and benefits of gain-of-function research, Ralph Baric spoke out against a moratorium on such research on influenza viruses and coronaviruses (SARS and MERS). In his view, GoF on coronaviruses was unlikely to produce a virus dangerous to humans, an assertion which contrasts with his earlier writings, in which he spoke of the bioterrorist potential of these techniques.

It is important to note that researchers Ralph Baric and Shi Zhengli are beginning to actively study the virulence factors of camel coronavirus (MERS-CoV), officially as of its emergence in 2012, as confirmed by a study published in 2015.[331] MERS-CoV, associated with MERS, has a high fatality rate, which accentuates the risks associated with any manipulation of this virus in the laboratory, and these risks are all the greater when it comes to gain of function experimentation.

In 2014, Baric admitted to having created a highly pathogenic chimeric SARS virus for mice and then having adapted it to human cells. This experiment crossed the red line in terms of degree of danger, as Marc Lipsitch, a senior CDC official, emphasized. In March 2021, Baric's collaborators published an update on the chimeric virus manufacturing technique, explaining how to reverse-engineer a SARS-CoV-2.[332]This technique is presented as a means of studying live attenuated vaccines, facilitating serodiagnosis, vaccine evaluation and antiviral screening.

In 2022, these teams went a step further, proposing a live attenuated vaccine consisting of modified SARS-CoV-2 to combat SARS-CoV-2 itself.[333] This proposal raises safety issues given the potential risks associated with the use of live attenuated viruses.

330. *Synthetic Viral Genomics, R. S. Baric, 2006. In: Working Papers for Synthetic Genomics: Risks and Benefits for Science and Society*, pp. 35-81. M. S. Garfinkel, D. Endy, G. L. Epstein, R. M. Friedman, editors, 2007.
331. *Two Mutations Were Critical for Bat-to-Human Transmission of Middle East Respiratory Syndrome Coronavirus*, Y. Yang, C. Liu, L. Du, S. Jiang, Z. Shi, R. S. Baric, F. Li, *J Virol*, 2015.
332. *Engineering SARS-CoV-2 using a reverse genetic system, X. Xie et al., Nat Protoc*, 2021.
333. *A live-attenuated SARS-CoV-2 vaccine candidate with accessory protein deletions, Y. Liu et al., Nat Commun*, 2022. Erratum in: Nat Commun, 2022 Oct, PMID 35896528.

This type of experimentation could also be at the origin of the Omicron variant. Indeed, many laboratories around the world were working on SARS-CoV-2 by infecting animals in search of virulence factors and to anticipate its evolution. Some laboratories investigated how Omicron might become more virulent and were manipulating the virus to this end.[334] Omicron may have been selected by passages of SARS-CoV-2 in mice, as I relate in my March 2022 article on the origin of the virus.

Pfizer is not to be outdone when it comes to GoF and admitted (while denying it!) to making GoF on SARS-CoV-2, by having it express the Spikes of the different variants in order to anticipate a more "effective" vaccine.[335]

Are we heading for SARS-CoV-3?

In November 2021, the CDC (US Centers for Disease Control and Prevention), a component of the US Department of Health and Human Services, amended its regulations on toxic agents and toxins. This amendment now includes SARS-CoV/SARS-CoV-2 chimeric viruses and describes certain genetic manipulations subject to this new regulation, suggesting that they were most likely already underway at that date. One example is the creation of a chimeric virus with the transmissibility of SARS-CoV-2 and the pathogenicity of SARS-CoV-1. The virulence factors of SARS-CoV-1 to be added to SARS-CoV-2 were described in detail. Such manipulations could lead to the emergence of a highly pathogenic and transmissible SARS-CoV-3.

Yet many virologists believe that gain-of-function research is incapable of preventing new pandemics. In their view, such efforts are an "absolute waste of time." There are an enormous number of viruses in wildlife and trying to predict which of them will emerge in humans is considered unfeasible. It amounts to using rare data to predict rare events, an approach which, according to these experts, simply doesn't work.[336]

In 2018, DARPA was already trying to anticipate the evolution of highly dangerous viruses such as Ebola, Lassa fever and Rift Valley fever.

334. *The altered entry pathway and antigenic distance of the SARS-CoV-2 Omicron variant map to separate domains of Spike protein*, T. P. Peacock et al., *bioRxiv*, 2021.
335. *Pfizer Responds to Research Claims*, Jan. 27, 2023, on Pfizer.com.
336. *The virome hunters, C. Schmidt, Nat Biotechnol*, 2018, PMID 30307913.

Let's hope that the COVID-19 pandemic will have tempered researchers' eagerness to make GoFs capable of rendering these viruses even more dangerous.

Vaccines: in a category of their own

The aim of these GoFs is to anticipate the evolution of viruses with pandemic potential and, at the same time, to develop laboratory-produced vaccines against them. The US National Science Advisory Board for Biosecurity (NSABB) is well aware of the risks. In March 2023, it published specific recommendations for closer monitoring of GoFs intended for the development of vaccines against future pandemic viruses. Such research had previously been excluded from the GoF moratorium, on the grounds that it was vaccine related. This exception raises questions, as it allows vaccines to escape the usual regulations, without clear ethical or scientific justification for this. However, the same NSABB insists on the importance of not allowing controls to delay such research.[337] This position potentially opens the door to all kinds of exemptions.

Aware that COVID-19 is neither the first nor the last pandemic disease to devastate the world, the WHO and Gavi, the Vaccine Alliance, are calling for heightened preparedness. They are encouraging scientists to speed up the manufacture of vaccines, with the ambitious goal of making them available within 100 days for the next pandemic.[338] The WHO and Gavi are drawing up a list of pathogens likely to emerge.[339] These include Rift Valley fever, hantaviruses, various coronaviruses, Congo hemorrhagic fever, Lassa fever, Marburg, yellow fever, H5N1 and H7N9 influenza, Chikungunya, Ebola and Nipah.

Gain-of-function research is a complex subject, requiring extensive knowledge of virology. I hope to have succeeded in making it accessible so that everyone can grasp the issues. This subject concerns the health of all mankind and as such, should be widely and publicly debated.

---

337. *Proposed biosecurity oversight framework for the future of science*, A Report of the National Science Advisory Board for Biosecurity, March 2023.
338. See the large number of articles for the tag *"next pandemic"* on the Gavi website, https://www.gavi.org/vaccineswork/tag/next-pandemic.
339. *WHO convenes experts to identify new pathogens that could spark pandemics*, UN NewsInfo, November 21, 2022.https://news.un.org/en/story/2022/11/1130897

4.3 Vaccines for the future

The vaccines we are going to discuss here concern coronaviruses, of course, but also other diseases, and are not yet all based on mRNA technology. I won't be exhaustive: the idea is to present a few examples showing that the vaccines of the future do not, at least for the time being, offer a favorable benefit-risk balance, despite the claims of their promoters and the hasty approvals of health agencies.

For example, Ralph Baric (and other teams) are developing vaccines against coronaviruses based on the measles virus. It may seem surprising, but the live, attenuated measles vaccine virus has been used for some years now to develop vaccines against other viruses. This involves constructing chimeras of the measles virus that express proteins from the targeted viruses on their surface. This technique has been used to immunize against SARS-CoV-1, MERS-CoV, HIV, hepatitis C and Chikungunya viruses... Baric has deposited the genome[340] of a virus modified from the vaccine strain (Edmonston B/Moraten) of measles, which expresses the Spike protein of SARS-CoV-2 on its surface. Another American team has even tested this vaccine on hamsters.[341]

With regard to vaccine promotion against future emerging viruses, the United States is launching an $88 billion national biodefense strategy to make vaccine development possible within 100 days. Unsurprisingly, mRNA vaccines are at the top of the list for their speed of production were a new virus to emerge.

The future of mRNA vaccines
Even before the COVID-19 pandemic, mRNAs were considered as the technical platform of the future for vaccines.[342] As already seen, in

---

340. *Mutant Measles morbillivirus strain MeVvac2-SARS2-S(H)*, Complete genome GenBank: MW090971.1.
341. *A safe and highly efficacious measles virus-based vaccine expressing SARS-CoV-2 stabilized prefusion Spike*, M. Lu et al., Proc Natl Acad Sci USA, 2021.
342. *Vaccines of the future [Les vaccins de demain]*, J. D. Lelièvre, Rev Francoph Lab. 2019; Bruno Pitard. Nanotaxi ® for RNA and DNA vaccines. medicine/sciences, EDP Sciences, 2019.

October 2019, at the Milken Institute Future of Health Summit, during a meeting about flu vaccines, the speakers (and in particular Anthony Fauci and Margaret Hamburg, Foreign Secretary of the US National Academy of Medicine), half-heartedly proposed to bypass clinical trials of mRNA vaccines and, with the help of a disruptive crisis, launch them on the market without undergoing 10 years of testing.

The healthcare industry is investing considerable funding in mRNA technology: anti-cancer therapy, metabolic diseases and infectious diseases are the three main areas of focus. As we have seen with GoFs, the public and private sectors are always closely associated in these investments, which are primarily concerned with the biopolitics of the future.

And yet, it was known before 2020 that mRNA vaccines are ineffective and toxic against infectious diseases. This is the case for candidate vaccines against influenza, rabies and AIDS, as I recall in my article on GTPs.[343] In her review of the literature on mRNA vaccines, geneticist Alexandra Henrion-Caude also highlights the failure of this technology applied to vaccines (*Les Apprentis sorciers*, Albin Michel).

Vaccines that chase variants
We have already mentioned the converging interests of the political-military-industrial complex. Among these, the interest in variants, whether in the case of influenza or coronaviruses, now enables the manufacture of vaccines to be relaunched in a never-ending race.

The genetic material for Moderna's booster vaccine, adapted to the Omicron variant, was manufactured by National Resilience, a company located in Ontario, Canada. National Resilience was founded relatively recently, in November 2020, and seeks to run its huge manufacturing plants with mRNA technology, whether for "vaccines" or gene therapies. Its executives are linked to the CIA, the Wellcome Trust, major banks, the Bill Gates Foundation, the Johns Hopkins Center, CEPI, Silicon Valley companies, Google, DARPA, the vaccine industry and... organized crime. This was revealed in August 2022 in an investigation by Whitney Webb for *Unlimited Hangout* magazine.[344]

---

343. *mRNA: Vaccine or Gene Therapy? The Safety Regulatory Issues*, H. Banoun, Int. J. Mol. Sci. 2023.
344. *RNA for Moderna's Omicron Booster Manufactured by CIA-Linked Company*, Whitney Webb, Unlimited Hangout, August 2022.

There are very strong links between Moderna, the FDA (and regulators in general), DARPA and the pharmaceutical industry.

In March 2023, it was learned that technology-focused biomanufacturing company National Resilience had obtained $410 million in funding from the US Department of Defense to manufacture one billion doses of vaccine for a future pandemic.[345]

The United States will spend $5 billion on a public-private partnership (Project NextGen) to develop long-term effective coronavirus vaccines, nasal vaccines and pan-coronavirus vaccines.[346]

The COVID-19 vaccine for autumn 2023 had already been chosen by health agencies worldwide[347] – mRNA-based and "adapted" to the XBB Omicron variant of spring 2023 (which had already been overtaken in frequency by the EG.5 and FL.1.5.1 variants since summer). A single dose for all (whether already vaccinated or not), except for children under the age of six, who will receive two or three doses! No new clinical trials will be required, although the regulators recognize the *immune imprinting* effect but are not certain. In other words, this means that the more you vaccinate against the same antigen, the more you restrain the immune system, preventing it from reacting to any new variant. For autumn 2024, the same lag time between the evolution of the virus and release of the vaccine was repeated: on the basis of animal trials alone, the FDA approved the vaccine adapted to variant KP.2, which had by then virtually disappeared from circulation in the US.

---

345. *National Resilience secures funding for domestic biomanufacturing capacity, Pharmaceutical Technology*, March 27, 2023.
346. Project NextGen, *Enhancing Preparedness for Future COVID-19 Strains & Variants with Next Generation Medical Countermeasures ASPR Administration for strategic preparedness and response.*
347. ICMRA (International Coalition of Medicines Regulatory Authorities), COVID-19 Omicron variant workshop, 8 May 2023. Co-chairs: Peter Marks (FDA, US) and Marco Cavaleri (EMA, EU).
Global regulators agree on way forward to adapt COVID-19 vaccines to emerging variants, EMA, May 30, 2023.

Other high-risk technologies

Intranasal vaccines

In 2023, Anthony Fauci discovered that respiratory viruses cannot be controlled by intramuscular vaccines, something that critical scientists have been repeating for years. We were delighted to read in 2023 what we explained in 2020: viruses replicating mainly in the respiratory mucosa don't produce viremia (don't circulate in the blood), therefore don't come into contact with the global immune system, and therefore not with antibodies, except in cases of severe illness.

Consequently, the production of blood antibodies by a vaccine injected intramuscularly cannot protect against a respiratory virus.

Fauci[348] suggested developing vaccines administered to respiratory mucous membranes, pointing out that we must first understand why reinfections are frequent with respiratory viruses before developing vaccines. Industry can be trusted to skip this step: mucosal vaccines are already in clinical trials.[349]

Yet we already know that intranasal vaccines present an increased risk of inflammation in the lungs in trials, animals have died after the second dose. Moreover, intranasal nanoparticles can penetrate directly into the brain.[350]

mRNA vaccines for animals

Animal vaccines are ahead of human vaccines, as always. mRNA vaccines had already been used against influenza in pigs since at least 2020, when the product was approved, but the information was well hidden. These are Merck's Sequivity products, which are mRNA vaccines, although this explosive term is not mentioned in the advertising.

There is talk of making "self-amplifying" mRNA vaccines against African swine fever, funded by the US government; "self-amplifying" means that the mRNA injected into a farm animal has the ability to multiply within that animal.[351]

Another technology, potentially risky for the environment,[352] is currently being studied for vaccinating wild animals. These are "self-disseminating" vaccines, which make it possible to vaccinate just a few subjects while protecting an entire population. This technology is being considered for vaccinating bats against the Ebola virus.

348. *Rethinking next-generation vaccines for coronaviruses, influenza viruses, and other respiratory viruses*, D. M. Morens, J. K. Taubenberger, A. S. Fauci, Cell Host Microbe, 2023, PMID 36634620.
349. *Nasal COVID-19 vaccine shows promise in early clinical trial*, NBC News, February 2023.
350. *The mRNA-LNP platform's lipid nanoparticle component used in preclinical vaccine studies is highly inflammatory*, S. Ndeupen et al., iScience, 2021, PMID 34841223.
351. *Genvax Technologies Secures $6.5 Million to Advance Novel Vaccine Platform*, Pork Business, August 9, 2022.
352. *As self-spreading vaccine technology moves forward, dialogue on its risks should follow*, Jonas Sandbrink, Bulletin of the atomic scientist, June 10, 2022.

New mRNA technologies applied to humans

CEPI is supporting the development of "self-amplifying" mRNA vaccines by an Indian company:[353] the vaccinee first multiplies the injected mRNA strands and then produces the protein encoded by the RNA, in order to reduce the quantity to be manufactured by the manufacturer. In this way, the vaccinated person works twice and for free, instead of the manufacturer. The avowed aim is to increase the quantity of antigen produced, and therefore of antibodies. This will further accentuate the unpredictability of the mRNA technique, for which the quantity of antigen produced is unknown.

Researchers who have raised security concerns associated with this new technology have not yet understood that mRNA does not remain where injected. An article[354] published in 2023 claims that these vaccines will not pose any problems for pregnant women, since the RNA remains in the shoulder. So, it's not looking good...

"Self-spreading" vaccine technology is also being considered for human use: it uses living viruses that will multiply in the vaccine recipient and be transmitted to other individuals. Even if these live viruses are attenuated, this presents risks. The document from the Johns Hopkins Bloomberg School of Public Health,[355] which discusses this technique, is hard to find, no doubt because it contains pertinent criticisms: how can we protect individuals who may have contraindications? How can we obtain the informed consent of those who will be vaccinated unknowingly through contact with a vaccine recipient?

Self-amplifying and self-disseminating vaccines will also be combinable, and we will soon have to familiarize ourselves with "SSSR" for Self-Spreading and Self-Replicating (vaccines)... Yet we must not overlook the associated risks, notably the possibility that live attenuated viruses may become dangerous again. For example, this is what

---

353. *CEPI to support development of self-amplifying mRNA vaccine technology for use against Disease X*, cepi.net, press release August 8, 2023.
354. *Rise of the RNA machines self-amplification in mRNA vaccine design*, J. D. G. Comes, G. P. Pijlman, T. A. H. Hick, Trends Biotechnol. 2023, PMID 37328401.
355. *Johns Hopkins Bloomberg School of Public Health Plans To Release Genetically Modified Self-Spreading Vaccines*, 2nd Smartest Guy in the World, February 16, 2023.
Technologies to address Global Catastrophic Biological Risks, PreventionWeb Publication, 2018 Report.

happens with live polio vaccines, which recombine in the digestive tract with the wild virus to produce pathogenic polio viruses.

Contraceptive vaccines

Also worthy of mention in these sorcerer's apprentice trials is the contraceptive vaccine based on hCG (chorio-gonadotrophic hormone),[356] which amounts to deliberately creating autoimmunity against a natural hormone.[357] It is supposed to be reversible, but this is highly unlikely.

Anti-cancer therapies called "cancer vaccines"

Public debate about these risky experimental techniques is essential. I tried to alert people to this in my article on GTPs, where I showed the inefficacy and toxicity (known even before 2020) of mRNA vaccines against infectious diseases: these include flu, HIV and rabies vaccines.

In the case of products designed to combat cancer, the results are equally disappointing and disturbing: most of the clinical trials registered were not published. It can be assumed that the results were negative. The only results published reported a lack of efficacy and notorious adverse effects, and concerned open-label trials, i.e. non-randomized trials of little value. One randomized clinical trial on prostate cancer patients reported nil benefit. Another trial on lung cancer showed the undesirable effects of mRNA technology.[358] The designation of "vaccine" raises apprehension that controls for these experimental products will be relaxed.

The headlong rush to dangerous "classic" vaccines

A new conventional vaccine has been approved against RSV (the virus responsible for bronchiolitis). It contains two recombinant RSV surface proteins (produced on hamster ovary cells). In the summer of 2023, we learned that Pfizer's Abrysvo had just been approved by the

---

356. Manufactured by the embryo shortly after conception and later by the trophoblast (a tissue of the placenta).
357. *Recherche. Le vaccin, prochaine grande avancée des méthodes contraceptives ? Courrier International*, May 18, 2023. Read also: *A Vaccine for Birth Control?* by Katherine J. Wu, *The Atlantic*, May 2023.
358. See my article on GTP and Alexandra Henrion-Caude's book *Les apprentis sorciers*, Albin Michel.

FDA for use in pregnant women,[359] after having been reserved for the over-60s. In July 2023, the EMA authorized Abrysvo for use in women over 60 and pregnant women.[360]

The RSV vaccine is not authorized for babies, but this point is a source of confusion: the aim is in fact to immunize babies, and this is supposed to be done passively by vaccinating the mother during pregnancy. This is not well understood by the general media, nor even by some health professionals, who fail to grasp that this amounts to indirect vaccination.

The FDA notice states that in the trial involving pregnant women, more premature babies were born in the vaccinated group than in the placebo group. Notwithstanding the obvious risks of prematurity, the health authorities seem to have neglected all precautionary measures.

The clinical trial on pregnant women is not accessible free of charge. This is an exception for Pfizer publications, which can afford an open-access article in the *NEJM*.[361] I get the paid version, but do not have access to the "supplementary material," which often carries surprises. According to the authors, the vaccine is effective in reducing the number of hospitalizations for bronchiolitis in infants during their first three months, but it does not sufficiently reduce the risk of this disease in infants during the same period.

As a point of information, another laboratory, GSK, is stopping the clinical trial of its RSV vaccine in pregnant women, precisely because it causes a high rate of premature births. This is why GSK's vaccine Arexvy is approved by the FDA only for people over 60. Arexvy is also under accelerated review by the EMA.[362] The European Agency authorizes it for the over-60s.

On the matter of vaccinating pregnant women, it is worth noting that pregnant women are now admitted as subjects of clinical trials,

359. *FDA advisers agree maternal RSV vaccine protects infants, but are divided on its safety*, Meredith Wadman, Science.org, May 17, 2023.
360. Committee for Medicinal Products for Human Use (CHMP), *Summary of opinion on Abrysvo for Respiratory Syncytial Virus (RSV) vaccine*, European Medicines Agency, 20 July 2023; *FDA Approves First Vaccine for Pregnant Individuals to Prevent RSV in Infants*, FDA, 21 August 2023.
361. *Bivalent Prefusion F Vaccine in Pregnancy to Prevent RSV Illness in Infants*, B. Kampmann et al., *New England J Med*, 2023.
362. EMA, *First vaccine to protect older adults from respiratory syncytial virus (RSV) infection*, April 26, 2023.

whereas they were previously totally excluded from such. This vulnerable population is now subject to various vaccine recommendations, whereas we senior healthcare professionals were taught that pregnant women should not be vaccinated.

Preventive therapies with monoclonal antibodies?

A novel concept is also emerging in the fight against bronchiolitis: preventive therapy, involving the direct injection of antibodies. In collaboration with AstraZeneca, Sanofi is marketing Beyfortus, a monoclonal antibody against RSV, for preventive injection in newborns. One of the clinical trials,[363] showed serious adverse reactions to the vaccine and three deaths in the vaccinated group versus 0 in the placebo group; according to the usual pitch, "the deaths were not attributed to the vaccine by the investigator," (totally impartial, of course).

The FDA recorded 12 deaths in all trials of this monoclonal antibody: four cardiac deaths, two cases of gastroenteritis, two sudden deaths, one case of cancer, one COVID-19, one fracture, one case of pneumonia, but none were considered treatment-related.[364] The EMA recorded three deaths in the placebo groups and 11 in the treated groups. The EMA issued a favorable benefit/risk balance ...[365]

Once again, the same population segments are targeted by dangerous products: newborns, pregnant women and the over 60s. It should be noted that these are the populations that are most closely monitored from a medical standpoint, and therefore easily vaccinated if the industry succeeds in persuading doctors of the benefits of its products. It will also be easier to conceal undesirable effects and deaths, since these subjects are considered to be at risk: pregnancy and aging are now considered as diseases. In France, the neonatal mortality rate

363. *Nirsevimab for Prevention of RSV in Healthy Late-Preterm and Term Infants, L. L. Hammitt et al., MELODY Study Group, New England J Med*, 2022, PMID 35235726.
364. FDA Biologics License Application (BLA) 761328 Nirsevimab Antimicrobial. Drugs Advisory Committee Meeting June 8, 2023. Division of Antivirals, Office of Infectious Diseases Center for Drug Evaluation and Research, https://www.fda.gov/media/169322/download.
365. EMA/786523/2022 Assessment report Beyfortus September 15, 2022, https://www.ema.europa.eu/en/medicines/human/EPAR/beyfortus.

has not dropped since 2005,[366] and the United States has the highest neonatal mortality rate in the developed world.[367] Newborns are also a high-risk population, so it will be easy to pass off vaccine deaths and adverse effects on account of the fragility of newborns.

As of September 15, 2023, the French Ministry of Health recommends injecting all newborns with Beyfortus before they leave the maternity ward:[368] would that be a mandatory injunction in disguise? Mothers don't always have an eye on their babies during their post-delivery hospital stay...

Also worth noting is the deliberate fuzziness surrounding how these new products are classified: the industry would like them to more or less be subject to the more flexible regulations for vaccines, to avoid complex and time-consuming clinical trials. For example, Beyfortus against RSV was fast-track approved as a vaccine. This is yet another reason for the imperative to grasp the full significance of the regulatory issues, which I have tried to highlight throughout this book.

366. https://www.insee.fr/fr/statistiques/7627069.
367. *US Has Highest Infant, Maternal Mortality Rates Despite the Most Health Care Spending*, Justina Petrullo, AJMC, January 31, 2023.
368. Banoun H. Analysis of Beyfortus® (Nirsevimab) *Immunization Campaign: Effectiveness, Biases, and ADE Risks in RSV Prevention*. Curr Issues Mol Biol. 2024 Sep 18;46(9):10369-10395. doi: 10.3390/cimb46090617. PMID: 39329969; PMCID: PMC11431526. https://pubmed.ncbi.nlm.nih.gov/39329969/

4.4 Biological weapons – seriously?

The virus was assuredly lab-leaked, but to assert that SARS-CoV-2 is a biological weapon, it would have to be proven that the leak was intentional and directed against an identifiable enemy. How could such a contagious virus be a select biological weapon, considering that it can turn against the aggressor? The virus spread rapidly across the planet, killing only the very old and the very frail, making it a rather ineffective and uncontrollable weapon.

In the context of a product of Sino-American collaboration, who would the aggressor be – China or the United States? If it were China, then China would not have leaked the virus from its own territory, and if it were the US, then they really messed up since more people died in the US than in China. Some imagine it to be a bioweapon after all, since SARS-CoV-2 was synthesized at the same time as the vaccines that were supposed to protect against it. Once again, if this is biological warfare, the result is rather pathetic considering vaccine inefficacy.

Yes, the pandemic was managed in military style, particularly in the United States, where the government response was described as a set of countermeasures against a biological weapon: why this hostile vocabulary in the context of a health issue? If anything, it stirred confusion and prevented understanding of this health issue in biopolitical terms. Biodefense experts asserted that the risk of COVID-19 being used as a large-scale weapon was low — its highly infectious nature would probably backfire on any group trying to spread it. They therefore recognized that SARS-CoV-2 was not a bioweapon but could become one in the hands of bioterrorists: there was no way the military was going to let management of the pandemic slip out of their control, they would rather concoct bad science-fiction scenarios.[369]

The Governor of the State of Florida, Ron DeSantis, also claimed that the COVID-19 vaccine was a biological weapon,[370] but then if indeed so, who designed it and who was the target? I would remind here that the manufacture of vaccines is supervised in the United States by the Department of Defense, via the PREP Act. If we follow the logic, this

---

369. *Officials probe the threat of a coronavirus bioweapon*, Politico, April 23, 2020.
370. *County GOP: COVID-19 vaccine is a bioweapon*, 12News, July 13, 2023.

would imply that the federal government deliberately orchestrated an attack against its own civilian population. This hypothesis becomes even more troubling when we consider that the country's armed forces, whose soldiers were also vaccinated, would also be targeted. In short, when examined more closely, this theory seems devoid of meaning or logic. On the other hand, it does make sense to admit that, in the history of vaccination, some collateral damage to civilian populations has been tolerated, in order to make way for new technologies considered essential to national security.

That said, I don't deny that certain elected and non-elected biopower officials display eugenicist or Malthusian tendencies, nor that there are apparent between the vaccine industry and such tendencies.[371]v Admittedly, the harmful results of virus and vaccine manufacture may vindicate their claims eventually. It is, however, difficult to reasonably imagine that this entire situation could have developed by Malthusian and eugenic design. We mustn't overestimate these individuals or regard them as more intelligent and Machiavellian than they actually are. They are, in fact, part and parcel of a larger system they serve to maintain.

There exist most certainly less convoluted and more effective strategies for reducing the population and inducing disease. I leave it to fans of conspiracy theories to imagine those scenarios.

Biopolitics of the future: conclusion
The spectacular occurrence that was COVID-19 may appear to be behind us: the media have moved on to other news stories and the politicians responsible for managing the pandemic are no doubt worrying about the legal consequences of their shenanigans, now becoming apparent to those seeking to understand. Yet biopower continues to push through its course for widespread vaccination and "preparedness" for future pandemics. An ever-growing number of viruses figure in this strategy to extend vaccination, whether they are declared mandatory or strongly promoted via publicity campaigns.

In 2019, the French government planned to make HPV vaccination mandatory for teenagers. This campaign was launched to test the waters in the wake of turbulent backlash to the 2018 introduction

---

371. *Developers of Oxford-AstraZeneca Vaccine Tied to UK Eugenics Movement, Unlimited Hangout*, December 26, 2020.

of eleven mandatory vaccines for infants. However, confronted with growing public distrust of vaccines in general, exacerbated by the COVID-19 pandemic, the government was obliged to reconsider its position. At the start of the 2023 school year, this initial mandatory requirement finally took the form of an intense promotional campaign, with HPV vaccination made available free of charge in all secondary schools in France, for girls and boys alike. And this despite the fact that this vaccine had been highly controversial since its introduction in 2006. In the United States, a long-running legal battle was being waged against the manufacturer of Gardasil,[372] with Merck accused of concealing serious side effects during clinical trials.[373]

Considering the recent developments in vaccinology, we urgently need public debate on functional gains and other dangerous experiments financed by governments. Also to be addressed is the matter of mRNA gene product regulation, in the form of both vaccines and gene therapy. These products and their formulation pose major safety and efficacy problems.

Western governments finance the transfer of mRNA technology to countries that do not have the means to develop it. The WHO sets up plants in Africa, France is the first country to finance mRNA technology transfer activities, and the European Union is also involved, in addition to its investments in Europe itself. Total investment expenditure slated for the period 2022 to 2027 by the EU Health Emergency Preparedness and Response Authority (HERA) is 5.76 billion euros. In South Africa, the EU is investing 40 million euros in mRNA vaccine factories... As you can see, this technology will play a key role in the vaccinology of the future.

---

372. See the website of the largest law firm involved in defence of victims: https://www.wisnerbaum.com/prescription- drugs/gardasil- lawsuit/
373. *Why is Slate questioning Gardasil?* Susan Mathews, December 17, 2017. https://slate.com/health-and-science/2017/12/why-slate-is-questioning-gardasil.html

Conclusion

Why yet another book on COVID-19? When I was advised to write a book compiling my scientific articles, I didn't at first see the point of another book on COVID-19 by a critical scientist, at a time when the crisis seemed to be behind us. But as I thought about it, I realized that a paper copy offers a refuge from digital censorship and the ephemeral nature of the web. I hope it will be of use to tomorrow's historians. The material and moral support provided by the BonSens. org association for this project is commendable and I wish to express my gratitude. BonSens.org brings together a large number of scientists and has done its very utmost to awaken our political leaders, while continuing to defend Science.

The writing of this book has enhanced my own understanding of what we have been through. This writing synthesizes and strives to give access to non-scientists the content of the articles that I have published over the last four years in peer-reviewed journals and on blogs over the last four years.

My work is not a comprehensive overview of how this health crisis was managed. This is why I have preferred to refer readers to the contributions of my colleagues, independent and critical doctors and scientists from a variety of disciplines, who have also published on this subject. Taken together, these critical analyses, in the perspective of Michel Foucault's concept of biopolitics, help us to grasp the coherence and logic behind what may initially appear to be a disastrous handling of public health since March 2020. I felt it necessary to look back to the pre-pandemic period to underscore this biopolitical explanation.

Those who had previously taken an interest in the history of public health will not be totally surprised by the turn that health policy has taken since March 2020, even though the accelerated pace of this biopolitical evolution may have surprised them.

Official announcements and ongoing scientific research give us clues as to the future management of infectious diseases, always in the same direction: risk-laden preparation for pandemics and widespread vaccination in response. Digital population surveillance, pandemic simulations, and bulk purchasing of "medical countermeasures" – i.e. drugs and vaccines – will become the norm in management, in line with international treaties and regulations, unless voices arise in opposition.

I was naturally predisposed to a critical analysis of COVID-19 management, thanks to my training and ongoing interest in biology in general, and evolutionary theory in particular. At the same time, my interest in epistemology has led me to tackle the scourge of scientism in this book. This ideology now predominates in all politically and economically sensitive disciplines, and biology is no exception. All COVID-19 research has been instrumentalized for the benefit of biopower.

Biopolitics, which today tends to impose health standards on all human populations, increasingly relies on vaccination as an alternative to caregiving in infectiology (and soon in other fields, such as oncology). Since the 18th century, "vaccinization" has acquired an authoritarian dimension, prioritizing vaccination coverage of populations to the detriment of the health of the individuals comprising these populations.

This ideology has been reinforced by the pharmaceutical industry's growing profits from the sale of vaccines, especially since the 1986 US law relieving manufacturers of any financial responsibility for adverse reactions.[374] This combination of ideology and the economic interests of vaccine manufacturers explains why biopolitics, which was initially designed to protect the health of populations, is now contributing to its considerable deterioration.

Like any medical intervention, vaccination should be subject to rigorous scientific scrutiny and assessment, particularly considering that it is administered to healthy individuals. Yet vaccines are subject to fewer controls than other drugs, those intended for the sick. The efficacy of traditional vaccines has not been sufficiently assessed by randomized, double-blind clinical trials, as highlighted in several specialist publications.[375]

The authoritarianism that has characterized vaccination management since the advent of the industrial era continues to intensify, whereas the potential adverse effects of this generalized practice are neglect-

374. National Childhood Vaccine Injury Act of 1986, https://en.wikipedia. org/wiki/National_Childhood_Vaccine_Injury_Act, https://www.congress.gov/bill/99th-congress/house-bill/5546
375. *Turtles All The Way Down: Vaccine Science and Myth (Paperback)* – July 16, 2022

ed. With the anti-COVID-19 vaccines, the lack of assessment and the intense pressure exerted on populations reached unprecedented levels, posing a serious risk of rapid deterioration to the global health of mankind.

Systemic censorship

Biopower today is exercised by an alliance of governments and health agencies with big industry. Official authorities work in collaboration with powerful non-governmental organizations to muzzle and discredit any criticism of biopolitics, equating it with the most ludicrous conspiracies. The mainstream media and social networks, channels totally subservient to biopower, are almost perfectly successful in censoring all critical opinion and even all analysis of official documents and scientific publications. This muzzling by the media in recent years raises profound questions about the way in which information is disseminated and controlled, particularly in the context of crisis. When dissident voices are silenced or marginalized, the plurality of viewpoints available to the general public is handicapped. Well-balanced information is essential to enabling people to make informed decisions, particularly when it comes to their health.

The question of origin

Like other independent teams (see *The Story of COVID-19: the pandemic of all fears*, first published in serial form in French on the *France Soir* website, between the end of August 2020 and the beginning of March 2021), I have shown that the pandemic is the result of gain-of-function experimentation on coronaviruses that began several decades ago with the aim of anticipating pandemics and the vaccinal response to them. These GoF experiments have been conducted since at least the 2000s in a collaboration between the United States and China, which brings us to the only reasonable question still unresolved about the geographical origin of SARS-CoV-2: Chinese, American or other?

Paternity of the virus must probably be attributed to US civil-military research (not forgetting the industrialists who developed the anti-COVID-19 vaccines and had already been involved for some years). The GoFs are designed to prepare us for pandemics. Their architects are well aware of the risks that such manipulations can present, as are most of the officials involved. The most lucid among them admit their role in the emergence of SARS-CoV-2 and affirm that it is impossible to anticipate future emerging viruses with pandemic potential in this way.

The highly probable emergence of SARS-CoV-2 dating from at least spring 2019 explains the progressive refinement over time of the pandemic anticipation scenarios. Reading them in terms of the progress of research, it even becomes clear that biopower has been anticipating a coronavirus pandemic since at least 2017. All the countermeasures that were decided during the COVID-19 crisis had been considered and discussed during these pandemic simulations, underscoring the importance of continued inquiry as these exercises remain relevant for our immediate future.

Biopower prescriptions and abusive treatment
From a diagnostic, therapeutic and epidemiological standpoint, COVID-19, the disease, has been subjected to political manipulation. Diagnostic tests (PCR, antigenic and serological tests, i.e. retrospective tests) were used mainly to fictitiously exacerbate the real severity of the disease by passing off numbers of "cases" for numbers of sick people. This manipulation is the logical continuation of the exaggeration that has been going on for years of the influenza burden.

Immunity assessment in individuals and populations by means of all-too-specific serological tests for such evaluation yielded a far too limited picture. All this was designed to prepare the population for the arrival of vaccines as the sole possible solution. I have shown how this was technically possible from the point of view of clinical biology (my official specialization). It was wrong to focus on antibodies as a diagnostic tool and standard of vaccine efficacy.

Antibodies have sometimes played a harmful role rather than a beneficial one, both historically and theoretically, based on the theory of evolution, and this was corroborated: they can exacerbate COVID-19 disease, depending on their level and quality. Two immunitary phenomena, "paradoxical" at first glance, may be responsible for this deterioration: the effects of ADE (antibody facilitation) and OAS (antigenic imprinting) may add up in this sense and also explain the facilitation and aggravation of post-vaccinal COVID-19. These phenomena were well known, and all the experts had warned against ADE at the start of the pandemic, but most of them then went silent or changed their tune to avoid hindering the development of vaccination campaigns.

I have reviewed studies of the potential reasons underlying why children and many adults were not affected by COVID-19, which were also ignored in order to dramatically amplify the danger attributed to the virus. In short, a "young" immune system (also in some adults, not only children) is the best guarantee against the serious effects of COVID-19 and is associated with high-quality intestinal microbiota. Consequently, these two factors ought to prevail as a first line of defense against viral infections in general. It is crucial to maintain the basic inflammatory condition of the body at a low level. This is one aspect of prevention that is not taken into account by biopolitics, because it is difficult to industrialize and hence unprofitable for Big Pharma.

We mustn't, however, overlook the fact that the SARS-CoV-2 virus is dangerous because of the manipulation of its Spike protein, which is toxic: this is why early treatment is essential in the event of symptoms indicating infection.

For this reason, I turned to the results of the many valiant doctors who had resolved to resist the government injunction against treating COVID-19 patients: scores of anonymous physicians, but also some very well-known doctors, such as Prof. Didier Raoult, Prof. Christian Perronne, Dr. Gérard Maudrux, the doctors at the IHU Marseille... Effective treatments exist, in fact, all of which are immunomodulators or antibiotics that act on the microbiota and co-infections. The ban on care still in force was a major setback, imposed at the outset on general practitioners, preventing them from fulfilling their crucial front-line role in the event of a pandemic, and later on all doctors, forbidding the use of effective anti-infectious treatments. The default of effective treatment can also be explained by the biopolitical interest in amplifying the disease burden of the virus. It should be remembered that the absence of treatment is the preamble-required condition for all emergency-use vaccine approvals and therefore a sine qua non for their validation. Similarly, the authorities denied the efficacy of supplements such as vitamin D and zinc.

I also briefly summarized my theoretical work on the evolution of the virus, which was published and earned me the right to review the work of other teams on this subject. The virus had attenuated as early as May 2020, as the doctors treating COVID-19 patients had noticed. The variants selected by the natural evolution of viruses generally follow this course: the most contagious and least aggressive viruses are more competitive, and this evolution is driven by the virus's interaction with the immune system of its host (the human population). On this issue, too, the media and the authorities tried to convince us at the start of the pandemic that the virus was not mutating, against all the evidence to the contrary.

In France, the IHU Marseille Méditerranée Infection Institute, which had the largest sequencing capacity in the country, was the first to identify the variants, but it was vilified on this point, no doubt because this institution was one of the few hospitals to treat patients on an outpatient basis, in defiance of the official ban on treatment. Still with regard to the political interference in the treatment of the disease, I also mentioned the mask masquerade, the futility of which was well known before COVID-19 in terms of limiting the pandemic spread of a virus. The large-scale use of masks by the general population merely confirmed this uselessness.

Flawed pharmacovigilance of high-risk vaccines
The COVID-19 context presented the ideal opportunity to develop mRNA vaccines in avoidance of the minimum 10 years of testing usually required. mRNA technology was targeted as the solution to the inefficacy of flu vaccines as early as 2010 (after the H1N1 pandemic).

I have compiled peer-reviewed evidence showing that natural immunity to coronaviruses is more robust and recedes more slowly than vaccine immunity. This fact, admitted for all diseases, was completely eclipsed. The reason? To promote vaccines. I was emphatic about the exaggerated role attributed to antibodies, both in the detection of immunity and as proof of protection against a disease. Antibodies are first and foremost witnesses to an encounter with a pathogen.

As far as COVID-19 is concerned, natural antibodies (acquired through infection), and especially vaccine antibodies, can exacerbate the disease. This was accepted by all experts on coronavirus vaccines at the start of 2020 (the ADE phenomenon), and it was later discovered that immune imprinting (OAS) made repeated injections of Spike vaccines even more harmful by weakening the response to variants. The ADE phenomenon partly explains the types of post-vaccination COVID-19 observed since clinical trials and in all observational studies in the commercial phase. OAS also partly accounts for the heightened susceptibility of vaccinees to successive SARS-CoV-2 variants.

Biopower naturally strives to conceal both the manifestation of these phenomena and their theoretical explanation. The majority of experts, doctors and even victims of the harmful effects of these vaccines are unable to recognize them, as they seem to be caught up in Orwell's doublethink mechanism. All COVID-19 vaccines and their modifications on the basis of the virus' Spike protein are likely to cause these adverse effects.

Clinical trials on adults had already revealed most of the adverse effects of all types of COVID-19 vaccines. These vaccine-associated pathologies are due to the inherent toxicity of the virus' Spike protein: it has been selected as the antigen for all vaccines. This is not malicious intent on the part of the manufacturers (they have not studied this toxicity): Spike is the most accessible and abundant antigen of the virus, and as such, the one that will produce the highest antibody levels, the gold standard of vaccinology. This is also why vaccine Spike has been modified compared to viral Spike: making it more stable, more antibody-producing, and even more toxic.

Trials on adolescents, children and infants have also clearly shown the inefficacy and high toxicity of mRNA vaccines. In 2020, no clinical trials were conducted on pregnant women, and later the results of the trial launched in February 2021 on only 726 women were only partially published in July 2023.[376] Women in the placebo group were vaccinated from the moment of delivery, preventing any long-term follow-up of adverse effects. These partial results show almost twice as many birth defects in the babies of vaccinated mothers and four times as many adverse effects compared with the placebo. Yet this population had been "targeted" from spring 2021 and, as expected, everything was done to conceal the effects of COVID-19 vaccines on pregnancy and unborn babies. The adverse effects on pregnant women, miscarriages, stillbirths, malformations and illnesses in infants, the drop in

---

376. *To Evaluate the Safety, Tolerability, and Immunogenicity of BNT162b2 Against COVID-19 in Healthy Pregnant Women 18 Years of Age and Older*, ClinicalTrials.gov. Detailed data: http://tiny.cc/NCT04754594.

birth rate, as well as disturbances to the menstrual cycle have been the focus of particular attention by the authorities: the aim is always to make them invisible and to accuse those who mention them of "misinformation."

The incidence of certain cancers after vaccination rose sharply in the 2021 statistics. Similarly, the risk of myocarditis in young people was significantly higher after vaccination than after infection with the virus itself, a fact also concealed.

Although it has not been clearly demonstrated that vaccine mRNA can integrate into the genome of a vaccinated person, this remains biologically plausible. This risk should have been given serious consideration before administering a product still in the experimental phase to billions of people, especially as we now know that anti-COVID-19 mRNAs are widely contaminated with DNA.

Conventional pharmacovigilance systems have proved ineffective in detecting the adverse effects of COVID-19 vaccines. Even though these were foreseeable before the vaccination campaigns began, everything has been done to avoid seeing them. And now, everything is being orchestrated to further exacerbate the burden of the virus and present it as more dangerous than the vaccines. Every publication along these lines contains biases that can easily be identified by any honest scientist.

I have reviewed the grounds showing that it is entirely possible for the vaccinated to contaminate the non-vaccinated through close contact: mRNA or vaccine Spike can theoretically be present in many bodily fluids. This hypothesis has met with much opposition, but no one has been able to contradict a single one of my arguments. Moreover, independent publications have shown the passage of vaccine mRNA into breast milk within eight days of injection.

I helped draft a document for magistrates in which we explain why it is important to order an autopsy after a post-vaccination death, whatever the pathology associated with the death may be and however long it has been since the injection. COVID-19 vaccines are, after all, experimental products, and a causal link can never be ruled out. It should not be up to the victims' families to prove this causal link. On the contrary, the onus should be on manufacturers and pharmacovigilance authorities to provide robust evidence exonerating their product.

The reckless race to gene therapy

Biopower will try to take advantage of the COVID-19 pandemic to continue advancement on two fronts: research into virus functional gains and acceleration of widespread vaccination.

The anti-COVID-19 mRNA vaccines are, in fact, gene therapies, and should have complied with the strict regulations associated with such products. By calling them "vaccines," health agencies have allowed their evasion of critical safety controls.

There is talk of extending mRNA technology to many vaccines and to treatment of genetic diseases and cancers. Without opposition from the public and elected representatives, there is reason to fear that these products will become widespread without sufficient pre-clinical and clinical trials: administration of all these mRNAs to healthy populations should be suspended until such time as a positive benefit/risk ratio for patients is demonstrated, which has not yet been done.

Undoubtedly at the origin of the pandemic, gain-of-function experiments on viruses continue unabated, as though nothing had happened: SARS-CoV-2 continues to be manipulated, as do other viruses that are more dangerous than coronaviruses. All this merits large-scale public debate.

When it comes to tomorrow's vaccines and future pandemics, enormous financial and technical resources are already being mobilized, also without any debate. mRNA factories are being built all over the world, and "enhancements" such as self-amplifying mRNAs are even being considered. Conventional vaccine techniques also promise nasty surprises if we fail to act. For example, there are plans for self-disseminating vaccines for animals (for the time being for animals!), contraceptive vaccines that are supposed to be reversible, and intranasal or skin vaccines.[377]

"Preventive therapy" for infectious diseases is a new concept, which will make it possible to relax the regulatory burden by passing these products off as vaccines, as we saw with Beyfortus, a monoclonal antibody against bronchiolitis in infants, already identified as ineffective and toxic, but authorized on an emergency use basis.

---

377. *Vaccines Delivered Via Dissolvable Skin Patches*, American Society for Microbiology, décembre 2022.

What will be our response to the trend of biopolitics ?

The ball is in the court of the general public and elected representatives, who must take up the critical work we are continuing to develop, in France for example, with the Conseil Scientifique Indépendant (CSI), the BonSens.org association and AIMSIB. Many such groups exist now worldwide, taking responsibility and enlightening those who dare to question. They must fight their way for access to independent, critical and honest information and analysis.

Knowledge is power

It is up to each and every one of us to find the right channels enabling us to be well-informed and active, and that starts with breaking down the wall of censorship in every way possible.

Abbreviations

ACE2	Angiotensin converting enzyme 2
ADE	Antibody-dependent enhancement
AE	Adverse event (or adverse effect)
AIMSIB	International Association for Independent and Caring Scientific Medicine
ANSM	French National Agency for Drug Safety (Agence nationale de sécurité du médicament et des produits de santé)
RNA	Ribonucleic acid
BMJ	British Medical Journal
BSL	Biosafety Lab, levels 1 to 4
CDC	Centers of Diseases Control (US)
CEPI	Coalition for Epidemic Preparedness Innovations
COVID-19	Coronavirus Disease 2019
CSI	Conseil Scientifique Indépendant ; French Independant Scientific Council
DARPA	Defense Advanced Research Projects Agency (US)
DoD	Department of Defense (US)
EHA	EcoHealth Alliance
EMA	European Medicines Agency
FDA	Food and Drug Administration (US)
FOIA	Freedom Of Information Act (US)
GoF	Gain of function
GTP	Gene therapy product
Insee	The national statistics bureau of France
NIAID	National Institute of Allergy and Infectious Diseases (US)

NIH	National Institutes of Health (US)
OAS	Original Antigenic Sin
PCR	Polymerase Chain Reaction
SARS-CoV-2	Severe Acute Respiratory Syndrome Corona-virus 2
Spike	SARS-CoV-2 surface protein
VAERD	Vaccine-Associated Enhanced Respiratory Disease
VAERS	Vaccine Adverse Event Reporting System
WHO	World Health Organization

Table of Contents

Complements

www.ingramcontent.com/pod-product-compliance
Lightning Source LLC
Chambersburg PA
CBHW031120020426
42333CB00012B/161